Philip Kerr & Ceri Jones

Straightforward

Level 2B

Student's Book

Lesson	Grammar	Vocabulary	Functional language	Pronunciation
1A Double lives p4	Stative & dynamic verbs			
1B Daily lives p6	Present simple & present continuous	Verbs with two meanings		
1C Identity p8	Subject & object questions	Self-image		
1D First impressions p10		Describing people	Describing people	Intonation (lists)
1 Language reference p12				
2A Around the world p14	Present perfect & past simple			
2B Unusual journeys p16		Phrasal verbs		Word linking
2C Down under p18	Present perfect for unfinished time			
2D Getting around p20		Verb collocations (travel)	Travelling	
2 Language reference p22				
3A Dream homes p24	Modals of obligation, permission & prohibition (present time)			
3B Unusual homes p26	*Make*, *let* & *allow*	Accommodation		
3C Bedrooms p28	Modals of obligation, permission & prohibition (past time)	Verb collocations (sleep)		
3D Dinner invitation p30			Requests	Intonation (requests)
3 Language reference p32				
4A Luck of the draw p34	Past simple & past continuous	Idioms (taking risks)		*Was* & *were*
4B Twists of fate p36	Past perfect simple	Injuries		
4C Bad luck stories p38		Time linkers		
4D Fancy that! p40		*Both* & *neither*	Talking about similarities & differences	
4 Language reference p42				
5A Hard sell p44	Comparisons 1	Adjectives (advertising)		
5B Cold calling p46	Comparisons 2	Adjectives (negative prefixes)		/s/, /z/ & /ʃ/
5C The office p48	Comparing nouns	Office activities		
5D Paperwork p50		Office supplies	On the phone	
5 Language reference p52				
6A Summer holiday p54	Future 1 (future plans)	Holidays 1		
6B Getting away p56	Future 2 (predictions)	Holidays 2		
6C Perfect day p58	Present tenses in future time clauses			
6D Travel plans p60		Collocations with *sound*	Indirect questions	Word stress
6 Language reference p62				
Communication activities p64	Audioscripts p68	Unit reviews p74		

		Reading & Listening	Speaking	Writing (in the Workbook)
1A	R	Liars! (Mad Men)	Discussing what people are most likely to lie about Talking about yourself	A description of a best friend
1B	L	Radio review of TV programme: How Michael Portillo Became a Single Mum	Describing daily routines **Did you know?** British political parties	
1C	R	Regional identity – what does it mean to you?	Discussing answers to an ASEAN quiz Devising a quiz about culture in your country	
1D	L	Dialogue about a new flatmate	Talking about first impressions Discussing making a good impression	
2A	R	Lawyer gives up job to cycle around the world	Discussing travelling	A description of a town or city
2B	L/R	Three unusual journeys	Talking about a film or book of a long journey	
2C	R	Excerpt from a blog about a trip around Australia	Talking about Australia Planning a journey across your country	
2D	L	Three dialogues about trying to get somewhere	Talking about daily transport in a city you know well **Did you know?** New York & London taxis	
3A	R	Paradise Ridge	Discussing where you live	Advantages and disadvantages
	L	Interviews with residents talking about disadvantages of living in Paradise Ridge		
3B	L	Three interviews with people who live in unusual homes	Designing a luxury holiday home	
3C	R	Six things you probably didn't know about beds and bedrooms	Talking about sleeping & dreaming	
3D	L	Dinner party	Describing a recent dinner party Roleplay: dinner party **Did you know?** Food in Britain	
4A	R	Lottery winners and losers	Inventing a story about a lottery winner	A narrative: lottery winner
4B	L	The world's luckiest man		
	R	Lucky Luciano		
4C	R	Three bad luck stories	Inventing a bad luck story **Did you know?** Superstitions in Britain	
4D	L	Dialogue at work: discussing things in common	Identifying & discussing coincidences	
5A	R	Catch them young	Planning & presenting an advertisement for a mineral water	An advertisement
5B	L	Phone call: credit card telesales	Carrying out a market research survey	
5C	R	Office stereotypes	Planning an office party	
5D	L	Ordering office supplies over the phone	Roleplay: phone dialogue ordering office supplies **Did you know?** London's Mayfair and Park Lane districts	
6A	R	Questionnaire: What kind of holiday person are you?	Making plans with other holiday makers	An extract from a holiday brochure
6B	L	Six short interviews at the airport	Planning a holiday for a family group	
6C	R	Emerald Tours	Discussing the perfect day out **Did you know?** Cork – European capital of culture	
6D	L	Enquiring about flights over the phone	Discussing the advantages of booking a holiday online or through a travel agent's	

1A Double lives

Speaking

1 Work in small groups. Look at the list and decide which things are the most important when you are describing who you are.

- name
- age
- job
- nationality
- marital status
- qualifications
- friends
- salary

2 Discuss these questions with your group.

- Which information in exercise 1 are you most interested in when you meet someone for the first time?
- Which of these things do you think people are most likely to lie about?
- Talk about the most honest person you know.

3 Put the following in order of seriousness (1 = most serious ➔ 6 = least serious).

- ☐ lying about why you are late for work/school
- ☐ lying about your age to get into a nightclub
- ☐ lying about your qualifications to get a job
- ☐ lying to your partner about another person
- ☐ lying to a friend about their new hairstyle
- ☐ lying to a member of your family about a present that you didn't like

Reading

1 Look at the headlines on the web page. Which of the following pieces of information do you expect to find?

1. what people do when they lie
2. why people lie
3. who lies more, men or women
4. examples of famous liars
5. examples of liars in films and on television
6. examples of favourite lies

2 Read the web page to check your answers.

Liars!

How to spot them

He thinks he's getting away with it, but his body and his voice are giving him away. He's stumbling over his words. He's fidgeting and nervous. His hands won't stay still and his palms are probably sweaty as well. He seems to be smiling, but there's a little bit of tension around his lips and his nose. Although the bottom half of his face is forming a smile, it hasn't reached his eyes. He's looking at you straight in the eyes and he appears to be 100% sincere, but the tone of his voice has dropped and the rhythm of his speech has slowed down. There's no doubt about it: he's lying.

Learn to spot the telltale signs.

Screen liars

It's 1960s New York. Don Draper is a successful advertising executive, a happily married man with a beautiful wife. But all of this is built on a lie, or better said, a series of lies. Even his name is a lie. He 'stole' it from an officer who was killed fighting in Korea. He returned to the States and turned his back on his past. With no experience and no qualifications he lied his way into a job with a successful advertising agency, where his talent in lying and selling lies makes him a big success. Everything seems to be going really well. Everybody respects and looks up to him, no one knows about his past. Until one day that is, when Don's half-brother suddenly appears …

Read more about screen liars.

The world's top ten lies

1. I love you.
2. You look great.
3. I'll call you tomorrow.
4. We never got the letter.
5. I'm not feeling very well.
6. I had no choice.
7. We had a lovely time.
8. I missed you.
9. It wasn't me.
10. I won't be long.

Read the top 100 lies.

Glossary
fidget *v* make small movements because you are nervous or bored
stumble *v* fall or almost fall

4

3 Read the texts again and say if the sentences are true (T) or false (F). Correct the false sentences.

1 It is possible to spot a liar because of his body language.
2 Liars sometimes speak more quickly.
3 Don Draper is good at his job.
4 Don Draper is not his real name.
5 He is proud of his past.
6 Most of the world's top ten lies are about money.

4 Work in pairs. Discuss these questions.

- What other sentences would you expect to see in the top 100 lies?
- Do you know of any other films where a liar is the central character? Tell your partner.

GRAMMAR: stative & dynamic verbs

1 Look at the verbs in italics. Circle the stative verbs and underline the dynamic verbs.

1 Every morning Gerald *puts on* a suit and tie, *kisses* his wife goodbye and *goes* to work.
2 Or, at least, that's what his wife *thinks*, and that's what Gerald *wants* his wife to believe.
3 In fact, Gerald *feeds* pigeons in the park or *does* crosswords in the local library.
4 His wife *goes* shopping every Saturday and *buys* new furniture for the house with her credit card.
5 She *doesn't know* that they *don't have* any more money.

Use dynamic verbs …
- in either the simple or the continuous form.
- to describe an action.
  He's **looking** at you.

Use stative verbs …
- in the simple form, not usually in the continuous form.
- to describe emotions, opinions, the senses and states that do not change.
  He **loves** his kids. Not ~~He's loving his kids~~.
  Everything **seems** to be going well. Not ~~Everything is seeming to be going well.~~

Common stative verbs:
agree   appear   be   believe   belong   cost
dislike forget   hate have   know   like   love
matter   mean   need own   prefer   realize
remember seem   think understand want

> SEE LANGUAGE REFERENCE PAGE 12

2 Walter Mitty is the hero of a short story by James Thurber. His life is sad and ordinary, but most of the time he lives in a dream world, as the heroic Captain Mitty. Correct three mistakes with stative or dynamic verbs in the two paragraphs from the story.

1 The weather is getting worse and the plane is not having enough fuel to return to base. But, Captain Mitty, who is sitting at the controls, is not knowing the meaning of the word *fear*. He is understanding that there is only one way to save everyone's life. 'We're going through,' he announces.

2 'I am being accurate at 100 metres. I never miss.' Mitty is holding a heavy automatic and the crowd believe him. The courtroom is in chaos. Mitty is needing to find a way out, but he is not wanting to use the gun.

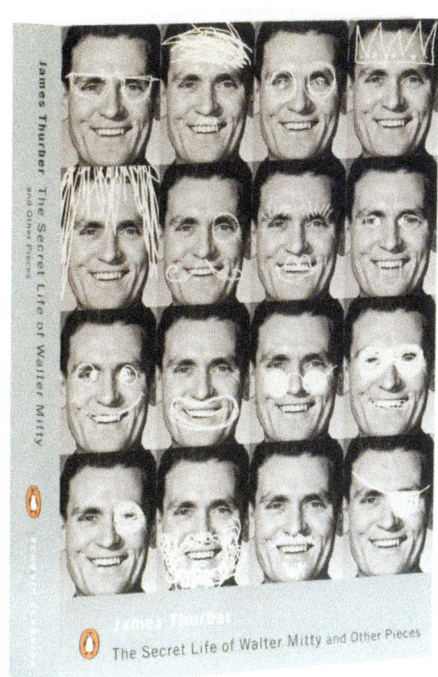

3 Work in pairs, A and B. You are going to describe a moment of Mitty's real and imaginary life using both dynamic and stative verbs.

A: Turn to page 64 and describe what is happening.
B: Turn to page 66 and describe what is happening in Mitty's imagination.

SPEAKING

1 Turn to page 64. Choose one sentence and complete it so that it is true for you. Complete the other sentences so that they are **not** true for you.

2 Work in pairs. Tell your partner your sentences from exercise 1. Can he/she guess which sentence is true?

1B Daily lives

LISTENING & SPEAKING

1 Work in pairs. Discuss these questions.
- What do you think the following people do on a typical working day?
  a) a mother of four small children
  b) a member of parliament
- Whose lifestyle is more similar to yours? In what ways?

2 Work in pairs. Read the TV review. What do you think the main differences between Michael Portillo and Jenny Miner's lifestyles will be?

TONIGHT • BBC2 9PM

In tonight's *How Michael Portillo Became a Single Mum*, a classic example of reality TV at its best, former politician, Michael Portillo, adds new skills to his CV. The son of a Spanish political refugee, Michael Portillo has had a long career in politics. He has been Secretary of State for Defence and he has stood for leadership of the Tory party, but in tonight's programme he takes on a whole new challenge. In his first appearance in the wonderful world of reality TV, he volunteers to look after Jenny Miner's four children for a week. It's a rare chance to see a politician at work in the real world.

3 🔘 1.01 Listen to the first part of a review of the TV programme. Check the answers you gave in exercise 2.

4 🔘 1.02 Listen to the second part of the review and answer the questions.
1 What did the reviewer think of Michael Portillo before the programme?
2 What did the reviewer think of him after the programme?
3 What was Tasha and her friends' reaction to him?
4 Which did he find more difficult: working in the supermarket or working as a classroom assistant? Why?
5 What was the biggest challenge Portillo faced on the programme?
6 Who was the reviewer's favourite character?

5 🔘 1.01–1.02 Listen again and complete the sentences.
1 Michael Portillo volunteered **to step into single mum Jenny Miner's** _____ for a week.
2 Life as a single mum is going to be **a real** _____-opener.
3 It is one of **the high** _____ of his week.
4 It looks as if **he's** _____ off more than he can chew.
5 All his people skills and lessons in political diplomacy **will get him** _____.

6 Work in pairs. Explain the meaning of the phrases in bold in exercise 5.

7 Which politician in your country would you like to see in a similar TV programme? Why?

GRAMMAR: present simple & present continuous

1 Choose the correct phrases to complete the rules below. Then choose examples from the sentences highlighted in audioscripts 1.01–1.02 on page 68.

> Use the *present simple / present continuous* …
> - to talk about facts (things that are always true) and permanent situations.
>   Example _____
> - to talk about habits and actions that happen regularly.
>   Example _____
>
> Use the *present simple / present continuous* …
> - to talk about actions that are happening at the moment of speaking.
>   Example _____
> - to talk about temporary situations and activities.
>   Example _____
>
> We usually use stative verbs in the *present simple / present continuous*.
> Example _____ Not ~~is wanting to~~

▶ FOR THE PRESENT SIMPLE AND THE PRESENT CONTINUOUS WITH FUTURE MEANINGS, SEE PAGE 62
▶ SEE LANGUAGE REFERENCE PAGE 12

6

Daily lives | 1B

2 Choose the correct verb forms to complete the article.

FAKING IT • BBC2 9PM

Faking it is the hit TV series where people learn a new job in just a few weeks and then try to persuade experts that it's their real job! In this week's episode, a volunteer (1) *has / is having* four weeks to learn a new skill. This week's volunteer, Tim Hutch, usually (2) *works / is working* as a music teacher in a secondary school. In *Faking it*, he becomes a rock star. When you see him in the programme, he (3) *plays / is playing* live on stage in a rock band! In his real job as a music teacher, he (4) *teaches / is teaching* kids to play classical guitar. That's the only instrument he can play. But in *Faking it* he (5) *learns / is learning* to play the bass guitar. Tim Hutch has many challenges to face, but the thing he most (6) *wants / is wanting* to learn is how to dance in time. Don't miss it!

3 Write six sentences about yourself using these time expressions.

| now | usually | once a week |
| this week | never | at the moment |

VOCABULARY: verbs with two meanings

Some verbs can be both stative and dynamic, but the meaning changes. You can use the verbs *think*, *see* and *have* in the simple and continuous forms, but with different meanings.

*I **see** what the problem is now.*
(= I understand what the problem is now.)
*I'm **seeing** a TV reviewer at ten tomorrow.*
(= I have arranged to meet her.)

> SEE LANGUAGE REFERENCE PAGE 12

1 Choose the correct verb to complete the sentences.

1 I *think / am thinking* this is probably the best programme I've seen all year.
2 I don't know if Portillo *thinks / is thinking* about starting a new career.
3 I *see / am seeing* what you mean.
4 I *am seeing / see* two politicians for a meeting tomorrow.
5 Jenny Miner *has / is having* four children.
6 Look at Portillo. He *has / is having* a really good time at the party.

2 Work in pairs. Explain the meaning of each use of the verbs in exercise 1.

3 Complete the sentences with *see*, *have* or *think* in the present simple or present continuous.

see
1 He _____ his doctor next week.
2 She _____ why he lied to her, but she isn't going to forgive him.

have
3 He _____ £5 in his pocket.
4 She _____ a party at her flat on Saturday.

think
5 He _____ about getting his hair cut this weekend.
6 She _____ reality TV shows should be banned.

4 Work in pairs. Use the three verbs from exercise 3 to make sentences that are true for you. Then tell your partner about yourself.

I think a lot of programmes on TV are very funny.
I'm thinking of going on holiday to Greece next year.

DID YOU KNOW?

1 Work in pairs. Read about British political parties and discuss the questions.

For nearly one hundred years, only two British political parties had governed Britain: the Labour Party, a socialist party whose leaders have included Tony Blair and Harold Wilson, and the Conservatives (also known as the Tories), traditionally a more right-wing party. Winston Churchill and Margaret Thatcher are perhaps the most famous leaders of the Tory Party. In the general elections in 2010 a third party, the Liberal Democrats, came into power for the first time, forming a coalition government with the Tory Party. The first Liberal Democrat leader to serve in government was the Deputy Prime Minister, Nick Clegg.

- What are the main political parties in your country?
- What are the differences between them?
- What other political parties are there?
- Who are the most famous members of those political parties?

1c | Identity

SPEAKING & VOCABULARY: self-image

1 Complete the sentences in column A with a phrase from column B.

A	B
1 I think of myself as *a Korean*,	a *an old-age pensioner* – I'm too busy for that.
2 I would describe myself	b as *quite fit for my age*.
3 I don't see myself as	c but *I've lived in the US for 25 years*.
4 I'm proud to be the	d *grandmother of two very clever girls*.
5 *My family* is the most	e important thing to me.
6 My neighbours probably see	f live in such a nice house.
7 I consider myself lucky to	g me *as a very friendly person*.

2 Change the words in italics in exercise 1 to make sentences that are true for you. Compare your sentences with a partner.

I think of myself as a Chinese, but I've lived in Myanmar for the last ten years.

READING

1 Read the article about regional identity. Which of the people 1–6 have positive feelings about regional identity?

2 Read the article again and answer the questions.
1 What does James want to see more of?
2 What does Putri want to happen?
3 What kind of people does Tam trust?
4 Where does Tam come from?
5 Who comes from Indonesia?
6 Who experienced a change in attitude towards regional identity?

3 Work in groups. Discuss these questions.
1 What do you feel about being a member of ASEAN?
2 How does ASEAN affect your life?

Regional identity
– what does it mean to you?

Last week, we asked Europeans what it means to be part of the EU. This week, it's the turn of people from Southeast Asia. What does regional identity mean to you?

1 We need to do more things together in Southeast Asia, and it's beginning to happen! We already have agreements for things like aviation, and we're moving towards a free trade system. With more trade between our countries, we will think of ourselves as real partners.
(James, bookshop owner)

2 I've read that there's a possibility the ASEAN countries could hold the FIFA World Cup™. A small country like Qatar is going to organize it, so why don't they give it to a whole region like ours? One country probably can't do it on its own, but together, why not? With the final in Jakarta, of course!
(Putri, advertising executive)

3 Who cares about regional identity? I don't think anyone thinks of themselves as Southeast Asian. You ask people where they come from and they say Thailand, or Myanmar, or Vietnam. They never say Southeast Asia! If you ask me where I come from, I'll say I'm a Thai. I'm proud of my country – that's the most important thing to me – not my region. You can only be sure of people who have the same culture as you.
(Tam, shopkeeper)

4 I hadn't felt a bond with other countries in the region until I won a scholarship to study in Singapore for two years. I met other students from all over the region, and we got on really well even though we spoke different languages and had different religions. It was the most amazing experience of my life!.
(Eyah, student)

5 I think it's important to have a sense of regional identity – for security, for trade and for prosperity. But what is happening in this part of the world? It seems that each year there are more and more disputes, more and more problems, and what are we doing about all these? We don't seem to agree about anything.
(Michelle, adminstrative assistant)

6 It's a good idea, but how many ordinary people know anything about other countries in the region? The politicians go to meetings, and there are sports competitions between countries and so on, but people don't seem to feel the importance of being part of the region. We need to do more about it.
(Adnan, editor)

Identity | 1c

GRAMMAR: subject & object questions

Questions
This is the usual word order in questions:

question word	auxiliary	subject	infinitive
How	does	it	affect me?
Why	don't	they	give it to us?

Subject questions
When the question word (*who, what, which* or *how many*) is the subject of the question, you do not need an auxiliary verb (*do, does* or *did*) with the present simple and past simple.

subject	verb
Who	cares about regional identity?
How many people	joined the meeting?

Object questions
If the question word is the object of a question, you use normal question word order with *do, does* or *did*.

object	auxiliary	subject	infinitive
Who	does	he	work for?
What	did	he	say?

> SEE LANGUAGE REFERENCE PAGE 12

1 Look at the questions in Reading exercise 2. Find two subject questions and four object questions.

2 Correct the grammatical mistakes in four of these questions.
1 What ASEAN stands for?
2 How many countries belong to ASEAN?
3 When decided the first five countries to form ASEAN?
4 Which was the last country to join ASEAN?
5 When Myanmar joined ASEAN?
6 What does the motto of ASEAN?

3 Use the prompts to make questions.
1 *Which language is the official language of ASEAN?*
1 Which language / be / the official language of ASEAN?
2 How many people / live / in ASEAN countries?
3 Which five countries / sign the ASEAN declaration first?
4 When / the first five countries / sign the ASEAN declaration?
5 Where / be / the office of the ASEAN secretariat?
6 Where / ASEAN / hold the 20th Summit in 2012?

SPEAKING

1 Work in pairs. Turn to page 64. Choose the correct answer to the questions in Grammar exercises 2 and 3. If you do not know the answer, guess!

2 Now work with a new partner. You are each going to see the answers for one exercise. Tell your partner if his/her answers are correct.

A: Turn to page 66. B: Turn to page 67.

3 Work in groups. Prepare six questions that test knowledge of your own country. Use the examples in Grammar exercises 2 and 3 and these topics to help you.

everyday life   famous people
history   important places

4 Work with students from another group. Ask them your test questions.

| 9

1D | First impressions

Police officer

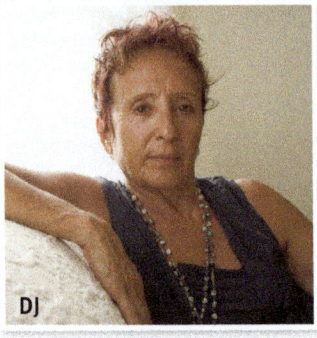
DJ

Student

Accountant

Speaking

1 Work in pairs. Look at the photos and the labels. What link is there between the photos and the title of this lesson? Discuss these questions.

- When and where was the last time you met someone new?
- Who was it?
- What was your first impression of them?
- Were your first impressions accurate?

2 Think of five situations when it is important to look good and make a good impression.

3 Explain the meaning of the saying below. Do you agree or disagree? Give examples to explain your opinion.

> *You can't judge a book by its cover.*

Listening

1 Look at the photo. What are the people doing? What do you think is the relationship between them? What do you think they're talking about?

2 🔊 1.03 Listen to their dialogue. Check your answers to exercise 1.

3 🔊 1.03 Listen again. Correct the mistakes in the sentences below.

1 Both girls have met the girl who might be their new flatmate.
2 She's the same age as them.
3 She's a businesswoman.
4 She really liked the bedroom.
5 She has already decided to take the room.

4 Look at the photos of the three women below. Which photo do you think shows the new flatmate?

5 Read the information and answer the questions.

> There are more than two million foreign students studying at universities in the UK. More than 50,000 come from China. More than any other one country.

- Do foreign students come to study in your country?
- If yes, where do they usually come from?
- Do you know any foreign students studying in your town?

VOCABULARY: describing people

1 Work in pairs. How many parts of the body can you name?

2 Match the groups of adjectives in column A to the nouns in column B.

	A		B
1	average/muscular/slim	a	eyes
2	bald/round/shaved	b	hair
3	blond/shiny/wavy	c	head
4	dark/narrow/wide	d	nose
5	healthy/pale/tanned	e	complexion
6	pointed/prominent/straight	f	build

3 Make a list of eight famous people with your partner. Choose one of the people from your list and describe his/her appearance. Your partner must guess who you are describing.

FUNCTIONAL LANGUAGE: describing people

1 Match the questions 1–3 to the answers a–f.

1 What is she like?
2 What does she look like?
3 What does she like?

a I think she's into Italian fashion.
b She seems very nice, relaxed and chatty.
c She's got long dark hair and dark eyes.
d She's young and wears really trendy clothes.
e She's very friendly.
f Rock music.

2 Work in pairs. Write the names of four people you know. Use the questions in exercise 1 to find out more about the people whose names your partner has written.

A: Who's Mark?
B: He's my brother.
A: What's he like?
B: He's cheerful and funny.

3 Complete the sentences in column A with a phrase from column B.

	A		B
1	She looks	a	a film star. (+ noun)
2	She looks like	b	quite friendly. (+ adjective)
3	She looks as if	c	she's going to a wedding. (+ phrase)

4 Complete the sentences with *like*, *as if* or –.

1 He doesn't look _____ very happy.
2 He looks _____ a doctor.
3 He looks _____ about 55.
4 He looks _____ he's just woken up.
5 He looks _____ he wants to be somewhere else.
6 He looks _____ the prime minister.

PRONUNCIATION: intonation (lists)

1 🔊 1.04 Listen to this extract from the dialogue in Listening exercise 2.

… the kitchen, the living room, the bathroom, her bedroom and the bedrooms.

Notice how the voice goes up for each item of the list and then down at the end of the list.

2 Practise reading these lists in the same way.

1 Monday, Tuesday, Wednesday and Thursday
2 who, what, where, when and why
3 Sue, Nick, Beth, John and me

3 🔊 1.05 Listen to the recording to check your pronunciation.

4 Work in pairs. Take it in turns to add one more item to the lists below. Repeat the whole list each time.

1 A: Britain, America, Australia and Canada
B: Britain, America, Australia, Canada and Ireland

1 Britain, America, Australia, …
2 eyes, ears, nose, …
3 intelligent, good-looking, kind, …
4 mother, cousin, grandfather, …
5 red, blue, yellow, …

> **Self-assessment (✓)**
> ☐ I can talk about first impressions.
> ☐ I can describe someone's appearance.
> ☐ I can understand descriptions of people's characteristics.
> ☐ I can describe similarities.

1 | Language reference

GRAMMAR
Stative & dynamic verbs

Some verbs can only be used in the simple form. These are called stative verbs. They often describe emotions, opinions, the senses and states that do not change.

I love you. Not *I am loving you.*
He seems friendly. Not *He is seeming friendly.*

Here are some common stative verbs:

agree	appear	be	believe	belong	contain
dislike	fit	forget	hate	know	last	like
love	matter	mean	need	own	prefer
realize	remember	seem	understand	want

We can use most verbs in both the simple and the continuous forms. These are called dynamic verbs.

*The weather **is getting** worse.*
*It often **snows** in January.*

It is possible for some verbs to be both dynamic and stative if they have two different meanings.

*He **has** a house in north London.* (have = own)
*She's **having** a few problems.* (have = experience)

Other common verbs that can be dynamic or stative (with different meanings) include:

be   feel   see   smell   think

Present simple & present continuous

We use the present simple …
- to talk about facts (things that are always true) and permanent situations.
  *She **lives** in a small flat.*
- to talk about habits and actions that happen regularly.
  *She **drives** the kids to school every day.*

We use the present continuous …
- to talk about actions that are happening at the moment of speaking.
  *He's **trying to** explain a problem to them.*
- to talk about temporary situations and activities.
  *She's **going** through a very rebellious phase.*

We can sometimes use both the present simple and the present continuous. Our choice depends on how we see the action.

*I **live** in Madrid.* (= I think this is permanent.)
*I'm **living** in Madrid.* (= I think this is temporary.)

See page 62 for information about the present tenses with future meaning.

Subject & object questions

The usual word order in questions is:

	auxiliary verb	subject	verb
Who	does	he	work for?
What	do	you	do on New Year's Eve?
Which party	did	you	vote for?

These questions are called object questions because the question words (*who, what, which party*) are the object of the verb.

In some *Wh-* questions, the question word (*who, what, which* or *how many*) is the subject of the verb. These are called subject questions. With a subject question, we do not need an auxiliary verb (*do, does* or *did*) with the present simple and the past simple.

subject (question word)	verb
Who	thinks regional identity is important?
What	happens on New Year's Eve?
Which party	won the last election?
How many people	voted for the government?

FUNCTIONAL LANGUAGE
Describing people

What is she **like**?
(= We are asking for a general description of the person.)

What does she **look like**?
(= We are asking for a description of the person's appearance.)

What does she **like**?
(= We are asking about the person's preferences or interests.)

	+ adjective
	intelligent.
She looks	*like* + noun
	like a doctor.
	as if/as though + phrase
	as if she needs a holiday.

Some English speakers use *like* instead of *as if/as though*. Many people, however, think this is incorrect.

*She looks **like** she needs a holiday.*

Language reference 1

WORD LIST

Self-image

consider (sb) + adj	/kənˈsɪdə(r)/
consider (sb) to be…	/kənˈsɪdə(r) tə ˌbiː/
describe (sb) as …	/dɪˈskraɪb ˌəz/
proud to + infinitive	/ˈpraʊd ˌtuː/
see (sb) as …	/ˈsiː ˌəz/
think of (sb) as …	/ˈθɪŋk əv ˌəz/

Describing people

average adj ***	/ˈæv(ə)rɪdʒ/
bald adj *	/bɔːld/
blond adj *	/blɒnd/
build n C *	/bɪld/
complexion n C *	/kəmˈplekʃ(ə)n/
dark adj ***	/dɑː(r)k/
healthy adj ***	/ˈhelθi/
muscular adj	/ˈmʌskjʊlə(r)/
narrow adj ***	/ˈnærəʊ/
pale adj ***	/peɪl/
pointed adj *	/ˈpɔɪntɪd/
prominent adj **	/ˈprɒmɪnənt/
round adj ***	/raʊnd/
shaved adj	/ʃeɪvd/
shiny adj *	/ˈʃaɪni/
slim adj **	/slɪm/
straight adj **	/streɪt/
tanned adj	/tænd/
wavy adj	/ˈweɪvi/
wide adj ***	/waɪd/

Other words & phrases

agency n C **	/ˈeɪdʒ(ə)nsi/
analyst n C **	/ˈænəlɪst/
arrest v **	/əˈrest/
arrogant adj *	/ˈærəgənt/
automatic n C/adj **	/ˌɔːtəˈmætɪk/
ban v **	/bæn/
base n C ***	/beɪs/
beefeater n C	/ˈbiːfˌiːtə(r)/
bite v **	/baɪt/
bottom n C/adj ***	/ˈbɒtəm/
career n C ***	/kəˈrɪə(r)/
cashier n C	/kæˈʃɪə(r)/
challenge n C ***	/ˈtʃælɪndʒ/
chaos n U **	/ˈkeɪɒs/
chew v **	/tʃuː/
citizen n C ***	/ˈsɪtɪz(ə)n/
clever adj **	/ˈklevə(r)/
clip n C *	/klɪp/
coalition n C **	/ˌkəʊəˈlɪʃ(ə)n/
courtroom n C	/ˈkɔː(r)tˌruːm/
crossword n C *	/ˈkrɒsˌwɜː(r)d/
cucumber n C	/ˈkjuːˌkʌmbə(r)/
decent adj **	/ˈdiːs(ə)nt/
deputy adj/n C ***	/ˈdepjuti/
dial v *	/ˈdaɪəl/
diplomacy n U	/dɪˈpləʊməsi/
election n C ***	/ɪˈlekʃ(ə)n/
emergency services n pl	/ɪˈmɜː(r)dʒənsiˌ sɜːvɪsɪz/
episode n C **	/ˈepɪsəʊd/
executive n C/adj **	/ɪgˈzekjʊtɪv/
expert n C ***	/ˈekspɜː(r)t/
eye-opener n C	/ˈaɪ ˌəʊp(ə)nə(r)/
face v ***	/feɪs/
fake v/adj/n C	/feɪk/
fidget v	/ˈfɪdʒɪt/
fireworks n pl	/ˈfaɪə(r)ˌwɜː(r)ks/
fit adj **	/fɪt/
flatly adv	/ˈflætli/
fuel n U ***	/ˈfjuːəl/
get away with (sth) v	/get əˈweɪ wɪð/
give (sb) away v	/ˌgɪv əˈweɪ/
govern v **	/ˈgʌvə(r)n/
headquarters n pl **	/hedˈkwɔː(r)tə(r)z/
hero n C **	/ˈhɪərəʊ/
honest adj **	/ˈɒnɪst/
imaginary adj *	/ɪˈmædʒɪnəri/
immigrant n C *	/ˈɪmɪgrənt/
impress v **	/ɪmˈpres/
impression n C ***	/ɪmˈpreʃ(ə)n/
instrument n C ***	/ˈɪnstrʊmənt/
invade v *	/ɪnˈveɪd/
invasion n C **	/ɪnˈveɪʒ(ə)n/
irrelevant adj **	/ɪˈreləvənt/
karaoke n U	/ˌkæriˈəʊki/
kid n C ***	/kɪd/
landlord n C **	/ˈlæn(d)ˌlɔː(r)d/
liar n C	/ˈlaɪə(r)/
lie v/n C ***	/laɪ/
lifestyle n C **	/ˈlaɪfˌstaɪl/
likeable adj	/ˈlaɪkəb(ə)l/
lip n C ***	/lɪp/
live off (sth/sb) v	/ˌlɪv ˈɒf/
look up to v	/ˌlʊk ˈʌp tu/
marital adj	/ˈmærɪt(ə)l/
modest adj **	/ˈmɒdɪst/
multiculturalism n U	/ˌmʌltiˈkʌltʃərəˌlɪz(ə)m/
mum n C **	/mʌm/
noodle n C	/ˈnuːd(ə)l/
old-age pensioner n C	/ˌəʊld eɪdʒ ˈpenʃ(ə)nə(r)/
palm n C **	/pɑːm/
parliament n C ***	/ˈpɑː(r)ləmənt/
patiently adv	/ˈpeɪʃ(ə)ntli/
patriotism n U	/ˈpætriəˌtɪz(ə)m; ˈpeɪtriəˌtɪz(ə)m/
phase n C ***	/feɪz/
pigeon n C *	/ˈpɪdʒ(ə)n/
political adj ***	/pəˈlɪtɪk(ə)l/
politician n C ***	/ˌpɒləˈtɪʃ(ə)n/
pretend v **	/prɪˈtend/
racism n U *	/ˈreɪˌsɪz(ə)m/
rare adj ***	/reə(r)/
reality TV n U	/riːˌæləti tiː ˈviː/
reaction n C ***	/riˈækʃ(ə)n/
rebellious adj	/rɪˈbeljəs/
refugee n C **	/ˌrefjʊˈdʒiː/
reviewer n C	/rɪˈvjuːə(r)/
rhythm n C **	/ˈrɪðəm/
right-wing adj *	/ˌraɪtˈwɪŋ/
salary n C **	/ˈsæləri/
series n C ***	/ˈsɪəriːz/
sincere adj *	/sɪnˈsɪə(r)/
single parent n C	/ˌsɪŋg(ə)l ˈpeərənt/
socialist adj/n C	/ˈsəʊʃəlɪst/
spot v **	/spɒt/
stage n C ***	/steɪdʒ/
stand for v	/ˈstænd ˌfɔː/
status n U ***	/ˈsteɪtəs/
stubborn adj *	/ˈstʌbə(r)n/
sweaty adj	/ˈsweti/
stumble v *	/ˈstʌmb(ə)l/
talent n C/U **	/ˈtælənt/
telltale adj	/ˈtelˌteɪl/
tension n U ***	/ˈtenʃ(ə)n/
till n C	/tɪl/
traditionally adv	/trəˈdɪʃ(ə)nəli/
typical adj ***	/ˈtɪpɪk(ə)l/
unfair adj **	/ʌnˈfeə(r)/
volunteer n C/v **	/ˌvɒlənˈtɪə(r)/

Abbreviations

n	noun	sth	something
v	verb	C	countable
adj	adjective	U	uncountable
adv	adverb	pl	plural
prep	preposition	s	singular
sb	somebody		

*** the most common and basic words
** very common words
* fairly common words

2A Around the world

Speaking

1 Work in pairs. Discuss these questions.

- What do you like and dislike about travelling?
- Who is the most widely-travelled person that you know? Where has he/she been? Why did he/she go there?
- According to an English saying, *travel broadens the mind*. Do you agree? In what ways has travel broadened your mind?

Reading

1 Work in pairs. You are going to read an article about a long journey. Look at the photos and headline. Think of two possible answers for each of the questions.

1 Why did the lawyer decide to cycle around South America?
2 Why is he dressed as a clown in the second photo?

Now read the article and find out if you were right.

2 Read the article again. What do the numbers in the box refer to?

| 100,000 | more than 60 | three |
| 30,000 | ten | more than five | 60 |

3 Match the highlighted phrasal verbs in the article to the words and phrases 1–6.

1 meets by chance
2 left
3 managing to survive
4 stayed
5 combining
6 started (a journey)

4 Work in pairs. Discuss these questions.

- Would you consider giving up your job or studies to do something like Alvaro did? Why or why not?
- Have you ever wanted to go on a long trip like Alvaro's? Where would you like to go?

LAWYER GIVES UP JOB TO CYCLE AROUND THE WORLD

More than ten years ago, a Spanish lawyer gave up a good job and left a comfortable life to cycle around the world. Ten years and almost 100,000 kilometres later, he's still very happy with his decision, 'You only live once and life in an office just isn't a life,' he says.

He began his journey in South America. The first country he visited was Bolivia. Since he first set out on his adventure he has visited more than 60 countries. The journey has already taken him to three continents and most of Asia still lies ahead. He is currently cycling through Mongolia and Japan is the next country on his route.

He spends two or three months in each country, but he has never stopped off for more than five days in any one place. Alvaro is getting by on a budget of three dollars a day, and has slept in fire stations, police stations and churches, in the mountains of Nepal and the dry Atacama desert of Chile.

He has given 60 performances to more than 30,000 people. 'My show includes juggling, music, magic, acrobatics and theatre. I perform to the poorest people and my sole purpose is to bring them a little happiness,' says Alvaro.

He explains that the trip is a way of bringing together the three things he loves most in life: 'Cycling's in my blood, I'm a born clown and I enjoy helping other people'. He is sponsored by his fans and his mission is to bring a smile into the lives of the people he runs into on his travels.

Around the world | 2A

GRAMMAR: present perfect & past simple

1 Look at the first three paragraphs of the article on page 14 again. Underline all the examples of the present perfect and past simple. Then answer the questions.

1 Which verb form do you use when the time is known?
2 Which verb form do you use when the time is not stated?

2 Choose the correct verb forms to complete the newspaper article.

From our Dublin Correspondent

The well-known writer and comedian, Tony Hawks, (1) *has accepted / accepted* a bet to hitchhike around Ireland with a fridge. He (2) *has begun / began* his journey in Dublin last week. He (3) *has almost given up / almost gave up* on the first day when his first lift (4) *has taken / took* him only three miles. But since then he (5) *has had / had* better luck. He (6) *has had / had* lifts in vans, cars and trucks, and yesterday he and his fridge (7) *has taken / took* a fishing boat to Tory Island. So if you're driving around in the Sligo area and see a man hitchhiking with a fridge – stop and give him a lift!

Use the past simple ...
* with questions that ask about the time of an event.
  *When **did** you last **catch** a taxi?*
* to talk about past actions when you know when the event happened.
  *He **caught** a taxi to the airport yesterday to meet a friend.*
* with certain time expressions, eg *yesterday, last week, one night, the last time, when.*

Use the present perfect ...
* to talk about past actions when the time is not stated. The event happened in the past, but the time is not important.
  ***Have** you ever **travelled** alone?*
  *I've **travelled** alone on business, but I've never **been** on holiday on my own.*
* with certain time expressions, eg *ever, never, already, yet, since, just.*
  *I've **just** come back from Dublin.*

> SEE LANGUAGE REFERENCE PAGE 22

3 Complete the questions. Put the verbs in brackets into the present perfect or the past simple.

1 How many countries _____ you _____ (visit)?
2 What's the most interesting place you _____ (be) to?
3 How many times _____ you _____ (go) away last year?
4 Where _____ you _____ (go) for your last holiday?
5 What's the furthest you _____ ever _____ (fly)?
6 When _____ you _____ (fly) for the first time?
7 What's the strangest form of transport you _____ ever _____ (use)?
8 _____ you ever _____ (travel) on your own?

4 Work in pairs. Ask and answer the questions in exercise 3.

15

2B | Unusual journeys

LISTENING & READING

1 🔊 **1.06–1.08** Listen to three stories about unusual journeys. Match each journey to two of the photos A–F.

A

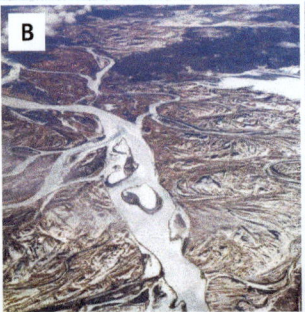
B

C

D

E

F

2 🔊 **1.06–1.08** Listen again and answer the questions.

Journey 1
1 Where did he finish his journey?
2 Who rescued him in the Alps? Why?

Journey 2
3 How long did their journey last?
4 What were they looking for?

Journey 3
5 How many people took part in the trip?
6 How long did it take the winners to complete the trip?

3 Read these texts about the three journeys. Find two mistakes in each text and correct them.

4 🔊 **1.06–1.08** Listen again to check your answers.

5 Which journey sounds the most interesting or enjoyable? Why?

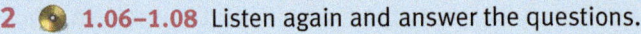

1 YOUR NEWS!
Swedish student wins web competition
21-year-old Tommy Kallstrom has won this month's Web Travel Site of the Month competition. His winning website contains details of his four-month trip through fifteen European countries on a Vespa that he used to deliver pizzas in his home town of Uppsala.

2 HUNTING THE TIGER • CHANNEL 6, 9PM
Tonight's documentary in the *Wildlife on 6* series takes a fascinating look at the animals of Siberia. Award-winning filmmakers, Chiara and Luca Colucci, spent six months in the far east of Russia looking for the rare Siberian tiger. There are only about 300 of these beautiful animals in the wild. With the help of a baby fox cub they found early on the trip, the Coluccis explore the beautiful River Amur region in their search for the tiger. An unforgettable journey and an unforgettable film.

3 University teachers hitchhike for charity
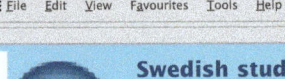
A group of teachers have hitchhiked the length of Britain to raise money for the charity, Oxfam International. The teachers had to get from Land's End to John O'Groats in less than two days. Only four of the teachers completed the trip in time.

16

VOCABULARY: phrasal verbs

Phrasal verbs have two parts: a verb and a particle, eg *get by, set out, stop off*.

Separable phrasal verbs
With some phrasal verbs, the object can come either before or after the particle.
   *He **sorted out** the problem.*
   *He **sorted** the problem **out**.*

If the object is a pronoun, eg *him, her, it*, the object always comes before the particle.
   *He **sorted** it **out**. Not He sorted out it.*

Inseparable phrasal verbs
With some phrasal verbs, the verb and the particle always come together, so the object always comes after the particle.
   *They **looked after** the bear cub.*
   *They **looked after** it.*

> SEE LANGUAGE REFERENCE PAGE 22

1 Match the phrasal verbs in bold in 1–6 to the definitions a–f.

1 He was able to **sort** the problem **out**.
2 They **came across** the bear near a river.
3 Tizio **got over** his injury.
4 Their friends and families **saw** them **off**.
5 A van **picked** her **up** after only five minutes.
6 The van **dropped** her **off** near the finishing line.

a felt well or happy again after something bad
b found an answer to a problem
c took someone or something in a car
d let someone get out of your car
e met or found by chance
f said goodbye to someone who was going on a journey

2 Which two phrasal verbs in exercise 1 are inseparable?

3 Put *it* in the correct place in the sentences.

1 I sorted *it* out before I left work.

1 I sorted out before I left work.
2 I'm sure you'll get over soon.
3 I've never come across before.
4 I've tried to give up many times.
5 Why don't you pick up on your way home?

4 Now think of a noun to replace *it* in each sentence.

1 I sorted the problem out before I left work.

5 Work in pairs. You are going to ask and answer questions using the phrasal verbs in exercise 1.

   A: Turn to page 64.   B: Turn to page 66.

PRONUNCIATION: word linking

1 🔘 1.09 We often join two words when an initial vowel sound follows a final consonant sound. Look at these examples from the listening exercise, then listen and repeat.

1 arrived‿in‿Athens
2 gave‿it‿all‿up
3 film‿of‿another‿incredible
4 still‿exist‿in
5 it's‿Alex‿and‿Isabelle
6 part‿of‿a‿group

2 Practise saying the phrases in exercise 1 quickly.

3 🔘 1.10 Listen and write the four phrases.

4 Practise saying the phrases. Remember to link the words.

SPEAKING

1 Think of a film or book you have seen or read recently that described a long journey. Prepare to tell a partner about it. Use the questions below to help you.

• Where was the film/book set?
• Who was going on the journey and why?
• What were the main events?
• Would you like to go on the same journey? Why or why not?
• Would you recommend the film/book to your partner? Why or why not?

2 Work in pairs. Tell your partner about the film/book.

2c | Down under

Speaking

1 Work in groups. Look at the photos on the blog below and share all that you know about Australia. Use the ideas in the box to help you.

> sports, film and music personalities
> climate   history   cities   things to do
> animals   well-known sights and landmarks

2 Now prepare a short quiz about Australia. Use your questions to test students from another group.

3 Work in pairs. Turn to page 65 and read about Uluru (Ayer's rock), one of the most famous landmarks in Australia. Discuss these questions.

1 Where is it?
2 What does it represent for the local people?

Reading

1 Read the first part of a blog about a trip around Australia and answer the questions.

1 Who is the author? What does she do?
2 What is she going to do?
3 What is the purpose of her blog?

2 Share your ideas with the class.

3 Find the adjectives in the blog that Nerina uses to describe these things.

1 the people that she has met   *incredible*
2 her experiences during the trip
3 the Rock at the start of the day
4 the Anangu caves and sacred art
5 the way that the Rock changes colour

Nerina Klein's travel blog

During my 35 years as a travel writer, I've visited more countries than I can count. I've backpacked
5 through Asia, cycled through Europe, driven across Africa, but I've never explored my own home, Australia. So the time has come to put
10 this right. Over the next six weeks, I'm planning to cover as much of the outback as I possibly can in a second-hand four-wheel drive, and I'll
15 be accompanied by my two grandchildren. They, unlike me, want to get to know their own country before they start exploring the rest of the
20 world. What follows is a diary of our travels and adventures. I hope it inspires people to leave the coast and find out what the real Australia is all
25 about.

Day 33 We camped out last night near the best place to watch the sunrise. After a few drinks and an hour or two of looking at the stars, we turned in and got some sleep before the climax of our six week trip: our first glimpse of Uluru (Ayer's Rock).
30 In the last five and a half weeks we've seen and done some amazing things. We've been blinded by the salt lakes of Curara Soak, we've relived history in the goldfields of Kalgoorlie-Boulder, we've been guests at the campfires of Aboriginal communities. But nothing compares to the spectacular sight of the famous Uluru, shining purple in the light of dawn. Over the years I've heard
35 plenty of people talk about the wonderful changing colours of the Rock, but until you see it yourself, it's impossible to imagine. We were absolutely spellbound.

We spent a good part of the day walking the 9.4 kilometres around the base of the Rock. It's well worth it. The caves and rock art are fascinating. If you get a
40 chance to join one of the tours given by the Anangu guides, do it. They explain everything about Uluru and all its sacred sites.

At sunset, we settled down to watch the Rock turn red against the darkening sky and planned the last leg of our trip – 450 kilometres across the desert to the modern town of Alice Springs. We talked about all the
45 incredible friends we've made during our trip and about the things we're going to miss once we leave the bush behind.

Glossary
turned in *v* went to bed
glimpse *n* quick sight
spellbound *adj* really fascinated

18

GRAMMAR: present perfect for unfinished time

1 Look at the highlighted phrases in the blog. Choose the correct phrases to complete the notes.

- They are all expressions that refer to a (1) *specific time in the past / period of time that hasn't finished*.
- The verb form that we use with them is the (2) *present perfect / past simple*.

2 Mark the phrases finished time (F) or unfinished time (U).

in the last few days	last month
last year	up till now
two days ago	during the last two weeks
over the past year	yesterday

3 Complete the text. Put the verbs in brackets into the present perfect or the past simple.

We (1) _____ (arrive) in Alice Springs yesterday. It's the biggest town we (2) _____ (see) over the last two months. Up till now, we (3) _____ (camp) under the stars. Last night, we (4) _____ (sleep) in a four-star hotel. We (5) _____ (have) a hot bath before we went to bed. We (6) _____ (not / watch) TV in the last six weeks.

4 Use the time expressions in exercise 2 and these verbs to make five sentences that are true for you.

| do | eat | go to | have | make | see |

I haven't been to a café in the last few days.

5 Make questions from your sentences in exercise 4. Then work in pairs. Ask and answer the questions.

Have you been to a café in the last few days?
No, I haven't. Have you …?

Use the past simple to talk about actions in the past that happened at a finished time.
> We **camped** out last night.
> At sunset, we **settled** down to watch the Rock turn red.

Use the present perfect to talk about actions in the past that happened in a period of time which is unfinished.
> During my 35 years as a travel writer, I**'ve visited** more countries than I can count.
> (= She is still a travel writer now.)
> In the last five and a half weeks we**'ve seen** and **done** some amazing things.
> (= The last five and a half weeks includes now.)

Here are some common expressions to describe unfinished time:

during		
in	the last	few months/two years, etc.
over		

▶ SEE LANGUAGE REFERENCE PAGE 22

SPEAKING

1 Work in pairs. You are going to plan a journey across your own country. Discuss these topics and prepare your route.

- from where to where?
- transport: motorbike/car/train/bicycle?
- how long?
- how many stops?
- places to stay?
- things to see/do?

2 Describe your route to the class. Who has the most interesting route?

Useful language

Our route begins in …
We travel by …
Our first stop is in …
In … we visit the …

2D | Getting around

Speaking & vocabulary: verb collocations (travel)

1 Work in pairs. Think about transport in your town/city and discuss these questions.
- What's the quickest way of travelling around your town/city?
- What's the most popular form of transport for people going to work?
- What's the best way for a tourist to travel around your town/city to see the sights?

2 Choose the correct verbs to complete the information from a tourist guide about Edinburgh.

Welcome to Edinburgh

Getting there ...

By air
From the airport, you can (1) *catch / get out of* the Airlink 100 bus, which (2) *runs / takes* 25 minutes to the city centre. Alternatively, you can (3) *miss / take* a taxi. The advantage of this is that the taxi driver can (4) *drop / arrive* you off wherever you like, but of course it is more expensive than public transport.

By rail
If you (5) *arrive / catch* by train, (6) *drop / get off* at Waverley Station, which is right in the city centre. From there, you can (7) *walk / get on* to most of the major sights.

Getting around
A good way to get to know the city is with a city bus tour. You can buy special tickets for the double-decker buses which allow you to (8) *get in / get on* and off when and where you want. In the evenings, the buses (9) *run / take* late, but if you (10) *get out of / miss* the last one, you can always take a taxi.

3 Work in pairs. Change the information in exercise 2 so that it is true for a city you both know well.

From the airport you can take the metro into the city centre. It takes 40 minutes.

Listening

1 Look at the photos. Where are the people? What are they doing?

2 🔊 1.11–1.13 Listen and match the dialogues 1–3 to the photos A–C.

3 🔊 1.11–1.13 Listen again. Decide if the sentences are true (T) or false (F). Correct the false sentences.

Dialogue 1
1 The passenger doesn't have the right money.
2 She doesn't know where to get off.

Dialogue 2
3 The man is taking a taxi because his car has broken down.
4 He is going to take the taxi alone.

Dialogue 3
5 The woman's train has already left.
6 The woman will have to get a taxi.

20

Getting around | 2D

FUNCTIONAL LANGUAGE: travelling

1 Match the phrases 1–8 to the photos A–C in Listening exercise 1.

1 Can I get a *taxi* anywhere *round here*?
2 Can you tell me the time of the next *train* to *North Park*?
3 Has the *11.40* for *North Park* left yet?
4 Could you tell me when we get to the *bridge*, please?
5 Does this *bus* go to the *town centre*?
6 Have you got change for a *ten-pound note*?
7 I'd like a cab for the *Pizzeria Roma*, please.
8 A *single* to the *town centre*, please.

2 Match the responses a–h to the phrases 1–8 in exercise 1.

a That'll be one twenty, please.
b Certainly, sir. We'll send one right away.
c Yeah, we go there.
d No, sorry love. Exact change only.
e I'll let you know.
f Not if you hurry, it's still at the platform.
g Yes, madam. There's a taxi rank at the front of the station.
h The next one's at 2.35, madam.

3 Replace the words in italics in exercise 1 with alternative words and phrases.

1 Can I get a *bus* anywhere *near the airport*?

4 Work in pairs. Prepare then practise short dialogues for the following situations.

- You're in a city centre. Ask a passerby for the nearest taxi rank.
- You are at home. Phone for a cab to take you to the station tomorrow morning.
- You are a stranger in the town. You are getting on a bus. Ask the driver for tickets to the town centre. You are going to the theatre. You don't know where to get off.
- You are getting off the bus. Ask the driver when the last bus leaves to get home.
- You are on a train. Ask if you can sit in an empty seat.

DID YOU KNOW?

1 Work in pairs. Read about taxis in New York and London and discuss the questions.

- There are over 12,000 yellow cabs in New York City.
- There are 21,000 black cabs in London.
- Yellow cabs are the only taxis that can pick up passengers on the streets of New York.
- Black cabs are the only taxis that can pick up passengers on the streets of London.
- You have to pass an English language test to become a yellow cab driver.
- You have to pass a test called 'The Knowledge' to become a black cab driver. It usually takes four years to pass the test.
- Robert de Niro was nominated for an Oscar® for his role as a New York taxi driver.
- Not all black cabs are black!

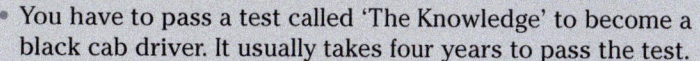

- Are taxis expensive in your town?
- Are they easy to find?
- Do they operate 24 hours a day?
- How often do you take a taxi?
- When was the last time you caught a taxi? Where were you going?
- Do you usually chat to the driver?

Self-assessment (✓)

☐ I can describe how to get around my town or city.
☐ I can ask for a taxi over the phone.
☐ I can ask for information about transport options.

2 | Language reference

GRAMMAR
Present perfect & past simple

When we talk about past actions, we can sometimes choose between the past simple and the present perfect.
We use the past simple …
- when we ask when the event happened (with *when*).
  *When **did** she **arrive** at Alice Springs?*
- when we say when the event happened (with time expressions like *yesterday, last week, one night*, that indicate a finished time).
  *She got there **two weeks ago**.*
  *He gave up his job **last year**.*

We use the present perfect …
- when the time is not stated. The event happened in the past, but the time is not important. We often use the present perfect to talk about general experience.
  ***Have** you ever **been** to Australia?*
  ***They've visited** many interesting places.*
- with time expressions that do not specify the exact time (eg *ever, never, already, yet, since, just, recently*).
  *He's **just** begun his journey.*
  *He's **already** visited six different countries.*
- when we talk about actions in the past that happened in a period of time which is unfinished.
  *She's made a lot of friends **in the last few weeks**.*
  (*in the last few weeks* includes present time)

Common expressions that refer to unfinished time are:

during	
in	the last few days/weeks/months/years
over	

Some time expressions can refer to both finished time and unfinished time.

*Have you done anything interesting **this morning**?*
(= It is still the morning.)
*Did you do anything interesting **this morning**?*
(= The morning is now finished.)

Other expressions that we can use with both tenses include *today, this week, this month*, etc.

Present perfect

affirmative	subject + *have/has* + past participle
negative	subject + *haven't/hasn't* + past participle
question	*have/has* + subject + past participle

Past simple

affirmative	Regular verbs: infinitive + *-ed* Irregular verbs: see list of irregular verbs on page 127
negative	Regular and irregular verbs: subject + *didn't* + infinitive
question	Regular and irregular verbs: *did* + subject + infinitive

Phrasal verbs

Phrasal verbs contain a verb and a particle (eg *get by, set out, stop off*). With some phrasal verbs, the particle is in two parts (eg *run out of, look forward to*). Phrasal verbs are either separable or inseparable.

With an inseparable phrasal verb, we cannot separate the verb and the particle.

*He finally **got over** his illness.*
Not *He finally got his illness over.*

With a separable phrasal verb, the object can come either before or after the particle.

*She **dropped off** her husband at the airport.*
*She **dropped** her husband **off** at the airport.*

If the object is a pronoun (eg *him, her, it*) the object always comes before the particle.

*Will you see **us** off?* Not *Will you see off us?*

FUNCTIONAL LANGUAGE
Travelling

Can I get a bus anywhere near/round here?
Could you tell me the time of the next train?
Could you tell us when we get to the station, please?
Does this bus go to the airport?
Has the 11.40 for North Park left yet?
Have you got change for a ten-pound note?
I'd like a cab for the Pizzeria Roma, please.
One single/A return to the town centre, please.

Language reference 2

Word list

Phrasal verbs

bring together	/ˌbrɪŋ təˈgeðə(r)/
break down	/ˌbreɪk ˈdaʊn/
come across	/ˌkʌm əˈkrɒs/
drop (sb) off	/ˌdrɒp ˈɒf/
get by	/ˌget ˈbaɪ/
get over (sth)	/ˌget ˈəʊvə(r)/
give (sth) up	/ˌgɪv ˈʌp/
look after (sb)	/ˌlʊk ˈɑːftə(r)/
pick (sb) up	/ˌpɪk ˈʌp/
pull out	/ˌpʊl ˈaʊt/
run into (sb)	/ˌrʌn ˈɪntuː/
see (sb) off	/ˌsiː ˈɒf/
set out	/ˌset ˈaʊt/
settle down	/ˌset(ə)l ˈdaʊn/
sort out	/ˌsɔː(r)t ˈaʊt/
stand up for (sth)	/stænd ˈʌp fɔː(r)/
stop off	/ˌstɒp ˈɒf/
turn in	/ˌtɜː(r)n ˈɪn/

Travel

catch a bus/plane/train	/ˌkætʃ ə ˈbʌs/ˈpleɪn/ˈtreɪn/
get in a bus/car/taxi	/ˌget ˌɪn ə ˈbʌs/ˈkɑː(r)/ˈtæksi/
get out of a bus/car/taxi	/ˌget ˌaʊt əv ə ˈbʌs/ˈkɑː(r)/ˈtæksi/
get off a bus/plane/train	/ˌget ˌɒf ə ˈbʌs/ˈpleɪn/ˈtreɪn/
get on a bus/plane/train	/ˌget ˌɒn ə ˈbʌs/ˈpleɪn/ˈtreɪn/
miss a bus/plane/train	/ˌmɪs ə ˈbʌs/ˈpleɪn/ˈtreɪn/
take a bus/taxi/train	/ˌteɪk ə ˈbʌs/ˈtæksi/ˈtreɪn/
take (time) to + infinitive	/ˈteɪk (taɪm) ˌtuː/

Other words & phrases

acrobatics n pl	/ˌækrəˈbætɪks/
act n C ***	/ækt/
adventure n C **	/ədˈventʃə(r)/
alternatively adv **	/ɔːlˈtɜː(r)nətɪvli/
amazing adj *	/əˈmeɪzɪŋ/
apparently adv ***	/əˈpærəntli/
award n C/v ***	/əˈwɔː(r)d/
backpack n C	/ˈbækˌpæk/
bear n C **	/beə(r)/
bet n C/v **	/bet/
blind adj/v **	/blaɪnd/
blood n U ***	/blʌd/
broaden v *	/ˈbrɔːd(ə)n/
budget n C ***	/ˈbʌdʒɪt/
bush n U **	/bʊʃ/
cab n C	/kæb/
campfire n C	/ˈkæmpˌfaɪə(r)/
cave n C **	/keɪv/
celebrate v ***	/ˈseləˌbreɪt/
charity n C/U ***	/ˈtʃærəti/
climate n C **	/ˈklaɪmət/
climax n C *	/ˈklaɪmæks/
clown n C	/klaʊn/
coast n C ***	/kəʊst/
comedian n C	/kəˈmiːdiən/
comfortable adj ***	/ˈkʌmftəb(ə)l/
competition n C ***	/ˌkɒmpəˈtɪʃ(ə)n/
continent n C **	/ˈkɒntɪnənt/
cub n C	/kʌb/
currently adv ***	/ˈkʌrəntli/
darken v	/ˈdɑː(r)kən/
dawn n C **	/dɔːn/
declare v ***	/dɪˈkleə(r)/
desert n C **	/ˈdezə(r)t/
double-decker adj/n C	/ˌdʌb(ə)l ˈdekə(r)/
eventually adv ***	/ɪˈventʃuəli/
exist v ***	/ɪgˈzɪst/
explore v ***	/ɪkˈsplɔː(r)/
extraordinarily adv *	/ɪkˈstrɔː(r)d(ə)nərəli/
fascinating adj **	/ˈfæsɪneɪtɪŋ/
fire station n C	/ˈfaɪə(r) ˌsteɪʃ(ə)n/
formation n C ***	/fɔː(r)ˈmeɪʃ(ə)n/
four-wheel drive n C	/ˌfɔː(r)wiːl ˈdraɪv/
fox n C **	/fɒks/
fridge n C *	/frɪdʒ/
glimpse v/n C *	/glɪmps/
goldfield n C	/ˈgəʊldˌfiːld/
headline n C **	/ˈhedˌlaɪn/
helicopter n C **	/ˈhelɪˌkɒptə(r)/
heritage n U **	/ˈherɪtɪdʒ/
hire v **	/ˈhaɪə(r)/
hitchhike v	/ˈhɪtʃˌhaɪk/
home town n C	/ˌhəʊmˈtaʊn/
in the wild adv	/ˌɪn ðə ˈwaɪld/
incredible adj *	/ɪnˈkredəb(ə)l/
injure v **	/ˈɪndʒə(r)/
injury n C/U ***	/ˈɪndʒəri/
inspire v **	/ɪnˈspaɪə(r)/
juggling n U	/ˈdʒʌg(ə)lɪŋ/
landmark n C	/ˈlæn(d)ˌmɑː(r)k/
lawyer n C ***	/ˈlɔːjə(r)/
length n C ***	/leŋθ/
lie ahead v	/ˌlaɪ əˈhed/
lift n C **	/lɪft/
local adj ***	/ˈləʊk(ə)l/
magic n U **	/ˈmædʒɪk/
mechanical adj **	/mɪˈkænɪk(ə)l/
mission n C **	/ˈmɪʃ(ə)n/
outback n U	/ˈaʊtˌbæk/
passerby n C	/ˌpɑːsə(r)ˈbaɪ/
perform v ***	/pə(r)ˈfɔː(r)m/
platform n C **	/ˈplætˌfɔː(r)m/
post v **	/pəʊst/
principality n C	/ˌprɪnsəˈpæləti/
purple adj *	/ˈpɜː(r)p(ə)l/
purpose n C ***	/ˈpɜː(r)pəs/
put (sth) right v	/ˌpʊt ˈraɪt/
raise v ***	/reɪz/
represent v ***	/ˌreprɪˈzent/
rescue v **	/ˈreskjuː/
rock n U/C ***	/rɒk/
sacred adj **	/ˈseɪkrɪd/
salt n U **	/sɔːlt/
search n C/v ***	/sɜː(r)tʃ/
second-hand adj *	/ˌsekəndˈhænd/
sight n C/U ***	/saɪt/
site n C **	/saɪt/
sole adj **	/səʊl/
solo adj / adv *	/ˈsəʊləʊ/
spectacular adj **	/spekˈtækjʊlə(r)/
spellbound adj	/ˈspelˌbaʊnd/
sponsor v **	/ˈspɒnsə(r)/
storm n C **	/stɔː(r)m/
stranger n C **	/ˈstreɪndʒə(r)/
taxi rank n C	/ˈtæksi ˌræŋk/
tiger n C *	/ˈtaɪgə(r)/
time limit n C	/ˈtaɪm ˌlɪmɪt/
tractor n C	/ˈtræktə(r)/
truck n C **	/trʌk/
unforgettable adj	/ˌʌnfə(r)ˈgetəb(ə)l/
van n C **	/væn/
widely-travelled adj	/ˌwaɪdli ˈtræv(ə)ld/
wildlife n U	/ˈwaɪldˌlaɪf/

23

3A Dream homes

Speaking

1 Do any of these phrases describe where you live?

- It's really convenient for the shops.
- It gets quite noisy at night.
- It can be a bit dull at times.
- The neighbours are really friendly.
- It's a bit small and we need more space.
- It's quite a long way from where I work/study.
- There's loads of space and plenty of light.

2 Work in pairs. Compare your answers in exercise 1 and discuss these questions.

- What are the advantages and disadvantages of living where you live?
- Would you like to live somewhere completely different? If yes, where?

Reading

1 Read the magazine article on page 25. Which section of the magazine does it come from?

a Advice for home buyers
b Alternative lifestyles
c Home improvements

2 Read the article again and tick the information that is mentioned.

1 Paradise Ridge opened over 20 years ago.
2 A lot of people want to live there.
3 It is very near a primary school and community college.
4 You are not allowed to drive your car in the cabin park.
5 Most of the residents work in Vancouver.
6 Everybody helps with the work of the community.
7 Meetings of the residents take place every month.
8 They grow vegetables in a community garden.

3 Work in pairs. List three advantages of living in Paradise Ridge. Then think of three possible disadvantages.

4 🔊 1.14–1.18 Listen to five residents of Paradise Ridge. Do they mention any of the disadvantages you listed in exercise 3?

5 🔊 1.14–1.18 Listen again and say who mentioned which topics. Match the residents 1–5 to the topics a–e.

a kids   c meetings   e isolation
b food   d shared work

6 Would you like to live in Paradise Ridge? Why or why not?

Grammar: modals of obligation, permission & prohibition (present time)

1 Complete the rules with words and phrases 1–4.

> To talk about permission, you use …
> To talk about prohibition, you use …
> To talk about obligation, you use …
> To talk about a lack of obligation, you use …
>
> 1 *don't have to* and *don't need to*.
> 2 *must* and *have to*.
> 3 *can* and *be allowed to*.
> 4 *mustn't*, *can't* and *not be allowed to*.

▶ See Language Reference page 32

2 Find one example in the article about Paradise Ridge for each of the rules in exercise 1.

3 Complete the house rules with words or phrases from exercise 1. Use your own ideas.

HOUSE RULES

1 You <u>don't have to</u> pay electricity and gas bills.
2 You _____ pay the rent on the first day of the month.
3 You _____ pay for phone calls.
4 You _____ smoke in the kitchen and lounge.
5 You _____ switch off the TV and CD player in the lounge at midnight.
6 You _____ have pets in the house.
7 You _____ do the housework.
8 You _____ have small parties on Saturday nights.
9 Visitors who stay the night _____ help with the housework.
10 Visitors _____ stay for more than three days.

Dream homes | 3A

4 Compare your rules with a partner. Whose rules are stricter?

5 Choose a place from the box and write four sentences about it using the words and phrases from exercise 1. Do not mention the name of the place.

church   hospital   library   museum
plane   prison   school   theatre

You aren't allowed to touch anything.
You don't have to go there, but it's usually interesting.
You often have to buy a ticket.
You have to leave your bag outside.

6 Work in pairs. Read your sentences to your partner. He/She must decide which place you are talking about.

7 Do you have to follow any rules where you live? Tell a partner about them.

We aren't allowed to put the rubbish out before 8pm.
We have to pay a monthly charge for the lift and the lights on the stairs.

Paradise Ridge

About 70 miles north-east of Vancouver is one of Canada's most beautiful tourist regions. Visitors come to enjoy fishing and water sports in the region's many lakes and rivers, to go skiing in
5 the winter or simply to enjoy the spectacular mountain scenery.

But while most people come for a short break, promising to return the following year, many people have decided to stay for good. One such visitor was a
10 Vancouver businesswoman, Kirsty Bourne, who first came to the region on a skiing trip.

Kirsty was looking for a place to live with her young family. 'Vancouver is fine for work,' she said, 'but, like all big cities, it's not a great place to live. I wanted
15 somewhere where everybody knows everybody else, where your neighbours are also your friends and all your problems are shared. Where parents don't have to worry about their kids when they're playing in the street and you don't need to lock your door at night.'

20 Just over twenty years ago, Kirsty founded Paradise Ridge, a cabin park in the heart of the Columbia Mountains, which is now home to 25 families. Each family owns their own small cabin, but they share ownership of the park and the common facilities. 'This
25 is a real, living community,' insists Kirsty, 'so residents aren't allowed to use their cabins as a holiday home. They can't come here just for their vacations.'

The heart of the Paradise Ridge community is a large wooden house that stands at the centre of the
30 25 cabins. Shared meals take place there three times a week and once a month there is a meeting when important decisions are made. 'Residents mustn't miss these meetings,' explains Kirsty, 'because it's important that we all share in the decision-making.' The most
35 important decisions usually concern new residents. Families can sell their homes if they want to leave, but the whole community must vote on new families before they are allowed to join.

'Keeping the community together is hard work,' says
40 Kirsty. 'Everybody has to lend a helping hand and take responsibility for the day-to-day running of the community. That includes doing repairs, looking after the kids, cooking the communal meals or leading one of the monthly meetings.' But it seems that there is no
45 shortage of families who want to join. There are more than 70 on the waiting list.

Glossary
for good *adv* permanently
lend a helping hand *v* share the work
running *n* management

25

3B Unusual homes

VOCABULARY: accommodation

1 Look at the photos. Which countries do you think these are? Why? What does your town look like from the air?

2 Complete the sentences in column A with a phrase from column B.

A	B
1 Most people in Britain own their homes, but about 30% live	a a house or a **flat** with their friends.
2 Accommodation in British town centres is usually	b in France.
3 It is quite common for young people to share	c in detached or **semi-detached** houses with gardens.
4 British families often prefer to live in the **suburbs**	d in **rented accommodation**.
5 About half a million British people own **holiday homes**	e in **apartment blocks** or rows of old **terraced** houses.

3 Match the words in bold in exercise 2 to the definitions 1–7.

1 two houses joined together
2 houses that are joined together in a line
3 homes that you live in for only part of the year
4 a home that is usually on one floor of a larger building
5 buildings that contain a number of separate flats
6 lived in by someone who pays money to the owner
7 parts of a town that are away from the town centre

4 Change the sentences in exercise 2 so that they are true for your country.

LISTENING

1 Work in pairs. Match the words in the box to the photos A–F. Would you like to live in any of them? Why or why not?

cave   houseboat   lighthouse
mobile home   tree house   windmill

A

B

C

D

E

F

26

2 🔊 **1.19–1.21** Listen to three people talking about their unusual homes. Where do they live? Choose your answers from the box in exercise 1.

3 🔊 **1.19–1.21** Listen again and make a note of the best and the worst things about where they live.

4 Match the sentences 1–8 to the three unusual homes in exercise 2. Then check your answers in audioscripts 1.19–1.21 on page 69.

1 We make dog owners leave their pets in the garden.
2 The local authorities make us move on.
3 We don't let little kids come up on their own.
4 They let us keep pets.
5 The farmers are happy to let us stay on their land.
6 The local people don't let us stay.
7 They don't allow us to have visitors.
8 We don't allow smoking.

GRAMMAR: *make, let & allow*

We can use the verbs *make, let* and *allow* to talk about obligation and permission.

Obligation   *make* + object + infinitive without *to*
Our teacher **makes us do** a lot of homework.
(= We must do a lot of homework.)

Permission   *let* + object + infinitive without *to*
The farmer **lets us stay** on his land.
(= We can stay on his land.)

allow + object + *to* + infinitive
They usually **allow us to stay** overnight.
(= We can usually stay overnight.)

allow + noun/verb + *-ing*
They **don't allow smoking** in the living room.
(= You can't smoke in the living room.)

> SEE LANGUAGE REFERENCE PAGE 32

1 Choose the correct verb to complete the sentences.

1 They *let / allow* us to put up our tent wherever we want.
2 They *make / allow* us park our cars in the car park.
3 They *let / allow* us use the washing machine in their kitchen.
4 They *make / let* us come and go when we want.
5 They *make / let* us pay £3 a night.

2 What is being described in exercise 1?

a) a hotel   b) a campsite   c) a holiday flat

3 Use the prompts to make sentences which are true for you.

| My | teacher
parents
boss
wife
husband
boyfriend
girlfriend | (doesn't)
(don't) | make(s)
let(s)
allow(s) | me
us | (to)
… |

My boss makes us work late on Fridays.
My girlfriend doesn't let me smoke in her car.

SPEAKING

1 Work in pairs. Discuss these questions.

- Is it common for people to have holiday homes in your country?
- Where are the most popular places to buy a holiday home? Why?
- Do people from abroad buy holiday homes in your country? Which countries do they usually come from?

2 Work in pairs. You are going to design a luxury holiday home. Discuss these questions.

- Where exactly is your holiday home?
- Is it a flat or a house?
- Is it old or new?
- How big is it?
- What facilities has it got? (eg garden, swimming pool, private beach …)

3 Talk to other pairs of students. Describe your holiday home and try to persuade them to book a holiday there.

Useful language

I think you'll really like it because …
It's just the thing you're looking for.
It's great for (families/couples/singles).
It's in the most fantastic spot …

3c Bedrooms

SPEAKING & VOCABULARY: verb collocations (sleep)

1 Complete the sentences with a verb from the box.

| fall | feel | go | have | make |
| remember | set | wake | | |

1 I often find it difficult to _____ up in the morning.
2 I always _____ the bed first thing in the morning.
3 I sometimes _____ a nap after lunch.
4 I sometimes _____ asleep in front of the TV.
5 I often _____ sleepy in the middle of the day.
6 I never _____ to sleep before ten o'clock.
7 I sometimes forget to _____ my alarm clock.
8 I can never _____ my dreams.

2 Change the sentences in exercise 1 so that they are true for you. Compare your sentences with a partner.

3 Work in pairs. Discuss these questions.

- Do you find it easy to get to sleep?
- What do you do when you can't get to sleep?
- Are you a heavy or a light sleeper?
- Do you usually remember your dreams the next morning?
- Can you remember a recent dream?

READING

1 Look at the photos on page 29. What do you know about the people?

2 Read the articles 1–6 and match them to the headings a–f.

a A week in bed   d Rules for healthy bedrooms
b Going nowhere   e Sleeping with strangers
c Sleeping on the moon   f A king's office

3 Read the articles again and match the phrases a–f to the end of each article.

a and it was never full!
b so he stayed where he was.
c because the green contained arsenic, a poisonous chemical.
d and they all suffered the physical effects of lack of sleep.
e where they recorded 'Give Peace a Chance'.
f with one hundred people in the room.

4 Find words in the article which match the definitions.

1 a decision by a court of law that someone is guilty of a crime
2 a man who looks after another man's clothes
3 a person who has to leave their country because it is dangerous for them to stay
4 a small hotel
5 a strong complaint or disagreement
6 a substance that gives a strong smell when it is burned
7 a bed made of rope or material that hangs between two posts or trees
8 an adjective used to describe things associated with the moon

GRAMMAR: modals of obligation, permission & prohibition (past time)

1 Read the sentences from the articles below. Then put the headings in the box in gaps 1–4.

| obligation | permission | prohibition | no obligation |

1 _____
Important friends **were allowed to** come into his room.

2 _____
You **had to** keep cooking smells away from bedrooms.

3 _____
Poorer travellers **didn't need to** get out of bed.
Louis XIV **didn't have to** worry about getting up in the morning.

4 _____
You **couldn't** put green wallpaper in bedrooms.
Mehran **wasn't allowed to** go through passport control.

> SEE LANGUAGE REFERENCE PAGE 32

2 Complete the text with modals from the grammar box.

A law of 1834 in Britain said that people (1) *couldn't* give money to the poor, unless they were old or ill. The government's solution to the problem of poverty was the building of workhouses around the country. Living conditions in the workhouses were very hard and you (2) _____ leave the building without special permission. Children under seven (3) _____ work, but everyone else (4) _____ do twelve hours a day. You (5) _____ have your own possessions and everyone (6) _____ wear a special uniform. You (7) _____ wash or shave only once a week. Husbands and wives (8) _____ speak to each other and they (9) _____ sleep in separate dormitories. The poor (10) _____ live in these workhouses, but, for many, there was not much choice.

Six things you probably didn't know about beds and bedrooms

1 In 19th century Britain, the Ladies' Sanitary Association published a list of rules for bedrooms. Bedrooms had to be fresh and airy, but not too airy in case people caught a cold. You had to keep cooking smells away from bedrooms, or burn incense to hide the smell. You couldn't put green wallpaper in bedrooms ...

2 Louis XIV of France was a busy man, but he didn't have to worry about getting up in the morning. His valet woke him up at 8.30 and important friends were then allowed to come into his room, where they could watch him wash and have breakfast. On some days when Louis was feeling sleepy, he didn't get up at all and he conducted the day's business from his bed ...

3 Astronauts on the first lunar missions in the 1960s and 1970s had big problems getting a good night's sleep. They had no hammocks in the lunar module and they had to sleep on the hard floor. They weren't allowed to take off their space suits because they took too long to get them back on. It was very difficult to get into a comfortable position ...

4 When people in Shakespeare's time stayed at an inn, they had to share their beds with complete strangers. When a rich traveller arrived at a busy hostel, he could take the place in bed of a poorer person. However, there was one inn in the small town of Ware where poorer travellers didn't need to get out of bed. The inn had a huge bed for eight people ...

5 After their wedding in 1969, John Lennon and Yoko Ono spent a week in bed at the Amsterdam Hilton hotel as a protest against the war in Vietnam. They wanted to repeat the protest two months later in the US, but Lennon couldn't get an American visa because he had a conviction for drugs. As a result, the couple had to go to Montreal ...

6 Political refugee, Alfred Mehran, lost his travel documents in Paris when he was on his way to London. Mehran wasn't allowed to go through passport control at Charles de Gaulle airport, so he made his bed on a plastic bench in the departure lounge and stayed there for eleven years until new documents finally arrived. When the documents arrived, Mehran wasn't sure he wanted to go home after all ...

3 Work in pairs. Look at the photo of a child's bedroom and discuss these questions.

- Did you sleep in a bed like this when you were younger?
- What was your bedroom like?
- What time did you have to go to bed?
- Were there any other rules that you had to follow as a child?

4 What were the rules in your home when you were a young child?

3D | Dinner invitation

SPEAKING

1 Think of the last time you had a meal at someone else's home and prepare answers to the questions.

- Whose home was it?
- How long ago was it?
- Was it a special occasion?
- Who was at the meal?
- What did you eat?
- What was the food like?
- What did you talk about during the meal?

2 Work in pairs. Describe the meal to your partner.

LISTENING

1 Work in pairs. Look at the pictures and describe what is happening in each one. What do you think the people are saying to each other?

2 🔊 1.22–1.25 Listen and match the dialogues 1–4 to the pictures A–D.

3 🔊 1.22–1.25 Listen again. Decide if the sentences are true (T) or false (F). Correct the false sentences.

1 The woman is doing something in the kitchen when the man arrives.
2 They go straight out to the garden.
3 The man hasn't been to the woman's house before.
4 The man likes sitting in the sun.
5 The woman doesn't want to go to the cinema.
6 The man's going to sit in the garden while the woman works.

Check your answers in audioscripts 1.22–1.25 on pages 69–70.

4 Imagine that you have invited a new friend for dinner in your home. What preparations will you make?

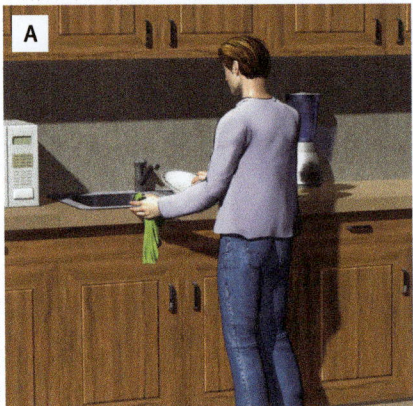
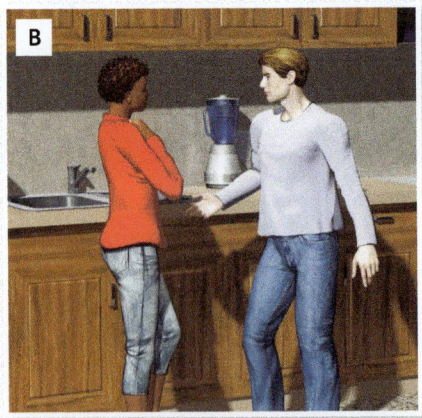

FUNCTIONAL LANGUAGE: requests
PRONUNCIATION: intonation (requests)

1 Look at audioscripts 1.22–1.25 on pages 69–70 again and underline examples of the phrases 1–8.

1 Can you …
2 Could I …
3 Could you …
4 Would you mind if I …
5 Do you think I could …
6 Do you think you could …
7 Is it all right/OK if I …
8 Would you mind + -ing …

2 Complete the table with the phrases in exercise 1.

asking someone to do something	asking for permission to do something
Could you possibly …	Can I …
Do you mind + -ing …	Could I possibly …
	I wonder if I could …
_____	_____
_____	_____
_____	_____

Which of the phrases are the most polite?

30

Dinner invitation | 3D

3 🔘 **1.26** Listen to these short exchanges. What is the problem with the responses?

1 A: I've got to do some work. Do you think I could do that first?
B: Yes.
2 A: Is it OK if I go out into the garden?
B: Yes.
3 A: Do you mind waiting? It'll only take me an hour or so.
B: No.
4 A: Would you mind if I moved the sunshade a little?
B: No.

4 Match the alternative responses a–d to questions 1–4 in exercise 3.

a Sure thing, be my guest. I thought we'd eat out there, actually.
b No worries, that's fine, could I wait out here?
c … feel free, do you need any help?
d … that's fine, do whatever you need to do.

🔘 **1.27** Listen to the recording to check your answers.

5 You can make requests more polite in two ways: (a) say *please* (b) use friendly intonation.

🔘 **1.28** Listen and repeat the example.

Could you take these plates out for me, please?

6 Work in pairs. Look at the requests in exercise 3 and the responses in exercise 4. Practise the dialogues, concentrating on making your intonation as polite as possible.

7 Work in pairs, A and B. You are going to act out a dinner party dialogue.

A: A friend has invited you for dinner in his/her home. Turn to page 64 for more information.
B: You have invited a friend for dinner in your home. Turn to page 67 for more information.

Did you know?

1 Work in pairs. Read about British food and discuss the questions.

Although in the past, Britain had a bad reputation for food, in the last ten years things have definitely changed for the better and this reputation is no longer deserved. There are over 30,000 restaurants in the country. In many cities, and even small towns, you can choose from Indian, Chinese, Italian, Japanese, Thai, French, Mexican, Turkish, Greek and Spanish food. There has even been a growth in new restaurants serving high quality traditional British food.

Cooking programmes on TV are incredibly popular and TV chefs like Jamie Oliver are well-known celebrities. Recipe books are often at the top of the best-seller list. Health food shops are everywhere and more and more people are eating organic food.

- Does your country have a good reputation for food? Is the reputation deserved?
- How often do you go to a restaurant or have a meal with friends?
- What are the most popular food books and TV programmes in your country?

Self-assessment (✓)

☐ I can make polite requests.
☐ I can respond politely to requests.
☐ I can describe a meal I ate at someone's home.

31

3 | Language reference

GRAMMAR
Modals of obligation, permission & prohibition (present & past time)

Permission

We use *can* + infinitive and *is/are allowed to* + infinitive to talk about permission in the present.

> You **can drive** in the UK when you are 17.
> The children **are allowed to watch** TV until ten o'clock.

We use *could* + infinitive and *was/were allowed to* + infinitive to talk about permission in the past.

> Many years ago people **could smoke** anywhere.
> She **was allowed to stay out** until twelve o'clock.

Obligation

We use *must* + infinitive and *has/have to* + infinitive to talk about obligation in the present.

> You **must arrive** 30 minutes before your flight.
> We **have to leave** soon.

We use *had to* + infinitive to talk about obligation in the past.

> He **had to pay** a lot of tax last year.

No obligation

We use *don't/doesn't have to* + infinitive and *don't/doesn't need to* + infinitive to talk about something that is not necessary (but it is allowed).

> You **don't have to come** if you don't want to.
> I **don't need to wear** a tie to work.

We use *didn't have to* + infinitive and *didn't need to* + infinitive to talk about an absence of obligation in the past.

> She knew the restaurant manager so she **didn't have to pay** for her meal.
> They **didn't need to get up** early because it was a holiday.

Prohibition

We use *can't* + infinitive, *mustn't* + infinitive and *isn't/aren't allowed to* + infinitive to talk about something that is not allowed.

> You **can't enter** the US without a passport.
> You **mustn't open** your papers before the exam begins.
> The students **aren't allowed to take** mobile phones to school.

We use *couldn't* + infinitive and *wasn't/weren't allowed to* + infinitive to talk about prohibition in the past.

> British schoolchildren **couldn't have** long hair in the 1950s.
> The monks **were not allowed to speak**.

Make, let & allow

Permission

We can use *let* + object + infinitive (without *to*) and *allow* + object + *to* + infinitive to talk about permission.

> She **lets her children do** anything they want.
> My father **let me use** his car.
> The teacher **allowed the students to ask** questions.

Obligation

We can use *make/made* + object + infinitive (without *to*) to talk about obligation.

> The company **makes the staff work** very hard.
> She **made me do** it again.

Prohibition

We can use *doesn't/didn't let* + object + infinitive (without *to*) and *doesn't/didn't allow* + object + *to* + infinitive to talk about prohibition.

> They **don't let me leave** until five o'clock.
> He **didn't let me speak**.
> They **don't allow animals to come** into the house.

FUNCTIONAL LANGUAGE
Requests: asking for permission

Requests

Can I (possibly) + infinitive …?
Could I (possibly) + infinitive …?
Do you think I could + infinitive …?
Is it all right/OK if I + present tense …?
I wonder if I could + infinitive …?

Responses

Yes, sure/of course/certainly/no problem/go ahead.
I'm sorry, but …
I'm afraid that …
If we want to refuse permission, we usually give an explanation.

32

Requests: asking someone to do something

Requests

Can you (possibly) + infinitive …?
Could you (possibly) + infinitive …?
Do you think you could + infinitive …?

Responses

Yes, sure/of course/certainly/no problem.
If we want to refuse the request, we usually give an explanation.

WORD LIST

Accommodation

apartment block *n C*	/əˈpɑː(r)tmənt ˌblɒk/
cabin *n C* **	/ˈkæbɪn/
campsite *n C*	/ˈkæmpˌsaɪt/
cave *n C* **	/keɪv/
communal *adj* *	/ˈkɒmjʊn(ə)l/
community *n C* ***	/kəˈmjuːnəti/
detached *adj* *	/dɪˈtætʃt/
dormitory *n C*	/ˈdɔː(r)mɪtri/
facilities *n pl* ***	/fəˈsɪlətiz/
flat *n C* ***	/flæt/
holiday home *n C*	/ˈhɒlɪdeɪ ˌhəʊm/
houseboat *n C*	/ˈhaʊsˌbəʊt/
lighthouse *n C*	/ˈlaɪtˌhaʊs/
local authority *n C*	/ˌləʊk(ə)l ɔːˈθɒrəti/
lock *v* ***	/lɒk/
mobile home *n C*	/ˌməʊbaɪl ˈhəʊm/
monthly charge *n C*	/ˈmʌnθli ˈtʃɑː(r)dʒ/
ownership *n U* **	/ˈəʊnə(r)ʃɪp/
rent *v/n U* ***	/rent/
resident *n C* ***	/ˈrezɪd(ə)nt/
semi-detached *adj*	/ˌsemidɪˈtætʃt/
suburb *n C* *	/ˈsʌbɜː(r)b/
tent *n C* **	/tent/
terraced *adj*	/ˈterəst/
tree house *n C*	/ˈtriːˌhaʊs/
wallpaper *n U* *	/ˈwɔːlˌpeɪpə(r)/
windmill *n C*	/ˈwɪn(d)ˌmɪl/

Sleep

fall asleep	/ˈfɔːl əˈsliːp/
feel sleepy	/ˌfiːl ˈsliːpi/
get to sleep	/ˌget tə ˈsliːp/
go to sleep	/ˌgəʊ tə ˈsliːp/
have a nap	/ˌhæv ə ˈnæp/
heavy sleeper *n C*	/ˌhevi ˈsliːpə(r)/
light sleeper *n C*	/ˌlaɪt ˈsliːpə(r)/
make the bed	/ˌmeɪk ðə ˈbed/
set the alarm clock	/ˌset ði: əˈlɑː(r)m ˌklɒk/
wake up *v* *	/ˌweɪk ˈʌp/

Other words & phrases

airy *adj*	/ˈeəri/
arsenic *n U*	/ˈɑː(r)s(ə)nɪk/
bench *n C* **	/bentʃ/
best-seller *n C*	/ˌbestˈselə(r)/
big deal *n C*	/ˌbɪg ˈdiːl/
bill *n C* ***	/bɪl/
candle *n C* **	/ˈkænd(ə)l/
chef *n C* *	/ʃef/
chemical *n C/adj* ***	/ˈkemɪk(ə)l/
conduct *v* ***	/kənˈdʌkt/
convenient *adj* **	/kənˈviːniənt/
conviction *n C* **	/kənˈvɪkʃ(ə)n/
crash *v* **	/kræʃ/
day-to-day *adj* *	/ˌdeɪtəˈdeɪ/
deserved *adj*	/dɪˈzɜː(r)vd/
dramatic *adj* ***	/drəˈmætɪk/
drawback *n C*	/ˈdrɔːˌbæk/
dull *adj* **	/dʌl/
effect *n C* ***	/ɪˈfekt/
enormous *adj* ***	/ɪˈnɔː(r)məs/
feel free	/ˌfiːl ˈfriː/
for good *adv*	/fə(r) ˈgʊd/
found *v* ***	/faʊnd/
growth *n U* ***	/grəʊθ/
half-way *adj/adv* *	/ˌhɑːfˈweɪ/
hammock *n C*	/ˈhæmək/
a helping hand	/ə ˌhelpɪŋ ˈhænd/
hostel *n C*	/ˈhɒst(ə)l/
incense *n U*	/ˈɪnsens/
inn *n C* *	/ɪn/
isolated *adj* *	/ˈaɪsəˌleɪtɪd/
isolation *n U* **	/ˌaɪsəˈleɪʃ(ə)n/
keep (sb) company *v*	/ˌkiːp ˈkʌmp(ə)nɪ/
living conditions *n pl*	/ˈlɪvɪŋ kənˌdɪʃ(ə)nz/
loads of **	/ˈləʊdz əv/
lounge *n C* *	/laʊndʒ/
lunar *adj*	/ˈluːnə(r)/
module *n C* ***	/ˈmɒdjuːl/
noisy *adj* *	/ˈnɔɪzi/
obviously *adv* ***	/ˈɒbviəsli/
organic *adj* *	/ɔː(r)ˈgænɪk/
owner *n C* ***	/ˈəʊnə(r)/
paradise *n C/U* *	/ˈpærədaɪs/
poisonous *adj* *	/ˈpɔɪz(ə)nəs/
poverty *n U* **	/ˈpɒvə(r)ti/
refugee *adj* **	/ˌrefjuˈdʒiː/
reputation *n C/U* ***	/ˌrepjuˈteɪʃ(ə)n/
responsibility *n U/C* ***	/rɪˌspɒnsəˈbɪləti/
ridge *n C* **	/rɪdʒ/
rubbish *n U* **	/ˈrʌbɪʃ/
sanitary *adj*	/ˈsænət(ə)ri/
scenery *n U* *	/ˈsiːnəri/
shortage *n C* **	/ˈʃɔː(r)tɪdʒ/
substance *n C* ***	/ˈsʌbstəns/
sunshade *n C*	/ˈsʌnˌʃeɪd/
task *n C* ***	/tɑːsk/
uniform *n C* **	/ˈjuːnɪfɔː(r)m/
vacation *n C*	/vəˈkeɪʃ(ə)n/
valet *n C*	/ˈvælɪt/ /ˈvæleɪ/
waiting list *n C*	/ˈweɪtɪŋ ˌlɪst/
wave *n C* ***	/weɪv/
wooden *adj* ***	/ˈwʊd(ə)n/
workhouse *n C*	/ˈwɜː(r)kˌhaʊs/

4A Luck of the draw

Vocabulary: idioms (taking risks)

1 Match the phrases in bold in sentences 1–6 to the definitions a–f.

1 **It's a bit of a gamble**, but I think we should give it a go.
2 **There's a lot at stake** here, I really don't think it's a good idea.
3 **It's against the odds**, but you never know – maybe we'll win. What do you think?
4 Well, I'm not sure. We could take a risk and win a million or we could **play safe** and keep what we have.
5 I never **try my luck** because I always lose.
6 **It's a lottery** – but if we don't play, we'll never win anything.

a you probably won't win
b take a risk
c there's a risk here, but it's only a small one
d if you lose, you could lose a lot
e it's a question of luck – anyone could win
f decide not to take a risk

2 Work in pairs. Discuss these questions.

- What are the risks involved in the following situations?
   a) asking your boss for a pay rise
   b) playing the lottery
   c) walking home alone in the dark
- Do you usually play it safe or do you like to try your luck?
- What was the last big risk that you took?

Reading

1 Look at the title of the article. Which of these words do you think you will find in the article?

addicts   celebrate   charities
governments   jackpot   low income
millionaires   schoolchildren

2 Read the article and choose the best ending, 1 or 2.

1 But when a ticket only costs a handful of small change, there is not much at stake. Why not try your luck?
2 The lottery clearly isn't the quick-fix solution to life's problems. It solves some; it causes others. But that isn't going to stop me buying my weekly ticket!

3 Explain in your own words who the lottery winners and losers are.

---

4 Saturday 6th August

Lottery winners and losers

Feeling lucky and want to try your luck on the lottery? The chances of becoming a millionaire are definitely well against the odds (1) _____. But millions of ordinary people, like you or me – or John Goodman*, this week's lottery millionaire – regularly buy our tickets, just in case. Maybe, we too will join the hundreds of people who win jackpots on national lotteries every week.

John Goodman, 42, an unemployed father of two from Swindon, is the latest to join the jet set. John was having a quiet drink (2) _____ when his winning numbers came up on the TV and he found out he'd won £17 million. According to locals, John is already planning to buy the pub.

But people like John and his fellow lottery millionaires aren't the only winners. The turnover for the gambling industry in the UK alone is over £42 billion per year – (3) _____. And over £1.5 billion of this goes to the government in taxes.

The lottery has always been popular with politicians as a way of raising money. When the British government was looking for ways to spend more on sport and the arts in the 1990s, it turned to the lottery. (4) _____, lotteries helped pay for the building of more than 50 universities, including Harvard and Yale. And over 2,000 years ago in China, the Great Wall was partly paid for with lottery money.

But where there are winners, there are also losers. It is well-known that the poor play the lottery more often than the rich and some critics of the lottery call it a tax on the poor. People on low incomes can end up spending hundreds of pounds a year on lottery tickets and some will become lottery addicts. Meanwhile, the rich play it safe by investing their money in less risky ways – (5) _____.

Large sums of government money go to charities every year and the charities certainly welcome it. But at the same time, when lottery money starts coming in, governments usually reduce the amount that they normally spend on good causes. This means that many charities, (6) _____, can suddenly find themselves with a lot less money.

So who actually wins in the end? It's something to think about next time you find yourself tempted to buy a lottery ticket.

*For legal reasons, this is not his real name.

4 Put the phrases a–f into the gaps 1–6 in the article.
a and especially the low profile ones
b (in fact you're more likely to be struck by lightning)
c buying stocks and shares, for instance
d in his local pub with his mates
e When America was recovering from the Civil War
f that's over £115 million a day

5 How do lotteries work in your country? Do you think that lotteries are a good way to raise money?

Grammar: past simple & past continuous

1 Work in pairs. Look at the sentence from the article below. Then complete the rules with *past simple* or *past continuous*.

> *John **was having** a quiet drink in his local pub when his winning numbers **came up** on the TV.*

Use the _____ for completed past actions.
Use the _____ for actions that were in progress at a particular time in the past.

You often use the past continuous with the past simple. Use the _____ for longer activities. Use the _____ for shorter, completed actions.

> *When America **was recovering** from the Civil War, lotteries **helped** pay for more than 50 universities.*

> See Language Reference page 42

2 Complete the two true stories. Put the verbs in brackets into the past simple or the past continuous.

Three friends (1) _____ (spend) the weekend in London when they were refused entry at a nightclub because they (2) _____ (not / wear) shirts and ties. They (3) _____ (go) to an all-night supermarket and (4) _____ (buy) some new shirts. While they (5) _____ (pay) for the shirts, they (6) _____ (decide) to buy a scratchcard and (7) _____ (win) £20,000. They (8) _____ (spend) the whole night celebrating in the nightclub!

A man (9) _____ (walk) under a tree when some bird droppings (10) _____ (fall) on his head. As this is supposed to be lucky, he (11) _____ (decide) to buy an instant lottery ticket and he (12) _____ (win) £24. The following week he (13) _____ (stand) under the same tree when the same thing (14) _____ (happen) again! So he (15) _____ (buy) another lottery ticket and won £444. He now spends time every week standing under that lucky tree, waiting for that little bird.

Speaking

1 Work in pairs. Make up a story about a lottery winner by answering the questions below. Then practise telling the story to another pair of students.

- Where and when did he/she buy the ticket(s)?
- How did he/she choose the numbers?
- Where and when did he/she hear about his/her lottery win?
- What was he/she doing at the time?
- What did he/she do next?

Pronunciation: *was & were*

1 1.29 Listen to the dialogue. Are the underlined words pronounced in their strong or weak forms? When do we use the strong forms of these words?

	strong	weak
was	/wɒz/	/wəz/
were	/wɜː/	/wə/

A: (1) <u>Was</u> that man standing under the tree again?
B: Yes, he (2) <u>was</u>. He (3) <u>was</u> with a friend this time.
A: What do you think they (4) <u>were</u> doing?
B: I asked them. They said they (5) <u>were</u> waiting for a bird.
A: A bird! I find that hard to believe.
B: They (6) <u>were</u>! They said it (7) <u>was</u> a lucky bird.
A: I knew he (8) <u>was</u> a bit crazy!

2 Work in pairs. Practise the dialogue with your partner.

4B Twists of fate

VOCABULARY: injuries

1 Match the injuries 1–8 to the pictures A–H.

1 He's bleeding.
2 He's got a big bruise.
3 He's got a black eye.
4 He's got a few scratches.
5 He's sprained his wrist.
6 He's suffering from shock.
7 He's twisted his ankle.
8 He's unconscious.

2 Work in pairs. Put the injuries in exercise 1 in order of seriousness (1 = most serious → 8 = least serious).

3 Work in pairs, A and B.

A: Choose an injury from exercise 1 and explain how it happened.
He was running for the bus when he fell over.

B: Listen to your partner's explanation and decide which injury he/she is talking about.

Then exchange roles.

The world's luckiest man?

Frane Selak, a retired Croatian music teacher, may well be one the luckiest people alive.

Click here for the full story. >>

LISTENING

1 Work in pairs. Discuss these questions.

- Do you know anyone who is particularly unlucky?
- When was the last time that you were unlucky?

2 Work in pairs. Look at the photo and headline to a news story. What do you think has happened to the man to make him 'the world's luckiest man'?

3 🔘 **1.30** Listen to the first part of a radio news story about Frane Selak and answer the questions.

1 What did he win?
2 What did he buy?

36

4 🔊 **1.31** Listen to the rest of the story. What other things have happened to him to make him the world's luckiest man?

5 🔊 **1.30–1.31** Listen again to the whole story and put the events in the correct order. Then answer the questions below.

☐ He bought a new house.
☐ He had a car accident in the mountains.
☐ He was burnt at a petrol station.
☐ He was hit by a bus.
☐ He was in a plane crash.
☐ He won the lottery.
☐ His bus fell into a river.
☐ His train fell into a river.

1 How many accidents was Selak involved in?
2 In what way is his latest piece of good luck different to all the other good luck stories?

6 Find the highlighted words and phrases in audioscripts 1.30–1.31 on page 70 and match them to the definitions 1–6.

| ploughed into | exploded | rails |
| corpses | haystack | sprayed |

1 crashed into
2 suddenly caught fire with a loud noise
3 threw liquid over something
4 dead bodies
5 the lines that a train runs on
6 large pile of dried grass

GRAMMAR: past perfect simple

> Use the past perfect to talk about completed actions in the past that happened *before* other actions in the past.
> He won the lottery with the first ticket he **had bought** for forty years.
> (= He bought a ticket and then he won the lottery.)
>
> Make the past perfect with **had/hadn't** + past participle.
>
> Look at the difference between the past perfect and the past simple.
> He was in hospital again. He **had had** another accident.
> (= He had an accident and so he went to hospital.)
> He was in hospital again where he **had** another accident.
> (= He had the accident when he was in hospital.)

⊙ SEE LANGUAGE REFERENCE PAGE 42

1 Complete the text. Put the verbs in brackets into the past simple or the past perfect.

In the late 1940s, the members of a church choir in Nebraska (1) _____ (*meet*) every Wednesday at 7.20 to practise their singing. But one day in 1950, it was already 7.25 and the choir (2) _____ (*not / arrive*). They (3) _____ (*be*) fortunate because at that moment a gas explosion (4) _____ (*destroy*) the church. The fifteen members of the choir (5) _____ (*have*) different reasons for being late. Two people (6) _____ (*break*) down in their car. Others (7) _____ (*decide*) to finish some work and another person (8) _____ (*fall*) asleep.

2 Read the short text. Use your imagination to answer the questions. Begin your answers with *Because he had ...*

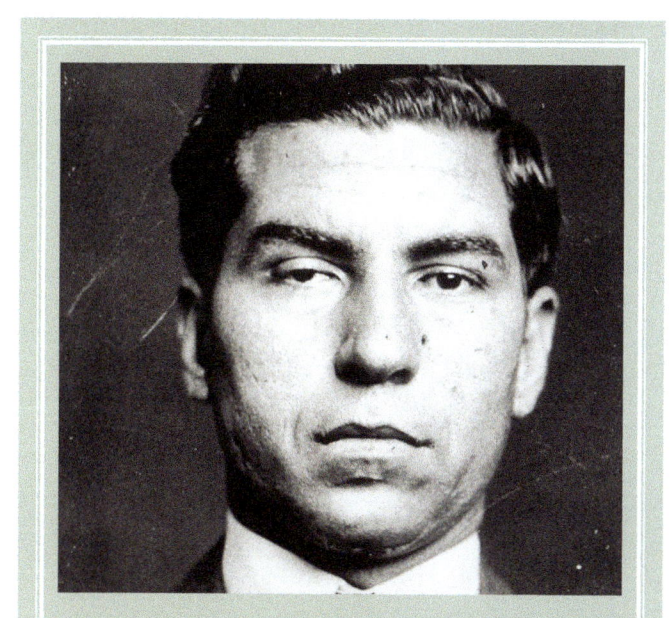

Lucky Luciano, an American gangster, was both famous and feared. Everybody recognized him because he had an injured eye and everybody wanted to be his friend. When America went to war in the 1940s, he didn't have to join the forces, but after the war finished he was forced to leave the country. He lived in Italy until his death in 1962.

1 Why was he called Lucky?
2 Why did he have a problem with his eye?
3 Why did he become famous?
4 Why were people frightened of him?
5 Why did he not have to join the army?
6 Why did he leave America?

🔊 **1.32** Listen to the recording to check your answers.

4c | Bad luck stories

A **MUM LEFT OUT IN THE COLD**
B *Mum pays for expensive joke*
C **Man loses job after mountain top adventure**

Reading

1 Read the news stories and match the stories 1–3 to the headlines A–C.

2 Read the stories again and answer these questions.

Story 1
1 How long was the man stuck on the mountain?
2 How did he survive?
3 Who found him?

Story 2
4 How long did the woman have to wait on the balcony?
5 Why did the woman go out onto the balcony?
6 How old was the little boy?

Story 3
7 How much will the mother have to pay?
8 How did the egg get on the roof of the car?
9 How long did it stay there before it was discovered?

3 Have you heard any bad luck stories in the news recently? If so, what were they?

1
A German man has lost his job because he was late for work. Thomas Milnik had survived five days in the Alps in freezing temperatures. But he lost his job because he had missed four days at work.

Thomas received a letter telling him that he'd lost his job while he was still in hospital. At the same time that he was reading his letter, the doctors were deciding whether to cut off six of his frostbitten toes!

The 41-year-old hiker was climbing in the Alps last Saturday when it suddenly started to snow. He was eventually rescued five days later when workers at a nearby research station heard his cries for help and called the mountain rescue services.

2
A local woman had to be rescued by police yesterday after her toddler son locked her out on the balcony.

The woman had gone outside on the balcony to hang out some clothes to dry. But her son, aged eighteen months, had pushed the door shut from the inside. The mother could only watch as her son walked to the sofa, climbed up on to it and then fell asleep!

After two hours of shouting for help, neighbours heard the woman's screams and called the police.

3
A mother will have to pay £675 because her teenage son fried an egg on the roof of his teacher's car. The boy, aged 14, had met up with friends at school one afternoon when the teachers were meeting inside to discuss their pupils' end of term reports. The three boys threw several eggs at the school windows of the conference room. One egg missed the window and landed on the roof of a teacher's Ford Mondeo.

Because of the summer sun, the roof was so hot the egg was immediately fried. And it continued to cook until the owner of the car discovered it two hours later. By the time he found it, the fried egg had burned into the paint.

Vocabulary: time linkers

Use *while*, *as* and *when* to show that two actions happen at the same time.
*A black cat crossed my path **while/as/when** I was walking down the street.*

Use *the moment*, *as soon as* and *when* to show that one action happens immediately after another action.
*I crossed the road **the moment/as soon as/when** I saw the black cat.*

Use *by the time* to show that one action has happened before another.
*I'd had three different accidents **by the time** I got home.*

▶ See Language Reference page 42

1 Look at the sentences below. One of the three time linkers in italics in each sentence is wrong. Underline it. Then explain why it is wrong.

1 Thomas Milnik found out that he'd lost his job *while / as / after* doctors at the hospital were deciding whether to cut off six of his toes.
2 The 41-year-old hiker was climbing in the Alps *as soon as / when / as* it suddenly started to snow.
3 He was eventually rescued five days later *the moment / after / when* workers at a research station heard his cries for help.
4 A woman had to be rescued by police yesterday *when / after / as soon as* her son locked her out on the balcony.
5 The mother could only watch *as / while / after* her son walked to the sofa, climbed up on to it and then fell asleep.
6 The egg continued to cook until the owner of the car discovered it two hours later. *By the time / When / The moment* he found it, the fried egg had burned into the paint.

38

Bad luck stories | 4c

2 Complete the article with appropriate time linkers from the grammar box.

Police arrested two burglars last night (1) _____ they jumped into a police car thinking it was their getaway car.

Police say that the two men had planned to break into two houses on the same street that night. They had arranged to meet a third man on the corner of the street (2) _____ they had finished in the second house.

The policeman who was driving the car said: 'They only realized it was the wrong car (3) _____ they were actually sitting in the back of it. But (4) _____ they realized it was a police car, it was too late. I'd locked the doors, and they couldn't get out.'

Speaking

1 Work in groups. Look at the pictures. They show another bad luck story. What's happening in each picture? What do you think happened in between?

2 Look at the words in the box and imagine five unlucky things that happened to the girl in the story.

| broken glass | car | mobile phone |
| bus | rain | puddle | wrong address |

3 Work as a class. Take it in turns to tell the story one sentence at a time.

A: *Jane was getting ready for an important date.*

B: *She was putting her make-up on when suddenly the cat jumped onto the table.*

C: *Unfortunately, when the cat jumped onto the table, it smashed the mirror.*

Did you know?

1 Work in pairs. Read about superstitions and discuss the questions.

Superstitions in Britain

In Britain, there are many superstitions connected with cats. Black cats are good-luck animals, and you should welcome them into your house. A black cat sitting outside your front door means that you will be rich, and you will be very lucky if you see a cat sneeze. However, if a black cat crosses your path, you will have bad luck. The bad luck will go away if you walk backwards or spit on the ground in front of you.

- Which birds or animals in your country are considered to be lucky or unlucky?
- What other superstitions are common?
- How superstitious are you?

39

4D | Fancy that!

Vocabulary: *both* & *neither*

Use *both* and *neither* to compare two people or things.
We both have brown hair.
Neither of us has a car.
Jenny and Zoe both live in London.
Neither Jenny nor Zoe has a boyfriend.

Arnold Schwarzenegger
Actor and politician

Penélope Cruz
Hollywood actress

1 Look at the photos. Complete the sentences below with *both* or *neither*.

1 _____ are very successful.
2 They _____ have brown hair.
3 _____ of them live in the United States.
4 _____ of them is American.
5 _____ Arnold Schwarzenegger nor Penélope Cruz have university degrees.
6 _____ Schwarzenegger and Cruz look very serious in the photos.

2 Look at sentences 5 and 6 in exercise 1 again. Choose the correct words to complete the rules below.

We use a *plural / singular* verb and *and / nor* with **both**.
We use a *plural / singular* verb and *and / nor* with **neither**.

▸ See Language Reference page 42

3 Work in pairs. Ask your partner questions and find six things you have in common. Then tell the rest of the class about the things you have in common. Use *both* or *neither* with *we* or *us* in your sentences.

We both have a brother.
Neither of us has visited London.

Listening

1 🔊 1.33 Listen to two colleagues chatting at work. Put the topics below in the order in which they are discussed. Two of the topics are not discussed.

☐ sport
☐ food
☐ TV programmes
☐ what they're doing tomorrow evening
☐ where they live
☐ where they were born

2 🔊 1.33 Listen again. Make a note of five things they have in common.

3 What did they say about the following things?

1 The White Rose
2 squash lessons
3 Harlech Crescent
4 Chinese takeaway

4 Find these expressions in audioscript 1.33 on pages 70–71 and explain them in your own words.

1 it's worth it
2 it's a bit out of your way
3 you're kidding
4 small world
5 no rest for the wicked

Functional language: talking about similarities & differences

Similarities

So/Neither + auxiliary verb + subject

Use *so* after a positive sentence and *neither* after a negative.
  I'm very busy at the moment. **So am** *I.*
  I can't understand. **Neither can** *I.*

Use *do/does/did* if there's no auxiliary.
  I study English on Thursdays. So **do** *I.*
  I started two years ago. So **did** *I.*

Use *Me, too* and *Me, neither.*
  I like pizzas. **Me, too.**
  I'm not very good at squash. **Me, neither.**

Differences

Use subject + auxiliary verb, not *so* or *neither*.
  I'm very busy at the moment. **I'm not.**
  I can't understand Chinese. **I can.**

Use *do/does/did* if there's no auxiliary.
  I went to the meeting yesterday. **I didn't.**

> See Language Reference page 42

1 Find and underline five examples of *so/neither* + auxiliary verb + subject in audioscript 1.33 on pages 70–71. For each example, find the verb that corresponds to the auxiliary verb in the response.

So am I. – I'm going tomorrow.

2 Choose the best response to complete the exchanges.

1 A: I didn't like the concert much.
   B: *Neither did I. / Neither didn't I. / Neither I did.*
2 A: I love Beethoven's 5th Symphony.
   B: *I do. / I don't. / Neither do I.*
3 A: I wasn't feeling too well yesterday.
   B: *Neither I was. / Neither was I. / So was I.*
4 A: I work in an office.
   B: *So am I. / So can I. / So do I.*
5 A: I'll have a pepperoni pizza, please.
   B: *So do I. / So have I. / So will I.*
6 A: I'm a very good squash player.
   B: *I'm not. / Neither am I. / So I'm not.*
7 A: I'm sure we've met before.
   B: *I am. / Neither am I. / So am I.*
8 A: I haven't been to the park for ages.
   B: *Me, neither. / Me, too. / Neither I have.*

3 Work in small groups. Take it in turns to respond to the sentences.

1 I like hip-hop and rap music.
2 I haven't been on a date for ages.
3 I'm going to be famous one day.
4 I'll probably write a novel when I'm older.
5 I'm never late for anything.
6 I've got several unusual pets, including a snake.
7 I didn't understand maths when I was a kid.
8 I was very popular in my last job/at my last school.

1 A: *I like hip hop and rap music.*
   B: *I don't!*
   C: *Neither do I!*

Speaking

1 Work in pairs, A and B. You are going to read a text about two American presidents and find out about the things they have in common.

A: Turn to page 65.
B: Turn to page 67.

2 Work in pairs. Without looking back at the text about the two presidents, how many coincidences can you remember?

3 Do you know any other stories about coincidences?

Yes? Spend a few minutes preparing your story.
No? Spend a few minutes inventing a story about a coincidence.

4 Now tell your story to the rest of the class. They must decide if your story is true or if you invented it.

Self-assessment (✓)

☐ I can discuss similarities and differences.
☐ I can use both *neither* and *both* to compare people.
☐ I can recognize the main topics discussed in informal dialogues.

4 | Language reference

GRAMMAR
Past simple & past continuous

We use the past continuous for actions in progress at a particular time in the past. These actions are incomplete.

At nine o'clock last night, he was watching TV.

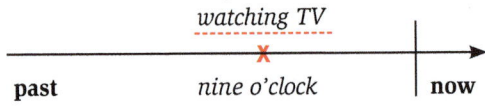

```
              watching TV
─────────────────┼──────────────┤
past         nine o'clock      now
                  x
```

We use the past simple for completed past actions.

*He **decided** to buy a lottery ticket.*

We often use the past continuous and the past simple together. We use the past continuous for longer, 'background' actions and we use the past simple for shorter, completed actions.

*Three friends **were spending** a weekend in London and they **decided** to go to a nightclub.*

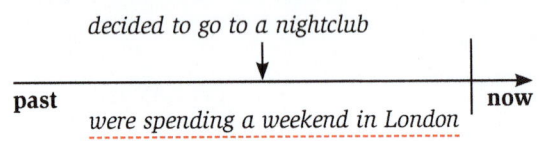

```
         decided to go to a nightclub
                    ↓
─────────────────────────────────────┤
past                                now
     were spending a weekend in London
```

Past continuous

affirmative
subject + *was/were* + verb + *-ing* ...
negative
subject + *was/were* + *not* + verb + *-ing* ...
question
Was/Were + subject + verb + *-ing*?

Past perfect simple

We use the past perfect to talk about completed actions in the past that happened before other actions in the past.

*Rescuers arrived, but Selak **had swum** to safety.*
(= Selak swam to safety and then rescuers arrived.)

We often use the past perfect and the past simple together to show the order in which two actions took place.

Compare the following pair of sentences:

*He **had married** her when he **won** the lottery.*
(= He married her and then he won the lottery.)

*He **married** her when he **had won** the lottery.*
(= He won the lottery and then he married her.)

affirmative & negative			
I/You/He/She/We/They	had / hadn't	broken	a leg.
question			
What	had	I/you/he/she/we/they	done?

Time linkers

We can use *while*, *as* and *when* to show that two actions happen at the same time.

*He was reading a letter **while/as/when** the doctors were deciding what to do next.*
***While/As/When** the doctors were deciding what to do next, he was reading a letter.*

We can use *the moment*, *as soon as* and *when* to show that one action happens immediately after another one.

*The boy fell asleep **the moment/as soon as/when** he climbed onto the sofa.*
***The moment/As soon as/When** the boy climbed onto the sofa, he fell asleep.*

We can use *by the time* to show that one action has happened before another.

*The party had finished **by the time** we arrived.*
***By the time** we arrived, the party had finished.*

FUNCTIONAL LANGUAGE
Talking about similarities & differences

Similarities
We can make short statements that begin with *so* and *neither* to show a similarity or agreement between what we think and a statement made by another person.

We use *so* after an affirmative statement, and we use *neither* after a negative statement.

I'm feeling tired.   **So** am I.
She's got a cold.   **So** have I.
They won't be happy.   **Neither** will you.
He hasn't finished.   **Neither** has she.

The auxiliary verb in the first statement is repeated in the statement that begins with *so* or *neither*.
If the first statement is in the present simple, the second statement will include *do/don't/does/doesn't*. If the first statement is in the past simple, the second statement will include *did/didn't*.

I like this place.   **So do** I.
I didn't understand.   **Neither did** I.

It is also possible to use *too* and *neither* after a pronoun.

He's Canadian.   Me, **too.**
She's not well.   Me, **neither.**

42

Language reference 4

Differences

When we want to say the opposite of another statement, we do not use *so* or *neither*. We use a pronoun followed by an auxiliary verb. We stress both the pronoun and the auxiliary verb.

> I can't swim. **I can.**
> I'm not hungry. **I am.**

If the first statement is in the present simple or the past simple, the second statement will include *do/don't/does/doesn't/did/didn't*.

> I don't like hamburgers. **I do!**
> He wants a divorce. She **doesn't**.
> They arrived early. You **didn't**!

Both & neither

We use *both* and *neither* to compare two people or things. The meaning of *both* is positive and the meaning of *neither* is negative.

> **Both** of them have a good job.
> (= He has a good job and she has a good job.)
>
> **Neither** of them has a good job.
> (= He doesn't have a good job and she doesn't have a good job.)

We use a plural verb when *both* is the subject of the sentence. We normally use a singular verb when *neither* is the subject of a sentence.
When we name the two subjects, *both* is used with *and*. *Neither* is used with *nor*.

> Both Ceri and Philip **speak** Spanish.
> Neither Ceri nor Philip **speaks** Slovenian.

Both can be used in two positions in a sentence.

> **Both** of them have children.
> They **both** have children.

WORD LIST

Idioms (taking risks)

a bit of a gamble /ə ˌbɪt əv ə ˈɡæmb(ə)l/
a lot at stake /ə ˌlɒt ət ˈsteɪk/
against the odds /əˌɡenst ði ˈɒdz/
give (sth) a go /ˌɡɪv ə ˈɡəʊ/
it's a lottery /ˌɪts ə ˈlɒtəri/
play safe /ˌpleɪ ˈseɪf/
try your luck /ˌtraɪ jə(r) ˈlʊk/

Injuries

ankle *n C* ** /ˈæŋk(ə)l/
black eye *n C* /ˌblæk ˈaɪ/
bleed *v* * /bliːd/
bruise *v/n C* * /bruːz/
burn *v/n C* *** /bɜː(r)n/
frostbitten *adj* /ˈfrɒs(t)ˌbɪt(ə)n/
scratch *n C/v* * /skrætʃ/
shock *n C/v* *** /ʃɒk/
sprain *n C/v* /spreɪn/
wrist *n C* ** /rɪst/
suffer from *v* *** /ˈsʌfə(r) ˌfrɒm/
twist *v* ** /twɪst/
unconscious *adj* * /ʌnˈkɒnʃəs/

Other words & phrases

according to *prep* *** /əˈkɔː(r)dɪŋ ˌtuː/
addict *n C* * /ˈædɪkt/
all-night *adj* /ˌɔːl ˈnaɪt/
balcony *n C* * /ˈbælkəni/
billion *n C* ** /ˈbɪljən/
burglar *n C* * /ˈbɜː(r)ɡlə(r)/
catch fire *v* /ˌkætʃ ˈfaɪə(r)/
choir *n C* /ˈkwaɪə(r)/
coincidence *n C* * /kəʊˈɪnsɪd(ə)ns/
corpse *n C* * /ˈkɔː(r)ps/
critic *n C* *** /ˈkrɪtɪk/
destroy *v* *** /dɪˈstrɔɪ/
droppings *n pl* /ˈdrɒpɪŋz/
end up *v* /ˌend ˈʌp/
explode *v* ** /ɪkˈspləʊd/
explosion *n C* ** /ɪkˈspləʊʒ(ə)n/
fancy *v* ** /ˈfænsi/
fry *v* * /fraɪ/
gamble *v* * /ˈɡæmb(ə)l/
gangster *n C* /ˈɡæŋstə(r)/
good cause *n C* /ˌɡʊd ˈkɔːz/
handful *n C* ** /ˈhæn(d)fʊl/
have (sth) in common /ˌhæv ɪn ˈkɒmən/
haystack *n C* /ˈheɪˌstæk/
hiker *n C* /ˈhaɪkə(r)/
icy *adj* * /ˈaɪsi/

income *n C/U* *** /ˈɪŋkʌm/
industry *n C* *** /ˈɪndəstri/
it's (not) worth it /ˌɪts nɒt ˈwɜːθ ɪt/
jackpot *n C* /ˈdʒækˌpɒt/
jet set *n C* /ˈdʒet ˌset/
jump *v* *** /dʒʌmp/
kidnap *v* * /ˈkɪdnæp/
knock *v* *** /nɒk/
legal *adj* *** /ˈliːɡ(ə)l/
leisure club *n C* /ˈleʒə(r) ˌklʌb/
lightning *n U* * /ˈlaɪtnɪŋ/
liquid *n C/U* ** /ˈlɪkwɪd/
local *adj/n C* *** /ˈləʊk(ə)l/
make-up *n U* * /ˈmeɪk ˌʌp/
nearby *adj/adv* ** /ˌnɪə(r)ˈbaɪ/
partly *adv* *** /ˈpɑː(r)tli/
pepperoni *n U* /ˌpepəˈrəʊni/
petrol station *n C* /ˈpetrəl ˌsteɪʃ(ə)n/
pile *n C* ** /paɪl/
plough into *v* /ˌplaʊ ˈɪntuː/
profile *n C* ** /ˈprəʊfaɪl/
puddle *n C* /ˈpʌd(ə)l/
pupil *n C* *** /ˈpjuːp(ə)l/
quick-fix *adj* /ˌkwɪk ˈfɪks/
rail *n C* *** /reɪl/
reduce *v* *** /rɪˈdjuːs/
regularly *adv* *** /ˈreɡjʊlə(r)li/
rescue *v/n C* ** /ˈreskjuː/
scream *v/n C* ** /skriːm/
smash *v* ** /smæʃ/
snake *n C* * /sneɪk/
sneeze *v* /sniːz/
solution *n C* *** /səˈluːʃ(ə)n/
solve *v* *** /sɒlv/
speedboat *n C* /ˈspiːdˌbəʊt/
spit *v* * /spɪt/
spray *v/n C/U* * /spreɪ/
squash *n U* /skwɒʃ/
stuck *adj* /stʌk/
sum *n C* *** /sʌm/
superstition *n C* /ˌsuːpə(r)ˈstɪʃ(ə)n/
survive *v* *** /sə(r)ˈvaɪv/
symphony *n C* * /ˈsɪmfəni/
tempt *v* ** /tempt/
toddler *n C* * /ˈtɒdlə(r)/
toe *n C* ** /təʊ/
turnover *n U* ** /ˈtɜː(r)nˌəʊvə(r)/
twist of fate /ˌtwɪst əv ˈfeɪt/
warehouse *n C* ** /ˈweə(r)ˌhaʊs/
wave *v* ** /weɪv/
wicked *adj* * /ˈwɪkɪd/
you're kidding /ˌjɔː(r) ˈkɪdɪŋ/

5A | Hard sell

VOCABULARY: adjectives (advertising)

1 Think of three different brand names that you know for each of the products below.

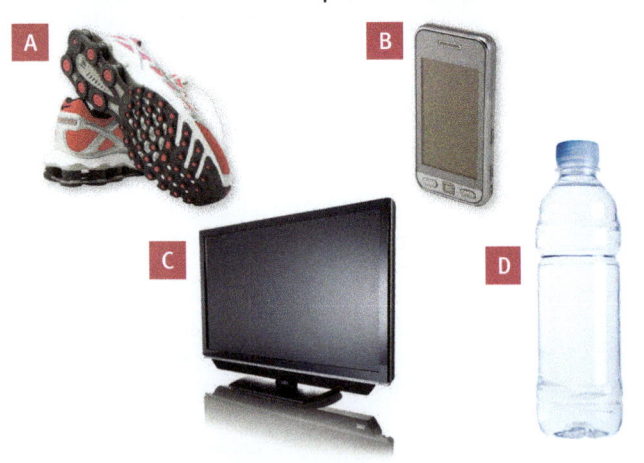

A
B
C
D

Which are your favourite brands for these products? Why?

2 Match the adjectives in the box to the products in exercise 1. Can you think of any other adjectives to describe them?

comfortable   delicious   efficient   fashionable
healthy   popular   reliable   strong   stylish

3 Think of another product and write six adjectives to describe it. Read your adjectives to the class. Can they guess what the product is?

READING

1 Look at this list of products that are often advertised with children in mind. How many more items can you add to it?

breakfast cereals, computer games, fast food, sweets …

Can you remember seeing any advertisements for these products? How did the advertisements appeal to children?

2 Read the article and answer the questions.

1 What is more important for American advertisers – the money that children spend now, or in the future?
2 How many different ways of catching children's attention are mentioned in the text?
3 Why is classroom advertising 'here to stay'?

CATCH THEM young

You want children to learn languages, computer skills, play the piano or become good, honest citizens. Any educationalist will tell you the simple answer: catch them young. You want children to buy your products and to develop brand loyalty? The answer is the same.

In 1997, children in America spent or influenced the spending of $500 billion and the figure is certainly much higher now. But far more important to the advertisers is what they will spend when they are adults. 'The kids we're reaching are consumers in training', said Joseph Fenton of Donnelly Marketing.

Kids spend 20% of their lives in school, so it is no surprise to find advertisers turning their attention to the classroom. What is rather more surprising is to learn how far advertisers have already gone.

- Over half of American students receive free covers for their text books with adverts for snacks and breakfast cereals.
- Many teachers use educational materials that are paid for by big business – mathematics worksheets with Disney characters, for example.
- Students who do better than others in their studies are given vouchers for free pizzas, burgers and French fries.
- Many school cafeterias serve and advertise brand name food. Schools also sell advertising space in school corridors and toilets, on the side of the school bus and school websites.
- Probably the least popular form of classroom advertising is Channel One. Eight million American teenagers have to watch a twelve-minute programme every day. This contains ten minutes of news and two minutes of commercials.

Not everyone is happy with the growth of classroom advertising, but it is almost certainly here to stay. The biggest problem facing most schools in America is a shortage of cash. Taxpayers don't want to pay more and other fund-raising programmes don't raise enough money. 'Advertising is not just the best way to raise money', said one school head. 'It's the only way.'

3 Read the first two paragraphs of the article again and complete the end of each line where it has been torn.

4 Is it right to advertise to young children? Why or why not?

GRAMMAR: comparisons 1

> Use comparatives to compare two things or people.
> *The figure is **higher than** ever before.*
> *Advertisers have **bigger** budgets **than** they used to have.*
> *Brand names are **more expensive than** other products.*
>
> Make negative comparisons with *less* + adjective + *than*.
> *Classroom advertising is **less common** in Europe **than** in the States.*
>
> Make the difference between the two things bigger or smaller with a modifier before the comparative adjective. For big differences, use *much, a lot, far*. For small differences, use *a little, slightly, a bit*.
> *The figure is **much higher** now **than** it used to be.*
> *Advertisements are **slightly longer** than they used to be.*
>
> Use superlatives to compare more than two things or people.
> ***The biggest** problem for schools is cash.*
> *Children are one of **the most important** markets for advertisers.*
>
> Make negative comparisons with *the least* + adjective.
> ***The least popular** form of advertising is Channel One.*
>
> ▶ SEE LANGUAGE REFERENCE PAGE 52

1 Write the comparative and superlative forms of the adjectives in the box.

| bad | big | good | happy |
| healthy | strong | surprising |

2 Complete the sentences. Put the words in brackets into positive or negative comparative or superlative forms. Remember that you may also need to include *than* or *the*.

1 I usually buy famous brand names because they are a lot _____ (*reliable*) other brands.
2 I always do my shopping at _____ (*cheap*) shops in town.
3 I prefer to go shopping during the week when it is _____ (*busy*) the weekend.
4 I think that _____ (*good*) time to go shopping is during the sales.
5 Small shops are often a bit _____ (*expensive*) big supermarkets, but they are much _____ (*interesting*).

3 Work in pairs. Think of three shops in your town. Make comparative and superlative sentences about them using the prompts.

cheap/expensive   stylish/old-fashioned
popular/crowded   bad/good quality
bad/good service   wide range of goods
friendly staff   easy to get to

4 Compare your ideas with another pair of students.

SPEAKING

1 Work in small groups. Read the information.

> You work for an advertising agency. A company that produces a fizzy mineral water called *Life* has hired you to create an advertisement. It wants to sell the water to young people (16–25) as an alternative to cola and other fizzy drinks. It has decided to advertise on TV. The advertising slogan will be 'Natural and Healthy'.

2 Plan your advertisement. Follow the steps below.

- Make a list of seven images you associate with the words 'natural' and 'healthy'.
- Choose one image from your list that is fashionable and will appeal to young people.
- Choose the kind of music you want to use.
- Decide whether you want to use a famous personality.
- Decide when would be the best time to show the advert on TV (before or after which programme).

3 Present your advertisement to the class.

5B Cold calling

LISTENING

1 Work in pairs. Discuss these questions.

- Do you ever get emails, letters or phone calls from people who want to sell you something? If yes, do you ever reply? Why or why not?
- Do you think this kind of selling is a good idea? Explain your reasons.

2 Look at the advertising envelope. Find words or phrases which match the definitions 1–3.

1 a period of time when you don't pay extra for borrowing money
2 the maximum amount of money that you can borrow
3 the money (percentage) that you pay when you borrow money from a bank

3 🔊 1.34 Listen to a telephone dialogue and say if the sentences below are true (T) or false (F). Correct the false sentences. Explain your answers.

1 The people on the phone know each other.
2 The caller is rude and aggressive.
3 The person at the other end is not really interested.
4 The caller eventually persuades the person on the other end to try the new card.

4 🔊 1.34 Listen to the dialogue again. Find five differences between the credit card that the salesman describes and the credit card on the envelope.

5 Work in pairs. Repeat the dialogue. Use the information on the envelope to help you.

A: You are the salesperson. Be as persuasive as you can.
B: You are interested in finding out more about the card. Ask as many questions as possible.

6 Work in pairs. Repeat the dialogue.

A: You are very busy and you are not at all happy that a salesperson has called you at home. Ask the caller how they got your name and number.
B: Be as polite as possible, try to calm the other person down and continue with the call.

The all-new Spark Platinum card

Mr Thomas Jones
491 Western Avenue
Greenford

Low interest rate – only 5.5%
High credit limit – borrow up to £15,000
Six months' free credit
Reward points for every £500 you spend

Apply for your card now

The red seal of approval

GRAMMAR: comparisons 2

Use *the same as*, *as* + adjective + *as* ... or *similar to* to say that two things are the same, or almost the same.
This credit card is **the same as** that one.
This credit card is **as good as** that one.
His name is **similar to** mine.

Use *different from* or *not as* + adjective + *as* ... to talk about the differences between two things.
This credit card is **different from** that one.
The Platinum Card is **not as good as** the Gold Card.
(= The Gold Card is better.)

> SEE LANGUAGE REFERENCE PAGE 52

1 Find six grammatical mistakes in the text and correct them.

Yes, sir, this is slightly different as the Mark V. It looks same, but this one is black and white. The black and white sets are not as popular colour these days. If you've ever watched television in colour, you'll know that it isn't the same thing at all. Of course, it's not expensive as the colour set. However, it's certainly as reliable the Mark V, and you'll see that the style is similar the colour set.

2 Rewrite the sentences using the prompts so that they have the same meaning.

1 *Whizzo* is better than any other washing powder.
No other washing powder *is as good as Whizzo*.
2 *Whizzo* is different from other washing powders.
Whizzo isn't _____.
3 *Whizzo* washes whiter than all other washing powders.
Other washing powders don't _____.
4 *Whizzo* is the most popular washing powder.
Other washing powders aren't _____.
5 *Whizzo* is cheaper than other washing powders.
Whizzo isn't _____.

Cold calling | 5B

3 Work in pairs. Choose one product from the list and write four slogans similar to the ones in exercise 2.
- 'Life' mineral water
- 'Jump' training shoes
- 'Snap' digital cameras

Vocabulary: adjectives (negative prefixes)

1 Look at audioscript 1.34 on page 71 and find seven adjectives that begin with negative prefixes. Add them to the table below.

un-	in-	im-	dis-
unlucky	incorrect	impatient	disloyal

Decide which negative prefix goes with these adjectives and put them in the table. Use a dictionary to help you.

> accurate   honest   polite
> prepared   probable   successful

2 Complete the sentences with a negative adjective from the table in exercise 1.

Top Tips for Telesales Staff

1 Never be _____ about why you are calling.
2 Never give your customer _____ information.
3 Never be _____ – do some research into your clients before you call.
4 Don't be _____ to make a sale – you may need to call the same person three or four times.
5 Even when customers are _____, make sure you stay calm and friendly.
6 Accept the fact that you are going to be _____ some of the time.
7 Offer to call your client back if the time is _____.

Pronunciation: /s/, /z/ & /ʃ/

1 🔊 1.35 Listen to the underlined sounds in the sentence.

/z/   /ʃ/   /s/
Whi<u>zz</u>o is the most popular wa<u>sh</u>ing powder in <u>S</u>cotland!

2 Look at the underlined letters and put the words in the box into three groups /s/, /z/ & /ʃ/.

> ama<u>z</u>ing   bu<u>s</u>   ca<u>sh</u>   <u>c</u>ertain   cla<u>ss</u>
> cour<u>se</u>   ea<u>s</u>y   effi<u>c</u>ient   men<u>ti</u>on   per<u>s</u>on
> rai<u>s</u>e   <u>s</u>end   <u>sh</u>op   <u>s</u>ure   thou<u>s</u>and
> time<u>s</u>   u<u>s</u>ing   wa<u>sh</u>

/s/ bus
/z/ amazing
/ʃ/ cash

🔊 1.36 Listen to the recording to check your answers.

3 Look at the words in the box. Which two sounds from exercise 2 do they each contain?

> bu<u>s</u>ine<u>ss</u>   <u>c</u>iti<u>z</u>en   commer<u>c</u>ial<u>s</u>   deli<u>c</u>iou<u>s</u>
> in<u>s</u>uffi<u>c</u>ient   <u>s</u>ale<u>s</u>man   <u>s</u>urpri<u>s</u>e   <u>s</u>tyli<u>sh</u>

🔊 1.37 Listen to the recording to check your answers.

Speaking

1 Work in pairs. You are going to do a market research survey. Prepare a list of 6–8 questions to ask people about their spending habits.

How much do you spend on clothes?
Where do you usually shop for food? Why?

2 Do your survey with as many students in the class as you can.

3 Give a short report to the rest of the class on the results of your survey.

> **Useful language**
>
> *One or two people (spend more than …) …*
> *Most of the class (prefer to …) …*
> *Almost everyone (likes …) …*

5c | The office

Vocabulary: office activities

1 Match the verbs in column A to the phrases in column B in as many ways as possible.

A	B
1 do	an email
2 make	a phone call
3 receive	a report
4 send	a photocopy
5 write	some photocopying
	the filing
	the coffee

2 Work in pairs. Discuss these questions.

- How many of the activities in exercise 1 do you do every day?
- Which activity do you think is the most difficult to do in a foreign language?
- Do you ever have to do any of them in English?

Reading

1 Read the article below about different types of people who work in offices. Match the types of people a–d to the descriptions 1–4.

a The trainee   c The workaholic
b The office flirt   d The boss

2 Match the types a–d in exercise 1 to the activities 1–8.

Which office type …
1 has a habit of making terrible jokes?
2 does the most work and spends the most time in the office?
3 spends the least time at their desk?
4 is always very enthusiastic?
5 is friendly one minute and angry the next?
6 takes fewer days' holidays than anyone else?
7 usually makes the coffee for everyone else?
8 thinks that chatting is more interesting than working?

3 Here are three more common office types. What do you think their main characteristics are?

- The office joker • The lazy worker • The gossip

Office Stereotypes

Whether you love them or hate them, work just wouldn't be the same without them. Here is a description of some of the most common office types. Is there one in your office?

1 This person is always very keen to appear to be your 'friend'. They often ask you about your weekend or your family. But the next minute they're asking you whether you've written that urgent report. They often have the annoying habit of making jokes – very bad jokes – which you have to laugh at. But the worst thing is that their moods change so quickly. When there's a crisis in the office, the happy, joking 'friend' disappears and is replaced by a bossy bully.

2 For most people, the office is a place where you work from nine to five. But for this person, the office is their home. In fact they spend much less time at home than they do at their desk. If they have to take holiday, they always make sure they have their cell phone and laptop with them so they can send and receive emails. And they make more business calls than when they're at work.

3 He or she is usually the youngest person in the office, but is also the person with the most energy and enthusiasm. They've probably just finished school and are getting some work experience before they start university. No task is too boring for them and no job is too repetitive. They just love making coffee and really don't mind doing all that last-minute photocopying.

4 This person spends more time chatting with their colleagues than working. They find work boring and they are always trying to make life in the office a little more interesting. They've always got a smile and a compliment for visitors – especially if they're young and good-looking. They spend very little time at their desks and are usually to be found by the photocopier or the coffee machine, trying to get a date for the next office party.

The office | 5c

GRAMMAR: comparing nouns

Use *more* + noun + *than* to compare two things or people.
  *He spends **more time** at work **than** with his family.*

Use *less/fewer* + noun + *than* to make negative comparisons. Use *less* with uncountable nouns and *fewer* with countable nouns.
  *He spends **less time** with his family **than** he does with his boss.*
  *He takes **fewer holidays than** anyone else in the office.*

Use *the* + *most* + noun to compare more than two things or people.
  *People who do things too quickly often make **the most mistakes**.*

Use *the least/fewest* + noun to make negative comparisons.
  *The workaholic always takes **the fewest days' holiday**.*

> SEE LANGUAGE REFERENCE PAGE 52

1 Choose the correct words to complete the text. Then say which office type from Reading exercise 3 is being described.

They receive the (1) *more / most* emails of anyone in the office – usually funny messages from friends. They then share these jokes with everyone else, so they spend (2) *more / most* time walking round the office than at their desks. They do the (3) *less / least* work of anyone and think that their mission is to make sure that there are (4) *less / fewer* sad faces on a Monday morning.

2 Complete the sentences with words from the box so that they are true for you.

| more | fewer | less |
| the most | the fewest | the least |

1 I know _____ jokes than most of my friends.
2 I make _____ phone calls in the morning.
3 I do _____ work possible on Friday afternoons.
4 I have _____ free time than my friends.
5 I have _____ energy at the end of the week.
6 I do _____ work in the morning than in the afternoon.

3 Compare your sentences with a partner.

SPEAKING

1 Work in groups of four, A–D. Imagine that you work in an office. The company wants you to organize a party for the office staff.

A: Turn to page 65.   C: Turn to page 67.
B: Turn to page 66.   D: Turn to page 64.

Read the information on your role card and think about your answers to the questions below.

- What kind of party would you like: a meal in a restaurant, a disco, a buffet? Where would you like the party to be?
- What day of the week would you prefer to have the party? What time should it start and finish?
- Who should be invited to the party: only company staff, staff and their partners, staff and as many friends as they like?
- Who should pay for the party: the company, the staff, both the company and the staff?

2 Now work with your group. The boss has called a meeting to discuss the party. Share your opinions and decide what sort of party you are going to have.

49

5D | Paperwork

VOCABULARY: office supplies

1 Look at the photo above and tick the objects in the box you can see. What other objects can you see?

> biros   calculator   drawing pins   elastic bands
> highlighter   in tray   ink cartridge   mouse pad
> notepad   paperclips   pencil sharpener   phone
> Post-its®   rubber   scissors   Sellotape®
> stapler   Tipp-Ex®™

2 Work in pairs. Discuss these questions.

- What can you tell about the person who works at this desk?
- Do you work at a desk every day? If not, where do you work/study?
- What does the place where you work/study look like?
- What do you think it says about you?

LISTENING

1 🔘 1.38 Listen to a telephone dialogue. Someone is ordering some office supplies from the stationery department. What does he want to order? Can he get it all?

2 🔘 1.38 Listen again and complete the order form below.

> Office supplies request form
> Department _____
> Requested by (full name required)
> _____
> Authorisation code _____
>
> | item | quantity |
> |------|----------|
> | | |
> | | |
> | | |
>
> Order taken by: _Pippa_____

3 Complete the sentences below with an appropriate verb. Then look at audioscript 1.38 on pages 71–72 to check your answers.

1 I'd like to _____ an order, please.
2 I'm _____ from the IT department.
3 That's what it _____ on the form.
4 I'll _____ if I can find it.
5 Can you _____ on a sec?

50

Paperwork | 5D

FUNCTIONAL LANGUAGE: on the phone

1 How many phone expressions can you make from the words in the boxes below?

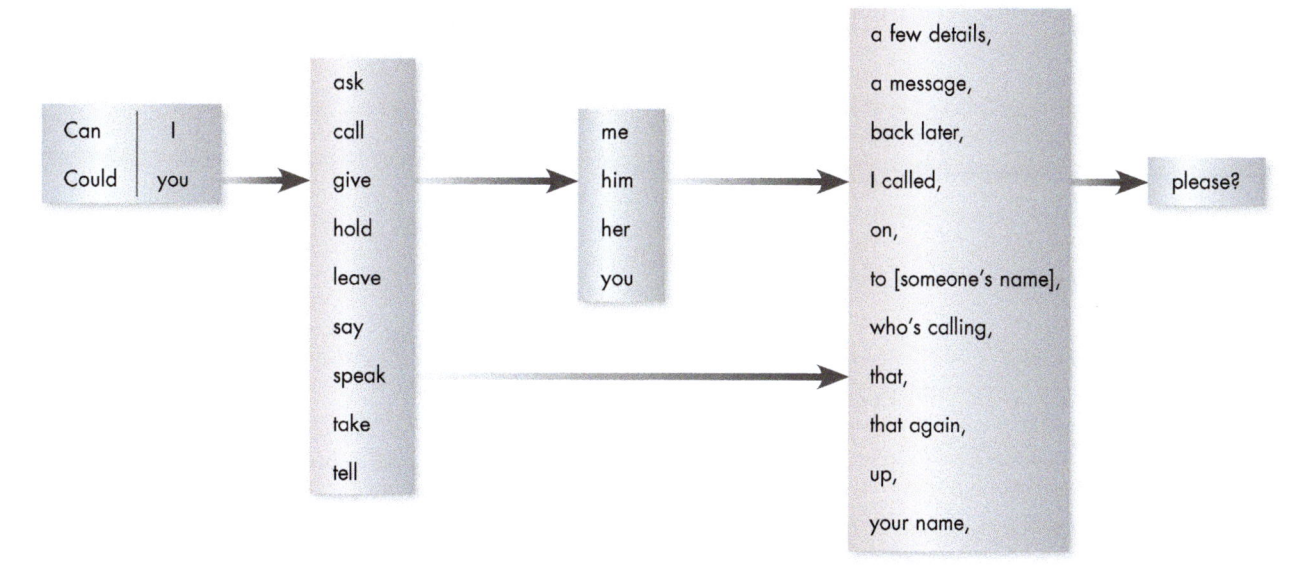

| Can / Could | I / you | ask, call, give, hold, leave, say, speak, take, tell | me, him, her, you | a few details, a message, back later, I called, on, to [someone's name], who's calling, that, that again, up, your name, | please? |

Can I leave her a message, please?
Could you say that again, please?

2 What questions from exercise 1 could you ask to get these replies?

1. Yes, the name's Bond. James Bond.
2. Yes, of course. I'll just get a pen and some paper.
3. Yes, I'll tell him as soon as he gets back.
4. Yes, but I don't think she'll be in the office until tomorrow morning.
5. Yes, OK. In about half an hour. Is that OK?
6. Yes, I'm sorry. It's a bad line, I think.

3 🔊 1.39 Listen to the recording to check your answers.

4 Work in pairs, A and B. You are going to act out a telephone dialogue with an office supplies company.

A: Phone the office supplies company and place an order for some stationery.
B: You work for the office supplies company. Answer the phone and use the order form in Listening exercise 2 to take the order.

Then exchange roles.

DID YOU KNOW?

1 Work in pairs. Read about offices in London and answer the questions.

> The most expensive offices in the world are in London's Mayfair and Park Lane districts – and these are also the most expensive properties in the game of Monopoly. Prices are almost twice as high as in the most popular parts of New York and Hong Kong. Besides having the most expensive offices and hotels, this part of London is close to the main shopping streets and some of the city's most fashionable squares.

- Where are most of the offices in your town/city? What is that part of your town/city like?
- Which is the best part of your town/city to work in?

Self-assessment (✓)

☐ I can answer the phone in a formal context.
☐ I can understand someone placing an order on the phone.
☐ I can place an order on the phone.
☐ I can describe an office.

5 | Language reference

GRAMMAR
Comparisions

We use comparatives to compare two things or people. We use *than* to join the two things we are comparing.

*The supermarkets are cheaper **than** my local shops.*
*Famous brand names are often more expensive **than** other brands.*

We can make negative comparisons with *less* + adjective + *than*.

*Orange juice is **less popular than** fizzy drinks.*

We can make the difference between two things bigger or smaller with a modifier before the comparative adjective. With big differences we use *much, a lot, far* and with small differences we use *a little, slightly, a bit*.

*Digital cameras are **much** more powerful these days.*
*The shop now has a **slightly** wider range of goods.*

We use superlatives to compare more than two things or people. We put *the* before the superlative adjective.

*She buys **the** cheapest clothes she can find.*
*It's **the** most fashionable brand at the moment.*

We can make negative superlatives with *the least* + adjective.

*Which shop is **the least friendly**?*

With short adjectives, we usually add *-er/-est*.

| fresh | fresher | the freshest |
| cheap | cheaper | the cheapest |

When an adjective ends in *-e*, we add *-r/-st*.

| wide | wider | the widest |
| late | later | the latest |

When an adjective ends in *-y* after a consonant, we change the *-y* to *-ier/-iest*.

| easy | easier | the easiest |
| busy | busier | the busiest |

When an adjective with one syllable ends with a consonant after a vowel, we double the consonant.

| big | bigger | the biggest |
| hot | hotter | the hottest |

With longer adjectives, we add *more/the most*.

| important | more important | the most important |
| reliable | more reliable | the most reliable |

Some adjectives have irregular comparative and superlative forms.

good	better	the best
bad	worse	the worst
far	further	the furthest

If we want to say that two things are the same, or almost the same, we can use the following structures:
1 *the same as*
  *Her trainers are **the same as** mine.*
2 *as* + adjective + *as*
  *Her trainers are **as old-fashioned as** mine.*
3 *similar to*
  *Her trainers are **similar to** mine.*

If we want to talk about the differences between two things or people, we can use the following structures:
1 *different from*
  *Her trainers are **different from** mine.*
2 *not as* + adjective + *as*
  *Her trainers are **not as nice as** mine.*
  (= My trainers are nicer.)

Comparing nouns

We can use comparative and superlative forms with nouns as well as adjectives.

We use *more* + noun + *than* to compare two things or people.

*In the US, there are **more classroom advertisements than** in Europe.*

We use *less/fewer* + noun to make negative comparisons. We use *less* with uncountable nouns and *fewer* with plural (countable) nouns.

*He does **less work** than his boss.*
*The company wants everybody to take **fewer days** off.*

We use *the most/the least/the fewest* + noun to compare more than two things or people. We use *the least* with uncountable nouns and *the fewest* with plural (countable) nouns.

*Who has **the most experience**?*
*Of all the people in the office, she spends **the least time** behind her desk.*
*Her department gets **the fewest complaints**.*

Language reference 5

FUNCTIONAL LANGUAGE
On the phone

Can/Could I …
   ask who's calling?
   ask your name?
   call (you) back later?
   give him/her a message?
   leave a message?
   speak to (name)?
   take a few details?
   take a message?
   take your name?

Can/Could you …
   call (me) back later?
   give him/her a message?
   give me a few details?
   give me your name?
   hold on?
   say that again?
   speak up?
   take a message?
   tell him/her who's calling?
   tell him/her I called?

WORD LIST
Adjective (advertising)

comfortable ***	/ˈkʌmftəb(ə)l/
crowded *	/ˈkraʊdɪd/
delicious *	/dɪˈlɪʃəs/
efficient ***	/ɪˈfɪʃ(ə)nt/
fashionable **	/ˈfæʃ(ə)nəb(ə)l/
healthy ***	/ˈhelθi/
popular ***	/ˈpɒpjʊlə(r)/
reliable **	/rɪˈlaɪəb(ə)l/
strong ***	/strɒŋ/
stylish *	/ˈstaɪlɪʃ/

Adjectives (negative prefixes)

dishonest *	/dɪsˈɒnɪst/
disloyal	/dɪsˈlɔɪəl/
dissatisfied *	/dɪsˈsætɪsfaɪd/
impatient *	/ɪmˈpeɪʃ(ə)nt/
impolite *	/ˌɪmpəˈlaɪt/
impossible ***	/ɪmˈpɒsəb(ə)l/
improbable	/ɪmˈprɒbəb(ə)l/
inaccurate	/ɪnˈækjʊrət/
inconvenient	/ˌɪnkənˈviːniənt/
incorrect *	/ˌɪnkəˈrekt/
insufficient **	/ˌɪnsəˈfɪʃ(ə)nt/
unbelievable	/ˌʌnbɪˈliːvəb(ə)l/
unlucky	/ʌnˈlʌki/
unprepared	/ˌʌnprɪˈpeə(r)d/
unsuccessful *	/ˌʌnsəkˈsesf(ə)l/

Office activities

do a report	/duː ə rɪˈpɔː(r)t/
some photocopying	/duː sʌm ˈfəʊtəˌkɒpiɪŋ/
the filing	/duː ðə ˈfaɪlɪŋ/
make a phone call	/meɪk ə ˈfəʊn kɔːl/
a report	/meɪk ə rɪˈpɔː(r)t/
a photocopy	/meɪk ə ˈfəʊtəˌkɒpi/
the coffee	/meɪk ðə ˈkɒfi/
receive an email	/rɪˌsiːv ən ˈiːmeɪl/
a phone call	/rɪˌsiːv ə ˈfəʊn kɔːl/
send an email	/send ən ˈiːmeɪl/
a report	/send ə rɪˈpɔː(r)t/
write an email	/raɪt ən ˈiːmeɪl/
a report	/raɪt ə rɪˈpɔː(r)t/

Office supplies

biro n C	/ˈbaɪrəʊ/
calculator n C *	/ˈkælkjʊˌleɪtə(r)/
drawing pin n C	/ˈdrɔːɪŋ ˌpɪn/
elastic band n C	/ɪˌlæstɪk ˈbænd/
highlighter (pen) n C	/ˈhaɪˌlaɪtə(r) (pen)/
in-tray n C	/ˈɪntreɪ/
ink cartridge n C	/ˈɪŋk ˌkɑː(r)trɪdʒ/
mouse mat n C	/ˈmaʊs ˌmæt/
note pad n C	/ˈnəʊt ˌpæd/
paper clip n C	/ˈpeɪpə(r)ˌklɪp/
pencil sharpener n C	/ˈpens(ə)l ˌʃɑː(r)p(ə)nə(r)/
Post-its® n pl	/ˈpəʊstɪts/
rubber n C	/ˈrʌbə(r)/
scissors n pl *	/ˈsɪzə(r)z/
stapler n C	/ˈsteɪplə(r)/
Tipp-Ex®™ n U	/ˈtɪpeks/

Other words & phrases

advertiser n C	/ˈædvə(r)ˌtaɪzə(r)/
aggressive adj **	/əˈgresɪv/
annoying adj **	/əˈnɔɪɪŋ/
appeal v ***	/əˈpiːl/
appreciate v **	/əˈpriːʃiˌeɪt/
approval n U ***	/əˈpruːv(ə)l/
big business n C	/ˌbɪg ˈbɪznəs/
blank adj **	/blæŋk/
bossy adj	/ˈbɒsi/
brand n C **	/brænd/
buffet n C	/ˈbʊfeɪ/
bully n C *	/ˈbʊli/
catch (sb's) attention	/ˌkætʃ əˈtenʃ(ə)n/
cereal n C/U *	/ˈsɪəriəl/
client n C ***	/ˈklaɪənt/
code n C ***	/kəʊd/
commercial n C *	/kəˈmɜː(r)ʃ(ə)l/
compete v ***	/kəmˈpiːt/
compliment n C *	/ˈkɒmplɪmənt/
consumer n C ***	/kənˈsjuːmə(r)/
corridor n C **	/ˈkɒrɪdɔː(r)/
cover n C ***	/ˈkʌvə(r)/
credit limit n C	/ˈkredɪt ˌlɪmɪt/
crisis n C ***	/ˈkraɪsɪs/
cutback n C	/ˈkʌtˌbæk/
digital adj **	/ˈdɪdʒɪt(ə)l/
district n C ***	/ˈdɪstrɪkt/
double v/adj ***	/ˈdʌb(ə)l/
educational adj ***	/ˌedjʊˈkeɪʃ(ə)nəl/
educationalist n C	/ˌedjʊˈkeɪʃ(ə)n(ə)lɪst/
energy n U ***	/ˈenə(r)dʒi/
enthusiastic adj **	/ɪnˌθjuːziˈæstɪk/
existing adj ***	/ɪgˈzɪstɪŋ/
fizzy adj	/ˈfɪzi/
flirt n C/v	/flɜː(r)t/
fundraising n U	/ˈfʌndreɪzɪŋ/
gossip v/n C/U	/ˈgɒsɪp/
influence v ***	/ˈɪnfluəns/
interest rate n C	/ˈɪntrəst ˌreɪt/
joker n C	/ˈdʒəʊkə(r)/
laser n C **	/ˈleɪzə(r)/
loyalty n U **	/ˈlɔɪəlti/
market research n U	/ˌmɑː(r)kɪt rɪˈsɜː(r)tʃ/
mood n C ***	/muːd/
ordinary adj ***	/ˈɔː(r)d(ə)n(ə)ri/
percentage n C **	/pə(r)ˈsentɪdʒ/
persuade v ***	/pə(r)ˈsweɪd/
platinum n U	/ˈplætɪnəm/
procedure n C ***	/prəˈsiːdʒə(r)/
process v **	/ˈprəʊses/
property n C/U ***	/ˈprɒpə(r)ti/
repetitive adj	/rɪˈpetətɪv/
reward v/n C **	/rɪˈwɔː(r)d/
sale n C ***	/seɪl/
seal n C **	/siːl/
slogan n C *	/ˈsləʊgən/
snack n C *	/snæk/
staff n U ***	/stɑːf/
stationery n U	/ˈsteɪʃ(ə)n(ə)ri/
survey n C ***	/ˈsɜː(r)veɪ/
sweet n C *	/swiːt/
taxpayer n C **	/ˈtæksˌpeɪə(r)/
terrible adj ***	/ˈterəb(ə)l/
trainee n C	/ˌtreɪˈniː/
urgent adj **	/ˈɜː(r)dʒ(ə)nt/
voucher n C	/ˈvaʊtʃə(r)/
washing powder n U	/ˈwɒʃɪŋ ˌpaʊdə(r)/
workaholic n C	/ˌwɜː(r)kəˈhɒlɪk/

53

6A Summer holiday

VOCABULARY: holidays 1

1 Choose the correct word or phrase to complete the collocations.

1 arrive *at the resort / a flight*
2 book *a flight / your way around*
3 check out of *the hotel / some holiday brochures*
4 choose *a destination / the packing*
5 do *the packing / the resort*
6 find *a deposit / your way around*
7 pay *a destination / a deposit*
8 pick up *the hotel / some holiday brochures*

2 What is the most logical order to do the things in exercise 1?

3 Work in pairs. Tell your partner about your last holiday. Use as many expressions as you can from exercise 1.

We chose our destination from a travel brochure. Then we …

READING

1 Read the questionnaire and answer each question for yourself.

2 Work in pairs and compare your answers. Do you have similar attitudes to travelling? Read your results on page 65 and see if you agree.

3 Find words or phrases in the questionnaire which match the definitions 1–8.

1 reading something to find specific information
2 happen unexpectedly or without planning it
3 a cheap holiday because you're booking late
4 do something after you've intended to do it for a long time
5 not take a lot of luggage
6 not prepare a long time ahead
7 made yourself comfortable
8 someone who looks after you when you're on holiday

4 Have you already decided what you're doing for your next holiday? Tell your partner about your plans.

Travel questionnaire
What kind of holiday person are you?

1 It's the end of February and lots of people are already planning their summer holidays. What about you?
a) I've already decided that I'm going back to the same place as last year and the year before.
b) I've bookmarked some useful websites and I'm going to spend the weekend looking through them and deciding where I want to go.
c) I really don't know yet. I fancy somewhere different, but I don't really care where. I know something will turn up, maybe a last-minute bargain or an invitation from a friend.

2 You've decided where to go and the next step is to book a flight. What are you going to do?
a) I've already printed my tickets and itinerary.
b) I'm planning to have a look for some cheap flights on the internet tonight.
c) It's too early to decide yet, I'll probably get round to it in a week or two.

3 When do you usually do your packing?
a) I've already started doing some shopping. I always like to get everything ready at least a day or two before I leave.
b) I'm going to do it all the night before. I know what I need to take already and I'm going shopping tomorrow to buy sunscreen and some film for my camera.
c) I'll probably do it the morning before I leave. It usually only takes about half an hour. I always travel light.

4 When do you plan to get to the airport?
a) A taxi's picking me up first thing in the morning. I want to check in at least two and a half hours before my flight leaves.
b) I've already checked in online, but I'd still like to be at the airport about an hour to an hour and a half before my flight leaves.
c) I'll probably get there just in time – I always leave things till the last minute.

5 You've just settled into your hotel. What are you going to do first?
a) I'm meeting the travel rep and the other new arrivals for a welcome cocktail in the bar.
b) I'm going to find the tourist information centre and ask about where I can hire a car.
c) I don't know yet. I'll just wait and see what there is on offer.

GRAMMAR: future 1 (future plans)

1 Look at question 5 of the questionnaire again and underline the future verb forms. Which verb form …

a) describes an intention?
b) suggests that no definite plans have been made yet?
c) suggests that a firm arrangement has already been made?

2 Choose the best verb forms to complete the dialogue.

A: Hello, we were on the same flight, I think.
B: Yes, we were sitting just behind you. How long (1) *will you stay / are you staying*?
A: We're here for two weeks. And you?
B: We're not too sure. (2) *We're going to stay / We'll stay* for a couple of days and then (3) *we're deciding / we'll decide* if we want to move on. Have you made any plans for tomorrow?
A: Yes, we've hired a car, (4) *we're picking / we'll pick* it up in the morning and (5) *we'll drive / we're going to drive* around the island. We want to find the best beaches. What about you?
B: We haven't made any plans yet. We'll probably wait to see what the weather's like tomorrow and then (6) *we're making up / we'll make up* our minds!
A: Well, there's plenty of room in our car if you fancy coming along. (7) *We'll leave / We're leaving* at 9.30, straight after breakfast.
B: OK, thanks. That sounds like a good idea. We'll let you know tomorrow.

3 Work in pairs. Write the three options for the last two questions in the quiz.

6 You know you should send some postcards. When are you going to write them?

7 It's your last day. Your plane leaves at 7.30 this evening. What are you going to do?

4 Find out if any of your classmates are doing anything special this evening/tomorrow/at the weekend.

Use *be going to* + infinitive to talk about intentions: things you definitely want to do, but you haven't made firm arrangements for yet.
We're going to book some tickets on the internet this evening.
(= This is what we intend to do, but we haven't done it yet.)

Use the present continuous to talk about things you've already decided to do and made some arrangements for.
We're meeting at the pizza house at 8.30.
(= We've already spoken to our friends and arranged a time and a place to meet.)

Use *will* + infinitive …
* to talk about the future when you haven't made any plans or arrangements.
* with *probably, possibly* or *perhaps*.
We haven't made any plans yet, we'll probably decide what to do when the others arrive tomorrow.

> SEE LANGUAGE REFERENCE PAGE 62

SPEAKING

1 Work in groups of three, A–C. It's your first morning in a hotel and you are sharing a breakfast table with some other guests. Find out what their plans are for the day.

A: Turn to page 65.
B: Turn to page 66.
C: Turn to page 67.

6B Getting away

Vocabulary: holidays 2

1 Read the information. Match the resorts to the photos A and B.

Our top two resorts in Jamaica

Negril

With eleven kilometres of beautiful white beaches, Negril is a very cosmopolitan resort, but manages to keep a laid-back atmosphere. It is ideal for a range of watersports and in the evenings you can dance to reggae in the lively clubs or join one of the crowded beach parties. Exotic, fun and completely unforgettable!

Port Antonio

Off the beaten track and away from the more well-known resorts, Port Antonio has some of the most exclusive and upmarket hotels on the island. With its romantic, secluded beaches and the picturesque scenery of the Blue Mountains, this is an area that you will never want to leave.

2 Read the information again and say if the sentences are true (T) or false (F). Correct the false sentences. Then underline the adjectives in the texts that helped you find each answer.

1 There are people from many different countries in Negril.
2 Negril has a very relaxed atmosphere.
3 The clubs in Negril are quiet and boring.
4 You will find Negril very similar to your home town.
5 Port Antonio is far from the places that people usually visit.
6 Port Antonio has cheap hotels.
7 The beaches in Port Antonio are all very crowded.
8 The Blue Mountains are very pretty.

3 Work in pairs. Discuss these questions.

- Would you prefer to go to Negril or Port Antonio? Why?
- What sort of holiday destination do you like? Use the adjectives in the texts about Negril and Port Antonio to describe it.

Buenos Aires is ideal for a range of cultural and fun activities. You can dance tango in La Boca or visit exclusive restaurants in Recoleta.

Listening

1 A radio reporter at Heathrow Airport asked six tourists the question: What are you most looking forward to on your holiday? Here are some of the things they mentioned. Which ones do you think were mentioned by men (M) and which by women (W)?

- the football
- the weather
- watersports
- romantic walks along the beach
- the shopping
- the beautiful women

2 1.40–1.45 Listen to the interviews to check your answers to exercise 1. Answer the questions below.

1 Where are they going?
2 How long are they staying?
3 What are they going to do?

3 1.40–1.45 Listen again. Complete the sentences with the correct number 1–6.

a Speaker _____ is travelling with his mother.
b Speaker _____ has some good news.
c Speaker _____ is going to spend a lot of money.
d Speaker _____ is going to be very tired by the time she gets home.
e Speaker _____ is interested in people-watching.
f Speaker _____ has just got married.

4 Look at the extracts below. What do the words in bold refer to?

Speaker 1: **That's** what everybody goes for, isn't it?
Speaker 2: We're planning to visit **every one**.
Speaker 3: What better place to see **them** than in the capital.
Speaker 4: That's definitely going to be **the highlight** of the four days.
Speaker 5: We're going to spend all of **it**.
Speaker 6: It looks like it's going to be wet and cold **here**.

1.40–1.45 Listen again to check your answers.

5 What do you most look forward to when you go on holiday?

GRAMMAR: future 2 (predictions)

Use both *will* and *be going to* + infinitive to make predictions about the future.
That'll definitely be the highlight of the trip.
That's definitely going to be the highlight of the trip.

Use *be going to* when you have present evidence for the prediction.
It's going to be hot today. (= The skies are blue and it's already 25°C at nine o'clock in the morning.)
You're going to be late. (= The class is about to start and you're still at home.)

Note that often the two forms have a very similar meaning.

> SEE LANGUAGE REFERENCE PAGE 62

1 Look at the pictures. Make two different predictions about what's going to happen next in each one.

2 🔊 1.46–1.47 Listen to the two dialogues. Were any of the predictions you made in exercise 1 correct?

3 Work in pairs. Look at the ideas in the box and predict five things for your partner.

| career | personal life | ten years from now |
| money | tomorrow | friends | exams | travel |

4 Tell your partner what your predictions are. Does he/she think they are possible?

SPEAKING

1 Work in groups of three, A–C. Read the information below.

> You work for a travel agency that specializes in 'made-to-measure' holidays for small groups. You have been asked to arrange a two-week summer holiday for a family group who are celebrating the grandparents' golden wedding anniversary.

2 Decide on the things below.
- destination
- accommodation
- possible activities and excursions
- facilities for the golden wedding party

You will find more information about the special needs and interests of different people in the group at the back of the book.

A: Turn to page 65.
B: Turn to page 66.
C: Turn to page 67.

3 Tell the rest of the class about the holiday you have planned.

Useful language

We've decided to … because …
We're going to arrange some …
They won't want to …
They'll probably be interested in …
They'd like to … so we're going to …

4 Now discuss the holidays with your group.
- Which holiday is …
  a) the most expensive?
  b) the most relaxing?
  c) the most fun?
- Which holiday do you think the family will choose?
- Which holiday would you enjoy most?

6c | Perfect day

Speaking

1 Work in pairs. Discuss these questions.
- Do you often go out for the day? Where do you usually go?
- Where's the best place to go for a day out in your area?

2 With your partner make a list of the five most important things for a good day out.

good weather, a nice restaurant ...

Reading

1 Read the article and match the headings 1–4 to the excursions A–D.

1 Time travel
2 Sports day
3 Bird's-eye view
4 Song and dance

Emerald Tours

Discover the best of Ireland in a day. We've put together an unbeatable selection of one-day excursions from Dublin.

Call now to make your reservation!

A Those of you who've had enough of sightseeing will love this action-packed day. In the morning, you can experience the thrills of rock climbing under the guidance of an experienced instructor. After lunch, there's sea-kayaking in Dublin Bay. To round the day off, there's a visit to the National Aquatic Centre, Europe's largest indoor waterworld. Or if you've had enough of water sports, our guide will take you for a pony ride along the sandy beaches of the Bay.

B For a taste of Ireland's ancient past, this excursion takes you to the magical area north of Dublin. As the sun sets, the highlight of the day will be a guided tour of the World Heritage Site of Newgrange, surrounded by its giant standing stones that are nearly 5,000 years old. Before we take you back into the depths of time, we will see the Hill of Tara, home of the ancient kings of Ireland, before the arrival of Christianity. This memorable day will begin with a visit to Slane Abbey where Saint Patrick brought the message of the Bible in the early 5th century.

C Ireland's west coast is one of the most beautiful and dramatic places on earth, and the ideal way to see it is from the air. In our brand new six-seater helicopter, you will first see the incredible lakes, mountains and rivers of Connemara. After you've had lunch in the pretty fishing village of Clifden, you'll be back in the air for breathtaking views of the wild Aran Islands. Don't forget to bring a camera with a zoom lens for once-in-a-lifetime shots of the seal colony.

D For those of you who like to lie in in the morning, the excursion to Dalkey leaves at the very respectable time of 11.30. Only a short drive from Dublin, the historic town of Dalkey has two castles and a little harbour, but it is also home to some of Ireland's best musicians (Bono, Van Morrison, Enya). Your day begins with a tour of three of the town's finest pubs, all with live music. Once you feel in the mood, our next stop will be a traditional Irish dancing club. Here you will learn the basic steps, in time for an evening of music and dance. The bus returns to Dublin at midnight, but you'll probably want to stay!

2 Read the article again and match the comments 1–8 to the excursions A–D.

1 Great fun, but I fell in twice and the sea was freezing!
2 I was very nervous at first, but the pilot was very kind and he took us to some amazing places.
3 In one place, there was a brilliant harp player. I bought the CD.
4 Ireland's history is so fascinating. We learnt so much.
5 It was my first time on a horse, but it certainly won't be my last!
6 The guide made it really interesting with his funny stories about Irish heroes.

7 The scenery was absolutely fantastic and we'll never forget the sight of the seal cubs.
8 We loved it so much that we decided to stay until the very end. We had to get a taxi back to our hotel.

3 Which excursion A–D should these people choose to go on? Explain your reasons.

1 a young couple on their honeymoon
2 a businessman who wants to impress a customer
3 a group of four retired holidaymakers from Florida
4 two students from a Dublin language school who want to celebrate their last weekend in Ireland
5 a family with two teenage children
6 a delegation of European politicians on a cultural visit

4 Work in pairs. Discuss these questions.

- Which day trip would you choose to go on?
- What do you think the people in exercise 3 would like to see and do in your area?

GRAMMAR: present tenses in future time clauses

1 Look at the highlighted sentences in the article and answer the questions below.

1 Do the sentences refer to the present or the future?
2 Which two verb forms are used after the words *if, after, before* and *once*?
3 Which verb form is used in the other part of the sentence?

2 Complete the text. Put the verbs in brackets into the correct form.

KING'S PARK HOLIDAY VILLAGE

Thank you for booking your weekend away at King's Park. When we (1) _____ (receive) your payment, we (2) _____ (send) you a brochure with details of all our fantastic offers. If you (3) _____ (want) to hire a bicycle during your stay, please let us know and we (4) _____ (make) sure it's waiting for you on your arrival. Once you (5) _____ (settle) into your cabin, one of our guides (6) _____ (come) over to see that everything is to your liking. And as soon as you (7) _____ (have) a chance to have a look around, our reception staff (8) _____ (be) more than happy to take your bookings for dinner and your choice of evening entertainment. If there (9) _____ (be) anything else you need during your stay *(morning newspapers, extra bedding, food or drink in your cabin)*, just let the staff know and they (10) _____ (help) you out as soon as they can.

3 Complete the sentences so that they are true for you.

1 I _____ as soon as I get some free time.
2 When I've done this exercise, I _____.
3 I _____ before I go to bed tonight.
4 Once I've _____, I _____.
5 I _____ as soon as I _____.

4 Compare your sentences with a partner.

> Use a present tense to talk about future time after conjunctions like *if, when, after, before, as soon as* and *once*. You often use *will* in the main clause of the sentence.
> **He'll get** in touch with you **as soon as he arrives**.
>
> Use the present perfect if you want to emphasize that the future action will have finished.
> **Once I've finished this, I'll give** you a call.

> SEE LANGUAGE REFERENCE PAGE 62

DID YOU KNOW?

1 Work in pairs. Read about Cork and discuss the questions.

In 2005, the city of Cork became the second Irish town (after Dublin) to become a European Capital of Culture. Visitors in search of culture can see the sculptures in the Crawford Gallery, go to a concert at the Opera House, take part in the Jazz and Blues festival, or simply find a bar in one of the historic streets and listen to some traditional Irish music. The most famous tourist attraction, however, is the Blarney Stone (just outside Cork). According to tradition, people who kiss the stone will become talkative and eloquent.

- What are the 'cultural capitals' of your country?
- What can you do in these cities?
- Which of these cities have you visited and what did you do there?

6D | Travel plans

Speaking

1 Work in pairs. Describe the photos.

2 Draw up a list of advantages and disadvantages of:
a) Making travel arrangements online
b) Booking through a travel agent's.

Think about the topics in the box.

> time   money   connections and routes
> special offers   unexpected problems   choice
> advice   group discounts

3 Work in a group. Which do you think would be better in the situations below: making travel arrangements online or booking through a travel agent's?

- an activity holiday for a large group of friends
- a package holiday for a family
- a long-distance flight to visit family
- a train to another town

4 When was the last time you booked a trip? Did you book it online or did you go to a travel agent's? Why?

Listening

1 🔊 1.48 Listen to a short dialogue. Match it to one of the situations in Speaking exercise 3. What kind of trip is being organized? Who is going where and when?

2 🔊 1.48 Listen again and complete the form.

Flight enquiry

Customer: Avril Goodman
Destination:
Option 1: airline
            cost
Option 2: airline
            cost

Travel plans | 6D

3 Work in pairs. Are the sentences below true (T) or false (F)? Correct the false sentences.

1 Avril knows the travel agent quite well.
2 She wants to book a flight for her boss.
3 Her boss knows the dates when he wants to fly.
4 The cost is more important than the flight time.
5 There isn't a big difference in cost between direct and indirect flights.
6 Avril gets all the information she wants.

4 🔊 1.48 Listen again to check your answers.

FUNCTIONAL LANGUAGE: indirect questions

> Use indirect questions when you are making polite enquiries. Direct questions can sometimes sound impolite.
>
> Begin indirect questions with introduction + *if* or question word + indirect question.
> *Do you know if he wants to go direct?*
>
> Here are some more common introductions to indirect questions:
> *I wonder …*
> *I'd like to know …*
> *Could you tell me …?*
> *Do you think you could tell me …?*
>
> Note that the word order in an indirect question is the normal affirmative sentence word order (subject + verb).
> *Can you tell me how long that takes?*
> Not … *how long does that take?*
>
> ❯ SEE LANGUAGE REFERENCE PAGE 62

1 Look at audioscript 1.48 on page 73 and find seven examples of indirect questions.

2 Change the questions below into indirect questions. Use different introductions.

1 Where can I buy an American or English newspaper?
2 How many cinemas are there in the town?
3 What time do banks open in the morning?
4 Is there an internet café in the city centre?
5 Which restaurant is the best in town?
6 Are there any non-smoking restaurants near here?

3 Work in pairs. Look at the questions you made in exercise 2. Decide what you would say if a tourist asked you these questions about your city.

VOCABULARY: collocations with *sound*
PRONUNCIATION: word stress

1 🔊 1.49 Listen to three short extracts from Avril's dialogue with the travel agent and tick the endings you hear.

1 That doesn't sound   a) much fun.
                             b) too bad.
                             c) very interesting.

2 Does that sound   a) all right?
                             b) like a good idea?
                             c) OK?

3 That sounds   a) fun.
                             b) great.
                             c) lovely.

2 Mark the adjectives positive (P) or negative (N).

1 amazing   5 fantastic
2 awful   6 horrible
3 dreadful   7 superb
4 excellent   8 terrible

3 Put the adjectives from exercise 2 under the correct stress pattern in the table.

•●	●●	•●•	●••
		amazing	

4 🔊 1.50 Listen to the exchanges and make a note of the intonation on the adjectives. Does it go up or down on the stressed syllable?

5 Tell your partner about three things that you have done today/that you did last week/that you are going to do at the weekend.

Your partner must respond using an expression with *sound*. Use an expression from the exercises above or choose a word from the box.

> boring   different   enjoyable   exciting
> fascinating   nice   painful   wonderful

A: Last week I had toothache so I went to the dentist's and he took out the tooth.
B: That sounds painful!

Self-assessment (✓)

☐ I can understand telephone travel enquiries.
☐ I can respond to personal news with appropriate phrases and intonation.
☐ I can use indirect questions to make polite enquiries.

6 | Language reference

GRAMMAR
Future 1 (future plans)

We use *going to* + infinitive to talk about future plans and intentions. These are things that we definitely want to do, but we haven't made firm arrangements yet.

We're going to get some brochures tomorrow.

affirmative & negative
They're going to hire a car.
He's going to visit his parents.
question
What is she going to do next?

We use the present continuous to talk about things we have already decided to do and made arrangements for.

We're getting the two o'clock flight from Heathrow.
(= We've already bought the tickets.)

We tend not to use *going to* + infinitive with the verbs *go* and *come*. We prefer to use the present continuous.

They're going to Corfu next summer.
What time are you coming?

We use *will* + infinitive to talk about the future when we haven't made any plans or arrangements. This is often used with *probably, possibly* or *perhaps*.

We haven't made any plans yet, we'll probably decide what to do when the others arrive tomorrow.

Future 2 (predictions)

We can use both *will* and *going to* + infinitive to make predictions about the future.

You'll really enjoy the trip.
You're really going to enjoy the trip.

We use *going to* + infinitive when we have present evidence for the prediction.

It's going to rain later this morning.
(There are black clouds in the sky.)
I'm not going to finish this today.
(I still have a lot of work and it's already late.)

In many situations, it is possible to use both *will* and *going to*.

Present tenses in future time clauses

We use a present tense to talk about future time after conjunctions like *if, when, after, before, as soon as* and *once*. We often use *will* in the main clause of the sentence.

As soon as everybody gets here, the coach will leave.
We will have lunch after we get to Dalkey.

Sentences which include *if*, a present tense to talk about future and *will* in the main clause are often described as *first conditional* sentences.

We use the present perfect if we want to emphasize completion of a future action.

Once we have seen the castle, we'll visit some of the pubs.

FUNCTIONAL LANGUAGE
Indirect questions

We use indirect questions when we want to make polite enquiries. Indirect questions usually sound more polite than direct questions.

I'd like to know if I can buy a return ticket.
Could you tell me if this is the right train for Dublin?
Do you know what time the next train leaves?
Can you tell me where the station is, please?

Indirect questions begin with an introduction.

Do you know …?
Can you tell me …?
Could you tell me …?
Do you think you could tell me …?
I wonder …
I'd like to know …

For *yes/no* questions, we use *if* (or *whether*) after the introduction.

In the second part of an indirect question (after the introduction), we use normal affirmative sentence word order (subject + verb).

Can you tell me what time it arrives?
Not ~~Can you tell me what time does it arrive?~~

62

Word list

Holidays

action-packed *adj*	/ˌækʃ(ə)n ˈpækt/
airline *n C* **	/ˈeə(r)ˌlaɪn/
beach *n C* ***	/biːtʃ/
bedding *n U*	/ˈbedɪŋ/
brochure *n C* *	/ˈbrəʊʃə(r)/
capital *n C* ***	/ˈkæpɪt(ə)l/
check in *v*	/ˌtʃek ˈɪn/
check out of *v*	/ˌtʃek ˈaʊt əv/
cosmopolitan *adj*	/ˌkɒzməˈpɒlɪt(ə)n/
deposit *n C* **	/dɪˈpɒzɪt/
destination *n C* **	/ˌdestɪˈneɪʃ(ə)n/
exclusive *adj* **	/ɪkˈskluːsɪv/
excursion *n C*	/ɪkˈskɜː(r)ʃ(ə)n/
exotic *adj* *	/ɪɡˈzɒtɪk/
find your way around	/ˌfaɪnd jə(r) ˌweɪ əˈraʊnd/
flight *n C* ***	/flaɪt/
fun *adj* **	/fʌn/
guided tour *n*	/ˌɡaɪdɪd ˈtʊə(r)/
itinerary *n C*	/aɪˈtɪnərəri/
laid-back *adj*	/ˌleɪdˈbæk/
off the beaten track	/ˌɒf ðə ˌbiːt(ə)n ˈtræk/
packing *n U* *	/ˈpækɪŋ/
postcard *n C* *	/ˈpəʊs(t)ˌkɑː(r)d/
picturesque *adj* *	/ˌpɪktʃəˈresk/
resort *n C* *	/rɪˈzɔː(r)t/
romantic *adj* **	/rəʊˈmæntɪk/
sandy *adj* *	/ˈsændi/
secluded *adj*	/sɪˈkluːdɪd/
sightseeing *n U*	/ˈsaɪtˌsiːɪŋ/
souvenir *n C* *	/ˌsuːvəˈnɪə(r)/
stop off *n C/v*	/ˈstɒp əv/ /ˌstɒp ˈɒv/
suitcase *n C* *	/ˈsuːtˌkeɪs/
sunscreen *n U*	/ˈsʌnˌskriːn/
tourist attraction *n C*	/ˈtʊərɪst əˌtrækʃ(ə)n/
travel agent *n C*	/ˈtræv(ə)l ˌeɪdʒ(ə)nt/
travel rep *n C*	/ˈtræv(ə)l ˌrep/
upmarket *adj*	/ˌʌpˈmɑː(r)kɪt/

Other words & phrases

abbey *n C*	/ˈæbi/
ahead *adv* ***	/əˈhed/
amazing *adj* **	/əˈmeɪzɪŋ/
ancient *adj* ***	/ˈeɪnʃ(ə)nt/
awful *adj* **	/ˈɔːf(ə)l/
babysitter *n C* *	/ˈbeɪbiˌsɪtə(r)/
bargain *n C* **	/ˈbɑː(r)ɡɪn/
battery *n C* **	/ˈbæt(ə)ri/
bay *n C* **	/beɪ/
bird's-eye view *n C*	/ˌbɜːdzaɪ ˈvjuː/
bookmark *v*	/ˈbʊkˌmɑː(r)k/
boring *adj* **	/ˈbɔːrɪŋ/
brand-new *adj* *	/ˌbrænd ˈnjuː/
breathtaking *adj* *	/ˈbreθˌteɪkɪŋ/
cabin *n C* **	/ˈkæbɪn/
catch up on *v*	/ˌkætʃ ˈʌp ˌɒn/
cocktail *n C*	/ˈkɒkˌteɪl/
colony *n C* **	/ˈkɒləni/
congratulations *n pl*	/kənˌɡrætʃʊˈleɪʃ(ə)nz/
delegation *n C* **	/ˌdeləˈɡeɪʃ(ə)n/
depth *n C* ***	/depθ/
dramatic *adj* ***	/drəˈmætɪk/
dreadful *adj* **	/ˈdredf(ə)l/
eloquent *adj*	/ˈeləkwənt/
enjoyable *adj* *	/ɪnˈdʒɔɪəb(ə)l/
exhausted *adj* *	/ɪɡˈzɔːstɪd/
fan *n C* **	/fæn/
fantastic *adj* **	/fænˈtæstɪk/
fascinating *adj* **	/ˈfæsɪneɪtɪŋ/
fate *n U* *	/feɪt/
firm *adj* ***	/fɜː(r)m/
flexibility *n U* **	/ˌfleksəˈbɪləti/
get round to (sth)	/ɡet ˈraʊnd tə/
giant *adj/n C* **	/ˈdʒaɪənt/
goalkeeper *n C* *	/ˈɡəʊlˌkiːpə(r)/
gorgeous *adj* *	/ˈɡɔː(r)dʒəs/
guidance *n U* **	/ˈɡaɪd(ə)ns/
harbour *n C* **	/ˈhɑː(r)bə(r)/
harp *n C*	/hɑː(r)p/
hero *n C* **	/ˈhɪərəʊ/
heritage *n U* **	/ˈherɪtɪdʒ/
highlight *n C* *	/ˈhaɪˌlaɪt/
hill *n C* ***	/hɪl/
honeymoon *n C* *	/ˈhʌniˌmuːn/
horrible *adj* **	/ˈhɒrəb(ə)l/
hyper-organized *adj*	/ˌhaɪpə(r)ˈɔː(r)ɡənaɪzd/
in particular	/ˌɪn pə(r)ˈtɪkjʊlə(r)/
in person	/ˌɪn ˈpɜː(r)s(ə)n/
indoor *adj* *	/ˈɪndɔː(r)/
instructor *n C*	/ɪnˈstrʌktə(r)/
kayak *n C*	/ˈkaɪæk/
knockout *n C*	/ˈnɒkaʊt/
last-minute *adj* *	/ˌlɑːst ˈmɪnɪt/
lens *n C* *	/lenz/
lie in *v*	/ˈlaɪ ˌɪn/
logical *adj* **	/ˈlɒdʒɪk(ə)l/
make up your mind	/ˌmeɪk ʌp jə(r) ˈmaɪnd/
memorable *adj*	/ˈmem(ə)rəb(ə)l/
option *n C* ***	/ˈɒpʃ(ə)n/
penny *n C*	/ˈpeni/
pilot *n C* ***	/ˈpaɪlət/
pony *n C*	/ˈpəʊni/
precise *adj* **	/prɪˈsaɪs/
range *n C* ***	/reɪndʒ/
reckon *v* ***	/ˈrekən/
respectable *adj* *	/rɪˈspektəb(ə)l/
rock climbing *n U*	/ˈrɒk ˌklaɪmɪŋ/
round (sth) off *v*	/ˌraʊnd ˈɒf/
saint *n C*	/seɪnt/
sculpture *n C* **	/ˈskʌlptʃə(r)/
seal *n C* **	/siːl/
settle into *v*	/ˌset(ə)l ˈɪntuː/
shot *n C* ***	/ʃɒt/
site *n C* **	/saɪt/
step *n C* ***	/step/
stunning *adj* *	/ˈstʌnɪŋ/
superb *adj* **	/sʊˈpɜː(r)b/
talkative *adj*	/ˈtɔːkətɪv/
terrible *adj* ***	/ˈterəb(ə)l/
thrill *n C/v*	/θrɪl/
unbeatable *adj*	/ʌnˈbiːtəb(ə)l/
unexpectedly *adv*	/ˌʌnɪkˈspektɪdli/
via *prep* ***	/ˈvaɪə/ /ˈviːə/
wild *adj* ***	/waɪld/
windsurfing *n U*	/ˈwɪn(d)ˌsɜː(r)fɪŋ/
zoom *v*	/zuːm/

Communication activities

1A Grammar exercise 3   page 5

Student A

1A Speaking exercise 1   page 5

I come from …	I have …	I'm feeling …
I live in …	I really like …	I always …
I work for …	I am looking for …	

1C Speaking exercise 1   page 9

Grammar exercise 2
1 a) Association of Southeast Asian Nations
    b) Assembly of Southeast Asian Nations
    c) Assembly of Southeast Asia Nations
2 a) 8   b) 9   c) 10
3 a) 1967   b) 1987   c) 1997
4 a) Brunei Darussalam   b) Cambodia
    c) Indonesia   d) Lao PDR
    e) Malaysia   f) Myanmar
    g) Philippines   h) Singapore
    i) Thailand   j) Vietnam
5 a) 1967   b) 1987   c) 1997
6 a) One Vision. One Region. One Community.
    b) One Vision. One Region. One Identity.
    c) One Vision. One Identity. One Community.

Grammar exercise 3
1 a) English   b) Malay   c) Thai
2 a) about 40 million
    b) about 600 million
    c) about one billion
3 a) Brunei Darussalam   b) Cambodia
    c) Indonesia   d) Lao PDR
    e) Malaysia   f) Myanmar
    g) Philippines   h) Singapore
    i) Thailand   j) Vietnam
4 a) 8 August   b) 18 August   c) 28 August
5 a) Thailand   b) Indonesia   c) Malaysia
6 a) Vietnam   b) Cambodia   c) Myanmar

2B Vocabulary exercise 5   page 17

Student A

1 Complete the questions with some of the phrasal verbs from page 17.

1 When was the last time you had to solve a difficult problem? What was it? How did you _____ it _____?
2 When was the last time you _____ someone _____ at an airport? Who was it? Where were they going?
3 Have you ever _____ any money in the street? What did you do with it?

2 Discuss the questions with your partner.

5C Speaking exercise 1   page 49

Student D

The lazy worker
You don't really want to go out with people from work on a Friday night or at the weekend – you've got better things to do. But if the company is going to pay for an expensive meal in a restaurant or a good party, you don't mind. In fact, you don't mind organizing everything – booking a place and making other arrangements. It would be a nice change from your usual boring job.

3D Functional language exercise 7   page 31

Student A

You've only just met. You haven't been to your friend's house before. Your friend is still in the kitchen preparing the food when you arrive. You really enjoy the evening. Your new friend is a great cook and a really interesting person. You'd like to get to know him/her better.

Think of four requests using the verbs in the box.

| close | give | have | leave | open | call |
| pass | put | smoke | take | use | do |

If you refuse a request, give a reason.

64

4D Speaking exercise 1   page 41

Student A

Ask questions to find out the missing information in the text.

Who is the second president?

There are a number of strange coincidences that link American presidents _____ and Kennedy. Both of them have seven _____ in their _____ and Lincoln had a secretary called _____ , while Kennedy's secretary was called Lincoln. Lincoln was _____ in 1860 and Kennedy one hundred years later in 1960, and the next president, in both cases, was called Johnson. Both men were _____ on a Friday, and both times, the men were with their wives. John Wilkes Booth shot Lincoln in a _____ and then ran to a warehouse; Lee Harvey Oswald shot Kennedy from a warehouse and then ran to a _____. Both killers have fifteen letters in their names.

5C Speaking exercise 1   page 49

Student A

> **The boss**
> A party is good for the staff because it is an opportunity for people to get to know each other better. For this reason, you don't mind paying as long as it isn't too expensive. You think that it is important that the staff decide what kind of party they want, but the final decision is yours.

6B Speaking exercise 2   page 57

Group A

- interested in water sports
- would like a babysitter a few evenings a week
- the younger children love anything to do with animals

6A Reading exercise 2   page 54

What kind of holiday person are you?

Mostly As

You are obviously hyper-organized and you like to make sure that you have everything under control months ahead of time. But have you ever thought that maybe you're a bit too organized? Sometimes it can be fun to make decisions at the last minute.

Mostly Bs

You know that planning ahead makes sense, and you like to make sure that the big decisions have been taken in plenty of time. But you still leave some space for flexibility and you are quite happy to change your plans if something better comes along.

Mostly Cs

You love to leave everything till the last minute. You think that way you can make the best of every opportunity that comes your way. But you may be missing out by letting fate and last minute bargains make your decisions for you. Why not try making your own decision for a change? You may like it!

6A Speaking exercise 1   page 55

Student A

> You're on holiday with a friend, but he/she isn't feeling well and has decided to stay in bed this morning. You'd like to wander around and explore the resort. You also want to do a bit of shopping. It would certainly be more fun with some other people. If your friend isn't feeling better later, you think you'll find out if it's possible to do some water-skiing.

2C Speaking exercise 3   page 18

> Uluru – also known as Ayer's Rock – is a large sandstone rock formation in central Australia. It stands more than 200 miles south west of the nearest large town, Alice Springs. It is of particular importance to the local Aboriginal people, the Anangu, who believe it is sacred. There are many caves with prehistoric cave paintings which are almost 10,000 years old. The Rock was declared a World Heritage Site in 1987.

1A Grammar exercise 3   page 5
Student B

1C Speaking exercise 2   page 9
Student A

Grammar exercise 2
1 a
2 c
3 a
4 b
5 c
6 c

6A Speaking exercise 1   page 55
Student B

You're staying in the hotel on business. You have a conference tomorrow, but today is free. You know the resort well. When you have free time, you often hire a speedboat, but it isn't much fun on your own. You also like windsurfing. But, first of all, you need to go to the shops to buy a new battery for your laptop.

2B Vocabulary exercise 5   page 17
Student B

1 Complete the questions with some of the phrasal verbs from page 17.

1 What's the best way to help someone _____ a disappointment?
2 Do you ever _____ hitchhikers _____ in your car? Why or why not?
3 When was the last time someone _____ you _____ outside your house? Why were you in their car?

2 Discuss the questions in pairs.

6B Speaking exercise 2   page 57
Group B

- *want somewhere warm and sunny*
- *don't want to be based in a town*
- *love camping*

5C Speaking exercise 1   page 49
Student B

The workaholic
You're not very keen on parties and you hate dancing, but a meal in a restaurant would be a good opportunity to talk to people from other departments. You certainly don't want a late night, because you like to get up early in the morning.

5C Speaking exercise 1   page 49
Student C

> The gossip
> You think a party is a great idea. A disco would be nice and you have lots of friends who would like to come. You know some very good clubs in the centre of town and you think that everyone would like them. These clubs are often closed on Monday and Tuesday nights, so the company could rent one. It could be a fantastic night out.

1C Speaking exercise 2   page 9
Student B

> Grammar exercise 3
> 1   a
> 2   b
> 3   c, e, g, h, i
> 4   a
> 5   b
> 6   b

3D Functional language exercise 7   page 31
Student B

> You've only just met. Your friend hasn't been to your house before. Your friend arrives early. You're still in the kitchen preparing the food when he/she arrives. You don't really enjoy the evening. Your new friend is a bit boring. You haven't really got a lot in common.

Think of four requests using the verbs in the box.

| close | give | have | leave | open | call |
| pass | put | smoke | take | use | do |

If you refuse a request, give a reason.

6B Speaking exercise 2   page 57
Group C

* good beaches very important
* like to visit markets and buy souvenirs
* want lots of night life

4D Speaking exercise 1   page 41
Student B

Ask questions to find out the missing information in the text.

Who is the second president?

There are a number of strange coincidences that link American presidents Lincoln and _____. Both of them have seven letters in their names and Lincoln had a secretary called Kennedy, while Kennedy's _____ was called Lincoln. Lincoln was elected in 1860 and Kennedy one hundred years later in 1960, and the next president, in both cases, was called _____. Both men were assassinated on a Friday, and both times, the men were with their _____. John Wilkes Booth shot Lincoln in a theatre and then ran to a _____; Lee Harvey Oswald shot Kennedy from a _____ and then ran to a theatre. Both killers have fifteen _____ in their _____.

6A Speaking exercise 1   page 55
Student C

> You're on holiday on your own because you think it's a good way to make new friends. You want to go into town to find out about hiring a car. You have read that there is a very interesting old town about 40 kilometres from your resort, and you would like to visit it. With a car you could also visit the most beautiful beaches which are further along the coast.

Audioscripts

1B Listening exercises 3 & 5
🔊 1.01

My choice for *Pick of the Week* this week is the BBC2 archive documentary *How Michael Portillo Became a Single Mum*. I think this is one of the best reality TV shows of all time.

For those of you who haven't seen it, Michael Portillo volunteers to step into the shoes of working mum, Jenny Miner, for a week, and look after her kids and her house and take over at her two part-time jobs.

He is obviously used to a very different lifestyle. He never cooks or cleans or does the shopping – he pays someone else to do that for him. And he doesn't have any children. Life as a single parent is going to be a real eye-opener for him.

Jenny has four children, the oldest is eleven and the youngest is eight. Every day, Monday to Friday, she drives the kids to school, and then she goes to her two part-time jobs, one as a classroom assistant and one as a supermarket cashier – and she doesn't pay anyone to do her housework for her!

1B Listening exercise 4 & 5
🔊 1.02

I always thought of Portillo as an arrogant and self-important man, but in this programme, Portillo comes across as very different. Very modest, very friendly, very likeable. He had a lot to learn in his week as a single mum. He had problems, and he wasn't afraid to admit it, but he never lost his sense of humour – and he even seemed to be enjoying himself at times.

At one point, Tasha, the eldest of the children, is having a karaoke party for her friends and Portillo is obviously having a good time. Tasha's friends are impressed by him and think he looks like George Clooney! It is one of the high points of his week.

In another clip, Portillo is working behind the cash till at the supermarket. He doesn't pretend to enjoy the work, but he says that the atmosphere is much nicer than in the Houses of Parliament.

His second job, in the primary school, is more difficult and, at the beginning, it looks as if he's bitten off more than he can chew. We see him in the classroom where he is working as a classroom assistant. At one point, he's having problems with some eight-year-olds. He's trying, and failing, to explain a maths problem to them. But he listens patiently to the teacher and by the middle of the week he's doing much better.

His greatest challenge is little Ellie, the youngest child. She's eight years old and very stubborn, and she's going through a very rebellious phase. She flatly refuses to listen to him and you can see that all his lessons in political diplomacy will get him nowhere. In one typical situation, Portillo is trying to persuade Ellie that it's bedtime, but she's being particularly difficult. Although you can see she's really tired and really wants to go to sleep, she's refusing to go.

I think in the end Ellie is my favourite character in the programme – but Portillo definitely came a close second.

1D Listening exercises 2 & 3
🔊 1.03

W1 = woman 1   W2 = woman 2

W1: So, did she come round?
W2: Who, the new flatmate? Yes, she did, this morning.
W1: And?
W2: And what?
W1: Well, what's she like? Is she going to fit in do you think?
W2: Well ... she's quite a bit older than the rest of us ... she's doing a Master's, I can't remember in what. I think she's about 35, maybe younger. She looks nice enough. She's smiley, chatty, friendly – and quite trendy. She looks like Tan, actually.
W1: Tan?
W2: Yeah, you know, she's got long dark hair and blue eyes, she was wearing make-up and her clothes looked kinda smart, she looked more like a businesswoman than a student.
W1: Mmm ... I'm not sure that's good ... Did she like the flat?
W2: Well ... I think she thought it was OK. I showed her the kitchen, the living room, the bathroom, her bedroom and the bedrooms. I think she likes the bedroom. I mean it is the biggest one, isn't it? I don't think she liked the wallpaper or the furniture though.
W1: Yeah, it does look a bit like an old granny's room.
W2: Yeah, and those horrible pink curtains! But I suppose she can change it, make it look a bit nicer.
W1: So is she going to move in?
W2: I don't know, she said she had to talk to the landlord and she'd let us know tomorrow at the latest.
W1: So, what do you think? Did she look as if she was going to say yes?
W2: Who knows! I guess, yes. She looked as if she was desperate to find somewhere as fast as possible, actually. She said she's living in a guest house at the moment. She said she'd let us know by tomorrow.
W1: OK, then I guess we'll just have to wait and see ...

1D Pronunciation exercise 1
🔊 1.04

the kitchen, the living room, the bathroom, her bedroom and the bedrooms

1D Pronunciation exercise 3
🔊 1.05

1 Monday, Tuesday, Wednesday and Thursday
2 who, what, where, when and why
3 Sue, Nick, Beth, John and me

2B Listening & reading exercises 1, 2 & 4
🔊 1.06–1.08

1 A Swedish pizza deliveryman has broken the record for the longest solo Vespa journey across Europe. Tommy Kallstrom, from Stockholm, arrived in Athens last week, after a four-month trip. Tommy visited fifteen countries on the way, including the principalities of Monaco and Liechtenstein. He kept a diary of his trip and, using his laptop computer, posted details and photos of his journey on his personal website. Tommy almost gave it all up when he had mechanical problems with his Vespa during a storm in the Swiss Alps. Fortunately, he was rescued by a farmer in a tractor who picked him up and took him to the nearest town, where he sorted the problem out. He eventually arrived in Athens on July 1st. Just in time to celebrate his 21st birthday! Tommy's website has won this year's Web Travel Site of the Year.

2 On TV later this week, you can see a documentary film of another incredible journey. Italian TV journalist Chiara Colucci and her husband, Luca, a wildlife cameraman, spent six months driving across Siberia in a Land Rover to make the film. They were looking for the rare Siberian tiger, of which only about two hundred still exist in the wild. However, the star of the film is a baby bear cub called Tizio that they came across near the River Amur. Tizio had been injured and the Coluccis took him with them so they could look after him. When Tizio got over his injury, he didn't want to leave the Coluccis, and the three became close friends. It's an extraordinarily beautiful film and you will not be able to stop crying when the Coluccis finally say goodbye to Tizio at the end of their journey in Vladivostok.

3
A: Hey, have you seen this?
B: What?
A: Here, look: 'University students hitchhike for charity'.
B: It's Alex and Isabelle! So what's the story?
A: Well, apparently they were part of a group of students who have hitchhiked from Land's End to John O'Groats to raise money for charity.
B: That's a long way to hitch ... and what charity was it?
A: Let's see ... yeah, a local children's hospital ... yeah, and it seems although ten of them set out together, only four of them actually arrived.
B: What do you mean, only four of them arrived? Did the others get lost or something?
A: No, the thing was they had a time limit; they had to get to John O'Groats in less than two days. See, there's a photo here of their friends and families seeing them off from Land's End last Friday, and it says here that they had to get to John O'Groats by midday on Sunday.
M: And they made it there in time?

68

Audioscripts

F: Yeah, not only that, they broke the record, too … it only took them ten hours and 20 minutes.
M: Ten hours? What did they do? Hire a helicopter or something?
A: Well, it says here that they were really lucky with their first lift. A van picked them up after only five minutes and took them almost all the way. It dropped them off just 20 minutes' walk from the finishing line.
B: And what happened to the others, then?
A: Looks like they gave up and turned for home.

2B Pronunciation exercise 1
1.09
1. arrived in Athens
2. gave it all up
3. film of another incredible
4. still exist in
5. it's Alex and Isabelle
6. part of a group

2B Pronunciation exercise 3
1.10
1. perform as a clown
2. lie in an office
3. set out on his adventure
4. hitchhike around Ireland

2D Listening exercises 2 & 3
1.11–1.13
1 D = driver   L = Linda
L: Hi. Does this bus go to the town centre?
D: Sorry, what was that?
L: Are you going into the centre?
D: Yeah, we go there.
L: Er, a single to the town centre, please.
D: That'll be one twenty, please.
L: Er, yeah. Er, sorry, have you got change for a ten-pound note?
D: No, sorry. Exact change only.
L: OK, just a second … erm … I don't think I've got it … oh yes, I have … .
D: Here you are.
L: Erm, I'm going to Bridge Street. Could you tell me when we get to the bridge, please?
D: Yup. I'll let you know.
L: Thanks.

2 A = male 1   B = male 2
A: How are you getting home? Have you got your car?
B: No, I didn't bring it … I'm going to get a cab. You live my way. Do you want to share one?
A: Well, OK, thanks, why not … I was going to get the bus, but, why not, if we're sharing …
B: Hello? Yes, I'd like a cab for the Pizzeria Roma, please. On West Road. Yes, on West Road. Er, as soon as possible, please. Five minutes? Perfect. Yes, the name is Harding. Yes, thanks, bye.

3 SA = Station Announcer
C = Camilla   I = Information Clerk
SA: Platform 14 for the 11.45 train to Brownsville. Platform 14 for the 11.45 train to Brownsville.
C: Excuse me, has the 11.40 for North Park left yet?
I: Not if you hurry, it's still at the platform, platform 10. It's running a bit late, you might catch it if you run … oh, no, that's it pulling out now.
C: Rats! Can you tell me the time of the next train to North Park?
I: The next one's at 2.35, madam.
C: 2.35! Oh no. I'm going to be so late. Can I get a taxi anywhere round here?
I: Yes, madam. There's a taxi rank at the front of the station. But you'll probably have a bit of a wait at this time of day.
C: Thanks, thanks.

3A Reading exercises 4 & 5
1.14–1.18
1. Disadvantages? I can't think of any, really. Maybe the monthly meetings that you have to go to. Some people never stop talking, and you have to sit there listening to people for hours. Er, I can't really think of anything else.
2. We're very happy here, but sometimes, yeah, I guess sometimes, it feels very small. I mean, everybody knows everything about everybody else. Sometimes it gets a bit too much.
3. We all have to help with repairs and things like that, but some folks do a lot more than others. The work isn't always divided very fairly. You know, it seems some families don't have to do as much as other families.
4. Every now and then, someone cooks a really horrible meal. You can't say anything. Well, you can, but nobody ever does. We all sit there and eat it and smile.
5. I think that most of us agree that one or two of the children are a problem. You know, just difficult kids, but their parents never do anything about them. They're allowed to do anything. But it's no big deal.

3B Listening exercises 2 & 3
1.19–1.21
1
A: The best thing? The sense of freedom, I guess. The fact that we can decide to go where we want when we want … if we get bored, we go somewhere new.
B: And the worst?
A: When the police or the local authorities make us move on. I mean, when we find somewhere where we want to stop, and we set up camp and make everything really nice and comfortable and then the police or the farmer or the local people don't let us stay. That happens quite often.
B: Do you have a favourite place to stop?
A: Yes, we've got two or three places we go back to every year, where we've got friends, where the farmers are happy to let us stay on their land. We usually go to pick fruit or do other odd jobs … .

2
A: The best thing? The views – no doubt about that. They're spectacular. And I love getting up to the sound of the sea. I particularly love the sea in winter, when the waves are enormous, and come crashing down on the rocks around the house. What other job lets you live somewhere so dramatic?
B: It certainly is dramatic, but doesn't it get a bit lonely out here sometimes?
A: Yes, that's the worst thing, it can get quite lonely. I usually spend three weeks here on the island and then I have three weeks off while my partner takes over. I love going home to see my friends and family. I miss them a lot! They don't allow us to have visitors, but the job keeps me pretty busy. And they let us keep pets. I've got three dogs, they keep me company!

3
A: Do you live here all year round?
B: No! It's a holiday home really. We usually spend a month or so here in the summer.
A: Isn't it a bit dangerous living halfway up a tree?
B: Obviously the biggest drawback of living in a tree is the danger of falling off! To start with, we were quite worried about it, especially when visitors came to stay … but nothing's happened yet. We don't let little kids come up on their own and we make dog owners leave their pets in the garden! And the other problem, of course, is fires … that really does worry us … so we don't allow any smoking.
A: It looks pretty small, too. Why on earth did you choose this as a holiday home?
B: Well, we wanted something different, but what we really like most of all is the idea … the feeling of, you know, of being part of nature. Hearing the birds, seeing all the animals …

3D Listening exercises 2 & 3
1.22–1.25
1 W = woman,   M = man
W: Hello. Come in, come in … .
M: Thanks … erm … these … are for you.
W: Oh, flowers … thank you, you shouldn't have. They're lovely! Come into the kitchen, I'm just finishing something …

2
M: Can I help with anything?
W: Oh, yes, please can you put these flowers in some water for me? Thanks.

69

M: No problem.
W: Can I get you something to drink? Some fresh lemonade maybe, I made some earlier this morning.
M: Erm … yes, yes thank you. That sounds great – just what I need, it's so hot today! Is it OK if I go out into the garden?
W: Sure thing, be my guest. I thought we'd eat out there, actually. The table needs laying, could you take these plates out for me?
M: Do you want me to take the glasses and the lemonade, too?
W: Yeah, thanks

3
W: Are you alright sitting in the sun?
M: Yeah … it is hot though! Would you mind if I moved the sunshade a little?
W: Feel free, do you need any help?
M: No, thanks, I think I can do it. There … that's better – wow, this is great, I love your flat, and this garden, it's just perfect.
W: Thank you, yes, I was really pleased when I found it … Would you mind passing the salad? Thanks!
M: How long have you been here?
W: Well, I moved in …

4
M: Thank you so much … that was great … hey, do you fancy going to the cinema later? That new Italian film's on … you know the one.
W: I'd love to, thing is, I've got to do some work. Do you think I could do that first?
M: Yes, that's fine, do whatever you need to do.
W: It'll only take me an hour or so. I mean, do you mind waiting?
M: No worries, that's fine, could I wait here … ?
W: Of course! Make yourself at home! And help yourself to whatever you want … Oh yes, do you think you could clear the table? Thanks!
M: Sure thing, and I'll do the dishes.

3D Functional language exercise 3
🔘 1.26

A = woman,   B = man
1
A: I've got to do some work. Do you think I could do that first?
B: Yes.
2
A: Is it OK if I go out into the garden?
B: Yes.
3
A: Do you mind waiting? It'll only take me an hour or so.
B: No.
4
A: Would you mind if I moved the sunshade a little?
B: No.

3D Functional language exercise 4
🔘 1.27

A = woman,   B = man
1
A: I've got to do some work. Do you think I could do that first?
B: That's fine, do whatever you need to do.
2
A: Is it OK if I go out into the garden?
B: Sure thing, be my guest. I thought we'd eat out there, actually.
3
A: Do you mind waiting? It'll only take me an hour or so.
B: No worries, that's fine. Could I wait out here?
4
A: Would you mind sharing if I moved the sunshade a little?
B: Feel free, do you need any help?

3D Functional language exercise 5
🔘 1.28

Could you take these plates out for me, please?

4A Pronunciation exercise 1
🔘 1.29

A: Was that man standing under the tree again?
B: Yes, he was. He was with a friend this time.
A: What do you think they were doing?
B: I asked them. They said they were waiting for a bird.
A: A bird! I find that hard to believe.
B: They were! They said it was a lucky bird.
A: I knew he was a bit crazy!

4B Listening exercises 3 & 5
🔘 1.30

Part 1 There's a great story in the news today about a 74-year-old retired teacher, Frane Selak. The headlines are calling him the luckiest man in the world – and it may well be true. Many of us buy our weekly lottery tickets and never win anything, but Selak recently won more than $1 million with the first lottery ticket he had bought in forty years. With the money, he bought a new house, a car, a speedboat and married his girlfriend.

4B Listening exercises 4 & 5
🔘 1.31

Part 2 But that's not the only reason why Selak is thanking his lucky stars. He is also lucky to be alive. A few years ago, he was driving his car in the mountains, when he saw a truck coming straight towards him. His car crashed off the road through the forest for a hundred metres, ploughed into a tree and exploded. Fortunately, Selak had jumped out. But this was not the first of his lucky escapes. In fact, Selak has become the master of lucky escapes. Back in 1962, he was travelling from Sarajevo to Dubrovnik when the train came off the rails and fell into an icy river. Rescue workers found seventeen corpses in the water, but Selak had swum to safety, suffering only shock, bruises and a broken arm. A year later, he was involved in a plane crash in which nineteen people died. But before the crash, Selak had jumped out of the plane and fallen in a haystack. Again, the only injuries were cuts and scratches and the usual shock. His next disaster was a bus accident when four people died. The bus left the road and Selak again found himself in a river. But he was becoming something of an expert at this sort of situation and again swam to safety. By this time, said Selak, his friends had stopped visiting him. A few years later, he suffered burns – and lost a lot of his hair – when his car caught fire at a petrol station. The petrol pump was old and had sprayed petrol all over the hot engine of his car. Then, in 1995, he was in hospital again. Another bus had knocked him over. And what does Selak think of all this good luck? He's just glad that he's been able to live long enough to enjoy his million-dollar lottery win.

4B Grammar exercise 2
🔘 1.32

Lucky Luciano was one of America's most famous gangsters and, for a time, he was even more powerful than Al Capone. He got his name when he was a young man because he had been so successful at choosing horses at the horse races. People recognized him immediately because he could not control one of his eyes. In 1929, rival gangsters had kidnapped him and cut his face with a knife. His eye never recovered. In the 1930s, Luciano became famous. He had made so much money that he could go anywhere and do anything. People were frightened of him, but everyone wanted to be his friend. Not surprising when you think that he had been responsible for the murders of about 500 people. In 1940, the Americans joined the Second World War, but Luciano did not have to fight. The police had arrested him four years earlier and he was in prison. He stayed there for ten years. Then, in 1946, he was put on a boat for Italy. The Governor of New York had given him his freedom – on condition that he left the country. Luciano stayed in Italy until he died in 1962.

4D Listening exercises 1 & 2
🔘 1.33

C = Clive   L = Linda
C: There you go.
L: Thank you – that should keep me busy for the rest of the afternoon! Hey Clive, were you at that new White Rose leisure club last night?
C: Yeah, why? Were you there too?

L: I thought it was you – you were in the car park, I shouted and waved and sounded the horn, but you didn't see me.
C: Really? Sorry about that.
L: So what do you think of it?
C: The White Rose? Not bad, the gym's pretty good. Pretty expensive but it's worth it. I mean, you have to keep fit, don't you? Are you a member?
L: Yeah, I joined last week. I signed up for the free squash lessons.
C: Really? You didn't! Me, too. Bit of a coincidence that, innit? Have you had your first lesson yet?
L: No, not yet.
C: No, me neither – not yet. I'm going tomorrow.
L: Really, so am I! At half seven
C: Me, too!
L: With Jeff?
C: Yeah, that's right.
L: Do you think we'll be in the same class, then? I thought it was women only. We'll be in the same class.
C: No, no, it's all mixed. Anyway, so … Amazing! What a coincidence! So how did you find out about the club, it's bit out of your way, innit? Don't you live the other side of town?
L: We did, but we moved last week. We live just round the corner now.
C: Yeah? So do we. Me and my wife I mean. Whereabouts?
L: Harlech Crescent
C: You're kidding! You live in Harlech Crescent!
L: Yes, why?
C: Well, so do we. We do, too. I mean, we live there, too. What number?
L: 48. Why?
C: Number 65, us. We live in 65.
L: Mm. No way! Small world. I didn't know we were neighbours!
C: Neither did I!
L: Hey, we'll have to get together some time. So you must be a regular at the Robin Hood?
C: That's right – it's my local. Not a bad pub, is it?
L: No, it's really nice. We've had a bit of a look around and it's definitely the best pub in the area.
C: So we'll be seeing you there then? Do you like pub quizzes?
L: Yes, from time to time – and Mark absolutely loves them. He went to the one last Monday.
C: Did he? Me, too. Me and some mates, we go every week. Who was he playing with?
L: I've no idea, I didn't go.
C: Neither did my wife – she wanted to see the film on TV.
L: Titanic?
C: Yes, that's it. You, too?
L: Yeah, me, too! It's a great film.
C: Listen, you'll have to … Why don't you come round one evening? Maybe we can get a takeaway in and a video. What do you reckon? Do you like Chinese?
L: Yeah, I love it. That place on the green is pretty good, isn't it? We had a meal from there last night.
C: You're not going to believe it, but so did we! We always do on Wednesdays.
L: Well, we'll have to do it together next time.
C: OK, I'll mention it to Joan, she'll love the idea. Right, got to go … no rest for the wicked and all that. See you around then … neighbour …

5B Listening exercises 3 & 4
🔊 1.34

J = Jones   S = Salesperson

J: Jones here,
S: Good morning, Mr Jones. My name's Michael Everest and I'm calling from Spark Financial Services. I'm sure you're a busy man, but I wonder if I could have a few minutes of your time, if it isn't too inconvenient …
J: Er, well I'm quite busy at the moment act …
S: We're doing a market research survey to find out more about people's credit card habits and I have a few questions that we would like to ask you. It'll only take a few minutes.
J: Er, well, OK, so long as it doesn't take too long.
S: Of course, if this is inconvenient, I could always call you back later.
J: Um, er …
S: That's very kind of you, Mr Jones. I appreciate your time.
J: Er …
S: Well, could I ask you first if you have heard of the new Spark Gold Card?
J: Er, no … I'm not really interested in a new credit card …
S: Ah well, if I may give you just a little bit of information, I'm sure you'll be as excited about the new Spark Card as we are. You may, for example, be interested to know that the interest rates with the new Spark Gold Card are not as high as most other cards. In fact, right now with the Spark Gold Card, the interest rate is an amazing three point seven per cent.
J: That sounds quite good actually …
S: What's more, if you transfer your balance from your other cards, as a new customer, we will give you nine months' free credit. That's nine months with no interest charges at all.
J: No interest charges?
S: No, none at all. Our market research shows us, too, that many people are dissatisfied with the credit limits on their cards. May I ask you if you sometimes find your credit limit is insufficient for your needs?
J: Er … well, no, not really … I'm quite happy with my card at the moment …
S: But we will take the credit limit on your existing card and double it. The maximum credit limit is twenty thousand pounds – much higher than most other card companies.
J: Oh, right, er … but I don't think I really need …
S: I wonder if there are any other reasons why you are unhappy with your present card. Did you know that the new Spark Gold Card also offers you reward points? For every £100 you spend with your card, we will give you five reward points. Isn't that just unbelievable?
J: Er, yeah, sounds good, I suppose. But it's very similar to what I've got already.
S: That's impossible! There are no other credit cards out there that can compete with the Spark Gold Card! Do you think you might be interested in having a new Spark Gold card? Are you sure I can't persuade you to try it out?
J: Er, well, no, not really … thanks.
S: But this offer is only available until the end of the month.
J: No, thanks a lot, but I'm just not interested. Goodbye
S: Well, maybe I could just take down a few details. It's Mr T Jones, is that correct?
J: Yes, that's right. T for Thomas. Tom Jones. The same as the singer.
S: You're a singer?
J: No, no, I said my name is the same as the singer. You know, er, Tom Jones.
S: Ah yeah, of course. And what do you do for a living, Mr Jones?
J: I'm, er, between jobs.
S: Between jobs?
J: Yes, you know, er, unemployed. That's not a problem, is it?
S: Er, no, no. Could you tell me which card you're using at the present time?
J: Oh, I haven't got one at the moment. But your Spark Card sounds exactly what I need. Could you perhaps send me two or three? Or four maybe? With different names on them?
S: I'm afraid that's impossible, sir, you can't hold a card in a different name.
J: Well, you don't need to tell anyone, do you? It could be our little secret.
S: I'm sorry, sir, but …
J: No, listen, you send me a pile of credit cards, all with different names – not with my name, of course, but names that are similar to mine. I'll take out lots of cash with them, right up to the credit limit. And then we divide the money between us. It's as easy as that. What do you say? Hello, anyone there? Hah! That got rid of him!

5B Pronunciation exercise 1
🔊 1.35

Whizzo is the most popular washing powder in Scotland!

5B Pronunciation exercise 2
🔊 1.36

/s/ bus; certain; class; course; person; send
/z/ amazing; easy; raise; thousand; times; using
/ʃ/ cash; efficient; mention; shop; sure; wash

5B Pronunciation exercise 3
🔴 1.37

business, citizen, commercials, delicious, insufficient, salesman, surprise, stylish

5D Listening exercises 1 & 2
🔴 1.38

P = Pippa   D = Dave

P: Hello? Good morning.
D: I'd like to place an order, please.
P: Yes, sir. Can I take your name, please?
D: Er, yes, it's Dave. I'm calling from the IT department.
P: Could I have your surname as well, please?
D: My surname? Yes, sure, but you won't need it. I'm the only Dave around here.
P: Sorry, but that's what it says on the form and the computer won't process it if any of the boxes are left blank.
D: Really? Must be a new procedure.
P: Yes, something to do with cutbacks I think.
D: Oh, right, yes, well, that would explain it.
P: So?
D: Oh, yes, er, sorry, it's Blackman.
P: Blackman? Can you spell that please?
D: Yes, of course. B-L-A-C-K-M-A-N.
P: Thank you. And can you tell me your department code, please?
D: I'll see if I can find it. Can you hold on a sec?
P: Yeah, sure.
D: Oh, yes, here it is. IT-007.
P: Thanks.
D: I just wanted six packs of paper for the printer and er, a couple of ink cartridges, colour.
P: Two colour cartridges.
D: Er yeah, that's it. The KS7.
P: Oh. I'm really sorry, but you can't order more than one colour cartridge at a time.
D: You're joking! OK, it'll have to be one then, and I'll just place another order tomorrow.
P: And the paper?
D: Er, yeah, six packs of laser paper, please.
P: I'm really sorry, but we haven't got any laser paper. We've only got the ordinary paper.
D: I'll er, just get some photocopying paper instead, then, thanks. Two packs of A4.
P: OK, so, a KS7 ink cartridge and two packs of white A4 paper. Anything else?
D: No, no, that's it thanks.
P: You're welcome. Bye.

5D Functional language exercise 3
🔴 1.39

1
A: Can I ask who's calling, please?
B: Yes, the name's Bond. James Bond.

2
A: Can I leave a message, please?
B: Yes, of course. I'll just get a pen and some paper.

3
A: Could you tell him I called, please?
B: Yes, I'll tell him as soon as he gets back.

4
A: Could you give her a message, please?
B: Yes, but I don't think she'll be in the office until tomorrow morning.

5
A: Can I call you back later?
B: Yes, OK. In about half an hour. Is that OK.

6
A: Could you speak up, please?
B: Yes, I'm sorry. It's a bad line, I think.

6B Listening exercises 2, 3 & 4
🔴 1.40–1.45

1   R = reporter   T = Tourist
R: Hello, can I ask you a quick question?
T1: Yeah, sure, go ahead.
R: Are you off on holiday?
T1: Yup, certainly am ... at last!
R: What are you most looking forward to?
T1: Oh, the windsurfing, definitely. I mean that's what everybody goes for, isn't it? We're planning to surf all day, every day. I mean, we're only going for a week and we have to make the most of what the Canaries have got to offer.
R: Sounds like you're going to need a holiday to get over your holiday – you're going to be exhausted with all that windsurfing.
T1: Yeah, probably! But we'll have plenty of time to catch up on our sleep when we get back home.

2
R: Hello, are you off on holiday today?
T2: Yeah, we are, well sort of ...
R: Do you mind if I ask you a quick question?
T2: Er, no, no, not at all.
R: What are you most looking forward to?
T2: Well, you see, we're off on our honeymoon ...
R: Congratulations!
T2: Thanks ... yeah, so I reckon what I'm most looking forward to is the romantic walks along the beaches. They say that Mauritius has got some of the most beautiful beaches in the world. And during the two weeks we're there we're planning to visit every one!
R: Well, I hope you have a great time.
T2: Thanks a lot, I'm sure we will!

3
R: And you, sir, what are you most looking forward to?
T3: The people-watching, I think.
R: The people-watching?
T3: Yes, you know, sitting in a street cafe watching the world go by.
R: Ah?
T3: Yeah, love it. And the women! You can't beat Italian women. Stunning. Gorgeous. Absolute knockout. And what better place to see them than in the capital?
R: Is that all you're planning to do during your holiday?
T3: More or less – unless I get lucky ... and a bit of sightseeing, too, of course: the Coliseum, the Vatican, that kind of thing. But I'm only going for the weekend, so there won't be much time to do anything else.

4
R: Can I ask you what you're most looking forward to on your holiday?
T4: Er ... I don't know really ... We've never been to Madrid before, so lots of things ... the city, the people, the sights, ... oh yeah, I do know what I'm looking forward to most – the football.
R: The football?
T4: Yeah, we've got tickets for the match on Sunday and that's definitely going to be the highlight of the four days.
R: And who are you travelling with?
T4: My mother ...
R: Your mother? And is she looking forward to the football, too?
T4: Yes, definitely ... she's more of a fan than I am! She really likes their goalkeeper.

5
R: And where are you off to, sir? Madam?
T5: We're off to New York.
R: On holiday or on business?
T5: Holiday.
R: What are you most looking forward to?
T5: The shopping! We've been to New York quite a few times, so we've done the sights. We go for the shopping. Best place for shopping in the world.
R: Are you looking for anything in particular?
T5: Well, the first thing we're going to buy is two large suitcases. To put everything else in that we buy.
R: That sounds like serious shopping!
T5: Yeah, definitely. We've got about er, £5,000 between us.
R: And you're going to ...
T5: Yes, we're going to spend all of it over the weekend. Every single penny.

Audioscripts

R: On anything in particular? Apart from the suitcases, of course.
T5: No, no. Whatever bargains we find, you know, electronic equipment, clothes, cowboys boots …
R: Well, happy shopping!
T5: Thanks!

6
R: And what are you most looking forward to on your holiday?
T6: Well, we're not actually going on holiday. We're going to visit my husband's parents in Melbourne for ten days.
R: Australia? That's a long way to go for ten days …
T6: Yes, it is, but we're going over to break some good news to the family …
R: Oh, yes … ?
T6: Yes, we're going to be parents. I'm expecting a baby in June.
R: Congratulations! And you haven't told them yet?
T6: No, we haven't. We wanted to break the news in person.
R: So that's obviously what you're most looking forward to …
T6: Yes, that, and the weather. It's summer over there and it looks like it's going to be cold and wet here.
R: It certainly does! Well, enjoy your trip and congratulations again on the good news!
T6: Thanks.

6B Grammar exercise 2
1.46–1.47

1 G1 = Girl 1 G2 = Girl 2
G1: Have you seen that bloke over there?
G2: The one sitting at the table?
G1: Yeah, not bad looking, is he?
G2: Yeah, and he's looking over.
G1: Do you think he's going to come over?
G2: No, he looks too shy … pity … .
G1: Yeah, real pity … .
G2: You're not going to go over and talk to him!
G1: Yeah, why not, let's give it a try …

2 B = Boy G = Girl
B: So, what do you think? Which one do you like?
G: Well, I like that one, but it looks really expensive.
B: Well, it's a special occasion; I don't think expense counts …
G: No, I suppose not. OK, that one, then. He'll love it!
B: Yeah, I think your dad's going to be really happy with his 60th birthday present.

6D Listening exercises 1, 2 & 4
1.48

J = June A = Avril
J: Good morning. T&A travel, how can I help you?
A: Hello, June, it's Avril here.
J: Avril! How are you? How was your weekend away?
A: Well, you know what the weather was like. Absolutely horrible. Awful. But the hotel was superb, and it was good for both of us to get away from that dreadful new woman at work. We had a lovely time, actually.
J: So, you're planning another bargain break weekend away?
A: No, wish I was. No, I'm making some enquiries for Derek my boss, actually.
J: Ah-ha. Derek, eh? What, is he off on a business trip or something?
A: Yes, something like that …
J: So where's he going this time?
A: Japan. But you mustn't tell anyone.
J: Japan? That's a long way to go for a business meeting. When's he going?
A: Well, he doesn't know yet … it's all very up in the air. No, he'd just like to know how much it costs for the moment. He isn't going for a business meeting actually, his son's getting married out there.
J: Really? When?
A: Next month.
J: OK. Do you know if he wants to go direct?
A: I think he's more interested in the cost, actually, at the moment. Do you think you could tell me what the cheapest options are? And then maybe we can look at the direct flights and compare costs.
J: OK. So, let's see. Do you know where he wants to fly to?
A: Yes, Tokyo.
J: OK, so leaving from London, arriving Tokyo. Let's see what we've got. OK, I've got a Finnair flight here for £650 return. There's a stop off at Helsinki.
A: Can you tell me how long that takes?
J: Yes, just a minute, here we are. As I said, it's via Helsinki and it takes … er … just over fourteen hours, fourteen hours and fifteen minutes to be precise.
A: Well, that doesn't sound too bad. What about direct flights, can you find out how much a direct flight costs?
J: Right, hold on a sec, here we are, there's a Japan Airlines flight at £884.80 – that takes eleven hours and 45 minutes.
A: Mmm … it's a big difference in price for a relatively small difference in time.
J: Hold on, there's another one coming up on the screen now … a Virgin Atlantic direct flight at £750 … Does that sound OK?
A: Maybe. Could you tell me how long it takes?
J: Well, the flight time's more or less the same, a little bit longer – twelve hours.
A: OK, so let me just check I've got that right. Finnair at £650 via Helsinki and Virgin Atlantic direct at £750. Can you tell me how long those two flights take again, please? Sorry, I forgot to write it down!
J: Yes, of course, fourteen hours fifteen minutes for the Finnair flight and twelve hours for the Virgin Atlantic direct.
A: OK, great, got that, thanks.
J: No problem.
A: Listen, I have to go now, see you over the weekend sometime?
J: Yeah, I'll give you a call. Bye.
A: Bye, but how about coming over for dinner at the weekend? My brother's going to be there, too.
J: Lovely. Are you going to introduce me to your mystery man?
A: Really, June! He's not a mystery man; it's just that we both want to be a little discreet. But yes, Derek will be there.
J: Well, I'd love to. That sounds lovely. I think it's fantastic that you two are, you know, er …
A: Yes, well, OK, I'll give you a call tomorrow. Must rush.
J: OK. Speak to you tomorrow. Bye.

6D Vocabulary & pronunciation exercise 1
1.49

1 J = June A = Avril
J: It's via Helsinki and it takes, er, just over fourteen hours, fourteen hours and fifteen minutes to be precise.
A: Well, that doesn't sound too bad.

2
J: There's another one coming up on the screen now. A Virgin Atlantic direct flight at £750. Does that sound OK?

3
J: Well, I'd love to. That sounds lovely.

6D Vocabulary & pronunciation exercise 4
1.50

1
A: Where did you go last summer?
B: We went camping. It was superb. We loved it.

2
C: What was the weather like?
D: Absolutely awful.

3
E: You know what? We had a car crash on the first day of our holiday.
F: Oh, you poor thing! That sounds dreadful!

4
G: We took a yacht round the Mediterranean last summer.
H: Really? That sounds amazing! I'd love to do that.

5
I: What did you think of Prague?
J: Fantastic! The kids enjoyed it, too.

6
K: You look brown! Where have you been?
L: The Algarve. It was excellent. Really, really good.

7
M: You have a good time in England?
N: No, not really. The food was horrible!

8
O: So, how was the skiing?
P: Terrible. There was no snow.

1 | Review

1 Correct the mistakes in the dialogue.

A: Paul, hi, it's me. Listen, are you wanting to come out for a meal this evening?
B: Yes, sure, of course. But aren't you spending your birthday with Scott?
A: No, he's busy. He's doing something else.
B: What? On your birthday?
A: Yes, he's working late at the office today.
B: He's seeming to have a lot of work these days.
A: Yes, maybe. But I'm not believing him.
B: What? You're meaning that he's lying?
A: Well, I'm knowing that he's not telling me the whole truth.
B: Are you thinking that he's seeing someone else?
A: Maybe. He's behaving a bit strangely at the moment.
B: How terrible! Poor you.

2 Complete the postcard below. Put the verbs in brackets into the present simple or the present continuous.

3 Read the short text and complete the comprehension questions for these answers.

The Church of England decided that women could be priests in 1992. Two years later, 32 women became the first female priests in the country. At the time, some male priests complained. They thought that it was the end of the church.

1 Who _____? The Church of England.
2 When _____? In 1992.
3 When _____? Two years later.
4 How many women _____? 32.
5 Who _____? Some male priests.
6 What _____? That it was the end of the church.

4 Complete the questions with a word from the box.

| as | of | to |

1 Do most people see you _____ an approachable person?
2 Do you consider yourself _____ be very patriotic?
3 Do you think _____ yourself as right-wing or left-wing?
4 How many people would you describe _____ very good friends?
5 Do you think you are lucky _____ live in the 21st century?
6 Which is more important _____ you – friends or family?

5 Work in pairs. Ask and answer the questions in exercise 4.

6 Complete the missing letters in the words.

1 He has a very p _ _ _ _ _ _ _ t nose, like a big carrot.
2 He looks ill and has a very unhealthy c _ _ _ _ _ _ _ _ n.
3 He prefers to have grey hair than to be b _ _ d.
4 He's got a very m _ _ _ _ _ _ r build – he must spend hours in the gym.
5 Her eyes look very n _ _ _ _ w in her new glasses.
6 He looks as if he's just got out of bed – his hair's a mess and he hasn't s _ _ _ _ d.
7 She looks very t _ _ _ _ d, but I think it's fake – some sort of cream.
8 Sometimes her hair is straight and sometimes it's w _ _ _ y.

I arrived in London yesterday and I (1) _____ (have) a good time already. At the moment, I (2) _____ (watch) a cricket match. Tom (3) _____ (play) cricket every Sunday afternoon and today his team (4) _____ (play) in Kew – near the famous gardens. I (5) _____ (not / understand) the rules, but it (6) _____ (not / matter) – it's good fun anyway. It (7) _____ (look) as if it's going to rain later (typical England!), but for the moment, the sun (8) _____ (shine). We (9) _____ (drink) warm beer and I (10) _____ (eat) a cheese and cucumber sandwich. England is everything I imagined! You'd love it!

Love
Claire xxx

Lauren Thompson
457 S. Monica Blvd.
Venice
CA
US

2 | Review

1 Choose the correct time expression to complete the questions.

1 Did you do anything special *last weekend / over the last few weeks*?
2 Have you booked your next holiday *yesterday / yet*?
3 Have you made many friends *during your time at this school / when you were at primary school*?
4 Have you seen any good films *one month ago / recently*?
5 How many times did you take a taxi *during the last year / last year*?
6 How often have you been ill *in the last six months / last month*?

2 Work in pairs. Ask and answer the questions in exercise 1.

3 Complete the article. Put the verbs in brackets into the past simple or the present perfect.

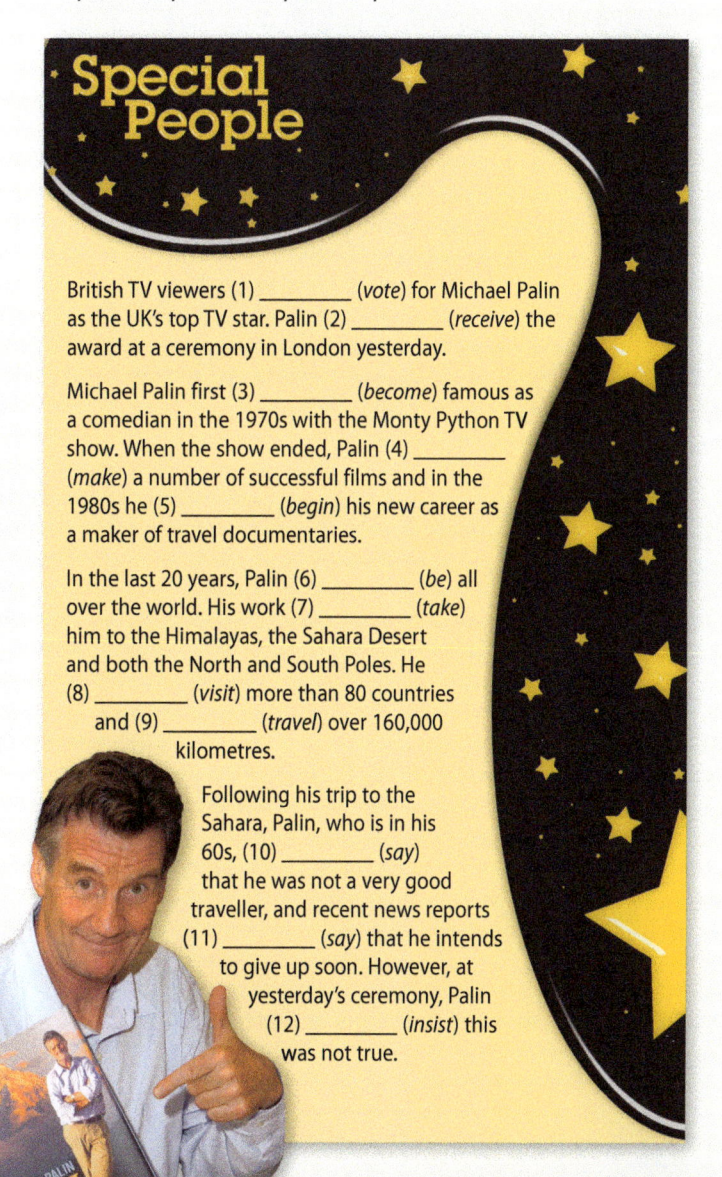

Special People

British TV viewers (1) _____ (vote) for Michael Palin as the UK's top TV star. Palin (2) _____ (receive) the award at a ceremony in London yesterday.

Michael Palin first (3) _____ (become) famous as a comedian in the 1970s with the Monty Python TV show. When the show ended, Palin (4) _____ (make) a number of successful films and in the 1980s he (5) _____ (begin) his new career as a maker of travel documentaries.

In the last 20 years, Palin (6) _____ (be) all over the world. His work (7) _____ (take) him to the Himalayas, the Sahara Desert and both the North and South Poles. He (8) _____ (visit) more than 80 countries and (9) _____ (travel) over 160,000 kilometres.

Following his trip to the Sahara, Palin, who is in his 60s, (10) _____ (say) that he was not a very good traveller, and recent news reports (11) _____ (say) that he intends to give up soon. However, at yesterday's ceremony, Palin (12) _____ (insist) this was not true.

4 Complete the sentences 1–8 with the phrases a–h.

1 A brown bear looks
2 He always drops
3 He often picks
4 I was surfing the net last night and came
5 It often takes a long time to get
6 She decided to give
7 She needs some help to sort
8 They've gone to see

a across a good site for hitchhikers.
b after her cubs for about two and a half years.
c off the kids at school on his way to work.
d off their friends at the airport.
e out a problem with a virus on her computer.
f over a serious illness like that.
g up hitchhikers in his truck.
h up the sport after her latest injury.

5 Rearrange the words to make sentences.

1 across before come him I never 've .
2 after her I if 'll like look you .
3 are picking them time up what you ?
4 came me nobody off see to .
5 could drop here me off please you ?
6 get it 'll over soon you .
7 give he it should up .
8 have it out soon sort to we .

6 Complete the dialogue with verbs from the box. More than one answer is sometimes possible.

catch   get   get off   get on   miss   run   take   walk

A: Excuse me, can you tell me how I can _____ to City Airport from here?
B: Yes, of course. The best way is to _____ a train to Stratford.
A: Thanks. How often do the trains _____?
B: Every ten minutes, so if you _____ one, you don't have to wait long. Platform 4.
A: Platform 4. OK. How long does it _____? Half an hour?
B: Oh no, only about fifteen minutes. You _____ the train at the last stop.
A: The end of the line. OK. And can I _____ to the airport from there?
B: No, you'll need to _____ the airport bus. It will be right outside the station.

7 Work in pairs. Practise the dialogue in exercise 6.

75

3 | Review

1 Choose the best explanation for the signs.

1. **Free car park for residents only**
   a) Everybody has to pay to park here.
   b) Nobody has to pay to park here.
   c) Residents do not have to pay to park here.

2. **Last check out 12.00**
   a) You don't have to check out before 12.00.
   b) You must check out before 12.00.
   c) You must not check out before 12.00.

3. **No guests in rooms**
   a) Guests are not allowed in the rooms.
   b) Guests must not leave their rooms.
   c) You can take guests to your room.

4. **Dogs welcome**
   a) You are allowed to bring a dog with you.
   b) You don't need to bring a dog with you.
   c) You have to bring a dog with you.

5. **Restaurant non-residents welcome**
   a) Non-residents can't eat here.
   b) You don't need to be a resident to eat here.
   c) You must be a resident to eat here.

6. **Swimming pool opening hours 08.00–20.00**
   a) Swimming is not allowed between 08.00 and 20.00.
   b) You can swim between 08.00 and 20.00.
   c) You mustn't swim between 08.00 and 20.00.

2 Complete the second sentence so that it has a similar meaning to the first.

1. In the Middle Ages, the church made most people give them one tenth of their money.
   In the Middle Ages, most people _had to give_ one tenth of their money to the church.
2. Only important people could wear purple clothes in 16th-century England.
   Only important people were _____ purple clothes in 16th- century England.
3. Between 1919 and 1932, Finnish people were not allowed to buy alcoholic drinks.
   Between 1919 and 1932, the Finnish government _____ its people buy alcoholic drinks.
4. Before 1963, American law let employers pay a man more than a woman for the same job.
   Before 1963, American employers _____ pay a man more than a woman for the same job.
5. The Soviet Union did not let some writers publish their work.
   Some writers _____ publish their work in the Soviet Union.

3 Correct the mistakes in the sentences.

1. Could you possibly leaving your dog outside?
2. Do you mind if I opening the window?
3. Do you think could you pick us up at eight o'clock?
4. I wonder if could I invite a few friends for dinner.
5. Is it all right when I leave work early tomorrow?
6. Would you mind to pass the mayonnaise?

4 Choose an appropriate response for the requests in exercise 3.

1. Yes, go ahead. / Yes, of course.
2. No, not at all. / Yes, sure.
3. No, that's OK. / Yes, no problem at all.
4. I'm sorry, but I'm busy tonight. / I'm afraid you can't.
5. No, that's fine. / Yes, that's fine.
6. Yes, here you are. / Certainly not.

5 Complete the questions in column A with a phrase from column B.

A	B
1 Can you get to	a alarm clock when you're on holiday?
2 Do you always make the	b asleep at school?
3 Do you ever set your	c bed every day?
4 Have you ever fallen	d nap and then decided to stay in bed until the next morning?
5 Have you ever had a	
6 How often do you wake	e sleep when there's a lot of noise?
7 What time do you begin to feel	f sleeper that you know?
	g sleepy in the evening?
8 Who is the heaviest	h up in the middle of the night?

6 Work in pairs. Ask and answer the questions in exercise 5.

4 Review

1 Choose the correct verb forms to complete the text.

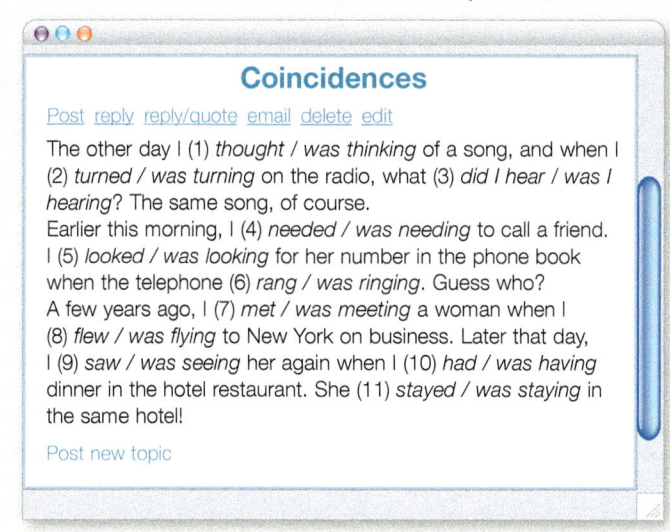

Coincidences

Post reply reply/quote email delete edit

The other day I (1) *thought / was thinking* of a song, and when I (2) *turned / was turning* on the radio, what (3) *did I hear / was I hearing*? The same song, of course.
Earlier this morning, I (4) *needed / was needing* to call a friend. I (5) *looked / was looking* for her number in the phone book when the telephone (6) *rang / was ringing*. Guess who?
A few years ago, I (7) *met / was meeting* a woman when I (8) *flew / was flying* to New York on business. Later that day, I (9) *saw / was seeing* her again when I (10) *had / was having* dinner in the hotel restaurant. She (11) *stayed / was staying* in the same hotel!

Post new topic

2 Complete the text. Put the verbs in brackets into the past simple, the past continuous or the past perfect.

Post reply reply/quote email delete edit

Last night I (1) _____ (*want*) to watch a film on TV, but my sister (2) _____ (*watch*) a quiz show. I (3) _____ (*agree*) to wait until the end of her show. The contestant (4) _____ (*sit*) in a big black chair. She (5) _____ (*answer*) nine questions correctly and she (6) _____ (*have*) one more question to get right for the jackpot. Her name (7) _____ (*be*) Emily – the same as me – and she (8) _____ (*wear*) exactly the same clothes as me! She (9) _____ (*have*) to give the name of the river in Budapest. I (10) _____ (*come*) back from a trip to Hungary only last week!

Submitted by Emily

3 Decide if the pairs of sentences below have the same (S) or different (D) meanings.

1 The fire started while he was at the petrol station.
 When he was at the petrol station, the fire started.
2 She bought a new house when she won the lottery.
 She won the lottery after she'd bought a new house.
3 She screamed the moment she saw him.
 As soon as she saw him, she screamed.
4 By the time we arrived, they had already left.
 They left before we arrived.
5 They called for help as soon as their car broke down.
 Their car broke down as soon as they called for help.
6 He had an accident while he was playing on the balcony.
 When he was playing on the balcony, he had an accident.

4 In four of the sentences below, one word is missing. Insert the missing words.

1 Both them like a bit of a gamble.
2 Neither my friends my family think it's against the odds.
3 Neither us feel like giving it a go.
4 We both want to try our luck.
5 There's a lot at stake for both the company the workers.
6 They both think it's a lottery.

5 Match the sentences 1–6 to the short responses a–f.

1 I bought a _____ last week.
2 I can't _____.
3 I like _____.
4 I wasn't _____ yesterday.
5 I'm going to _____ tomorrow.
6 I've never been to _____.

a Neither can I.
b Neither have I.
c Neither was I.
d So am I.
e So did I.
f So do I.

6 Complete sentences 1–6 in exercise 5 so that they are true for you.

Work in pairs. Read your sentences to your partner. Your partner must respond to your sentences truthfully.

7 Complete the sentences with a word from the box.

| ankle | black | bleeding | bruise |
| scratch | shock | sprained | unconscious |

1 He _____ his wrist playing squash.
2 He wouldn't explain how he got a _____ eye.
3 Her finger is _____ after she cut it with a knife.
4 Many people were suffering from _____ after the explosion.
5 She's got a _____ on her arm where the ball hit her.
6 The cat was frightened and tried to _____ me.
7 The doctors think he may remain _____ for a few hours.
8 The parachutist twisted her _____ when she landed.

| 77

5 | Review

1 Look at the information in the table and say if the sentences 1–8 are true (T) or false (F). Correct the false sentences.

A quick guide to local furniture stores			
Alum & Key	🛏️🛏️🛏️🛏️	£££	🙂
Bettabeds	🛏️🛏️	££	🙂🙂🙂
Home Comforts	🛏️🛏️🛏️	£	🙂🙂🙂🙂

1 Bettabeds is the least expensive of the three stores.
2 Home Comforts is slightly cheaper than Bettabeds.
3 Alum & Key is less friendly than the other shops.
4 The nicest staff are at Home Comforts.
5 Alum & Key has the biggest range of furniture.
6 It's easier to find what you want at Bettabeds than at Home Comforts.
7 On the whole, Bettabeds is better than Home Comforts.
8 Alum & Key is the worst place to go for good service.

2 Complete the sentences with a word from the box.

> as   from   not   the   to

1 The prices in superstores are similar _____ the prices in local shops.
2 Local shops are _____ as convenient as superstores.
3 The staff in superstores are _____ friendly as in local shops.
4 Opening hours at local shops are different _____ superstores.
5 One superstore is _____ same as another.

Work with a partner. Decide if you agree with the sentences in exercise 2.

3 Choose the best word to complete the sentences.

1 He gets the *fewest / more* complaints.
2 He has the *least / less* experience of all of them.
3 I have a lot *fewer / less* energy than him.
4 I've taken *fewer / least* holidays this year.
5 She has *less / more* projects than the others.
6 She probably has the *fewest / most* work to do.

4 Complete the dialogues with an appropriate phrase.

A: Hello. Could I (1) _____, please?
B: I'm afraid that Mrs Robinson isn't at home right now. Can I (2) _____?
A: Yes, please. This is Benjamin here.
B: I'm sorry. Could you (3) _____?
A: Yes. Benjamin. B-E-N-J-A-M-I-N. Could you (4) _____?
B: Yes, of course. I'll ask her to call you as soon as she gets back.

C: Sales and marketing. Can I (5) _____?
D: Yes, hello. Could I speak to Thomas, please?
C: I'm sorry, but Thomas isn't at his desk right now. I think he's at lunch.
D: Oh, right. Can I (6) _____? In about an hour?
C: Yes, I'm sure that he'll be back then. Could I (7) _____?
D: Yes, it's Mrs Laurence.
C: OK, Mrs Laurence. I'll tell him you called.

Work in pairs. Practise the dialogues.

5 Complete the sentences with a positive or negative form of the adjectives in the box.

> comfortable   correct   delicious
> polite   popular   satisfied

1 It was a very _____ restaurant so they had to book in advance.
2 It was a very stylish place, but the chairs were very _____.
3 Last time they went, the food was _____, but this time it was not so good.
4 In addition, they didn't enjoy the meal because the waiter was extremely _____.
5 The bill was _____ so they asked for it to be changed.
6 They were _____ with the service so they decided to complain to the manager.

6 Four of the sentences below are strange or illogical. Put a cross next to these sentences.

1 He made a few corrections with his pencil sharpener.
2 He ordered a couple of note pads from the stationery department.
3 Her secretary used a highlighter to show all the important information.
4 I need a new ink cartridge for my stapler.
5 She spent the day working in the filing cabinet.
6 She wrote an important biro to the new clients.
7 The photocopies were attached with a paper clip.
8 There are loads of reports in my in tray that I have to look at.

6 Review

1 Choose the best verb forms to complete the dialogue.

A: (1) *Are you going to do / Will you do* anything interesting this weekend?
B: Probably not. (2) *We're staying / We'll stay* at home, I guess. And you?
A: Yes, (3) *we're visiting / we'll visit* some friends at the coast. But according to the weather forecast, (4) *it's going to rain / it will rain*, unfortunately.
B: Well, I'm sure (5) *you're having / you'll have* a nice time anyway.
A: Yes, it doesn't matter too much. We're more worried about the traffic. It's a holiday weekend, so there (6) *are going to be / will be* a lot of cars on the road.
B: If you leave early, (7) *you're going to be / you'll be* OK.
A: Yes, but we can't leave until after nine because (8) *we're going to do / we'll do* a bit of shopping first.

2 Look at the dialogue in exercise 1 again. Which examples of *going to* can you replace with the present continuous?

3 Complete the sentences. Put the verbs in brackets into the correct form.

1 We're going to look for a hotel as soon as we _____ (*arrive*).
2 After we've checked in, we _____ (*find*) somewhere to eat.
3 We'll go for a walk around the city when we _____ (*eat*).
4 If the weather _____ (*be*) bad, we'll go on a bus tour.
5 Once we know the city a bit better, we _____ (*visit*) a museum or two.
6 We'll visit the National Gallery before we _____ (*leave*).

4 Correct the mistakes in the questions.

1 Do you know what will your next film be?
2 Could you tell us which actor or actress would you really like to work with?
3 Can you tell us what do you like most about making films?
4 We'd all like to know how much did you earn for your last film.
5 Can you tell us if you ever do watch your own films?
6 Our viewers would like to know you're going out with anyone at the moment.

5 Work in pairs. Imagine that you are a journalist and a famous film star. Ask and answer the questions in exercise 4.

6 Complete the sentences with a word or phrase from the box.

arrive   book   check out   choose
do   find   pay   pick up

1 Don't forget the sunscreen when you _____ the packing.
2 Guests must _____ of the hotel before eleven.
3 Please _____ your excursions 24 hours in advance.
4 Signs in the town are written in English so it's easy to _____ your way around.
5 There will be a welcome party when you _____ at the hotel.
6 We have hundreds of exotic destinations to _____ from.
7 We kindly ask you to _____ a 5% deposit when you make your reservation.
8 You can _____ a brochure at our shop during normal shopping hours.

7 Complete the text with the best answers, a, b or c.

The Philippines

Cebu Island, the Philippines' top tourist destination, has something for everybody. With both (1) _____ hotels and accommodation for travellers on a budget, you're sure to find the ideal place to stay. Cebu has many lively, (2) _____ resorts, where you can meet people from all over the world. These are perfect for (3) _____ holidays, with (4) _____ facilities for mountain biking, horse riding, trekking and water sports nearby.
Travellers looking for peace and quiet can choose one of the more (5) _____ holiday villages. And if you want to take things easy, you can relax on one of the hundreds of beautiful (6) _____ beaches, or go for a (7) _____ walk in the (8) _____ Cebu Mountains.

1 a) dreadful   b) painful   c) upmarket
2 a) awful   b) cosmopolitan   c) guided
3 a) shy   b) gorgeous   c) action-packed
4 a) dramatic   b) laid-back   c) superb
5 a) horrible   b) secluded   c) talkative
6 a) exhausted   b) sandy   c) unbeatable
7 a) memorable   b) discreet   c) ancient
8 a) exclusive   b) picturesque   c) respectable

John Waterman
Additional material
by Mike Sayer

Straightforward

Level 2B

Workbook

Contents

p84	1A–1D	Stative & dynamic verbs; Present simple & present continuous; Verbs with two meanings; Subject & object questions; Self-image; Describing people
p88	1 Reading	*You never get a second chance to make a first impression*
p89	2A–2D	Present perfect & past simple; Present perfect for unfinished time; Phrasal verbs; Travelling; Verb collocations (travel)
p93	2 Reading	*Eddie Izzard – the marathon man!*
p94	3A–3D	Modals of obligation, permission & prohibition (present time); *Make*, *let* & *allow*; Modals of obligation, permission & prohibition (past time); Accommodation; Verb collocations (sleep); Requests
p98	3 Reading	*Interview*
p99	4A–4D	Past simple & past continuous; *Both* & *neither*; Past perfect simple; Talking about similarities & differences; Injuries; Time linkers
p103	4 Reading	*A win on the horses*
p104	5A–5D	Comparisions 1; Comparisions 2; Comparing nouns; Adjectives (advertising); Adjectives (negative prefixes); Office activities; Office supplies; On the phone
p108	5 Reading	*Statistics*
p109	6A–6D	Future 1 (future plans); Future 2 (predictions); Present tenses in future time clauses; Indirect questions; Holidays 1; Holidays 2; Collocations with *sound*
p113	6 Reading	*What is the real price of tourism?*

Writing

p114	1	A description of a best friend
p116	2	A description of a town or city
p118	3	Advantages and disadvantages
p120	4	A narrative: lottery winner
p122	5	An advertisement
p124	6	An extract from a holiday brochure

Useful language to improve your writing p126   **Irregular verbs** p127

1A Double lives

STATIVE & DYNAMIC VERBS

1 Choose the correct verb form to complete the sentences.

1 You're lying! I *don't believe / 'm not believing* what you're saying.
2 Clara *thinks / is thinking* of changing her job.
3 I *want / am wanting* to watch *Mad Men* on TV.
4 She says that she *likes / is liking* me, but I'm not sure.
5 This day out at the funfair *costs / is costing* me a fortune.
6 I *hate / am hating* people who lie.

2 Find and correct six grammatical mistakes in the verbs in the advertisement.

> **Are you believing your partner when they say they're working late at the office?**
>
> **How are you knowing if he or she is telling the truth?**
>
> **Easy!**
>
> ▸ Buy the person you are loving the Lie Detector.
> ▸ This unique device can tell if a person is lying or not.
> ▸ It is asking a simple question. If the person is lying, they get an electric shock. If they are telling the truth, nothing happens.
>
> **It couldn't be easier.**
> So if you think about what you are wanting to buy your loved one, think no more – **Trickster Toys** has the perfect gift for him or her.
> **Every couple should have one.**

VOCABULARY FROM THE LESSON

3 Underline the word or phrase that does not go with the verb.

1 **lie**   about why you're late   to a friend
         about your age   by a member of your family
2 **have** no choice   a lovely time   sincere
         no qualifications
3 **look** ahead someone   up to someone   great
         at someone straight in the eyes
4 **be**   dating someone   fidgeting and nervous
         honesty   a liar
5 **tell** the truth   about a story   a lie
         your partner something

4 Complete the dialogue with words from the box.

| fidgeting | sweaty | liar | date | great | nervous |

Meena: You look fantastic, Gabrielle.
Gabrielle: Oh, you (1) _____!
Meena: I'm not lying! You look (2) _____.
Gabrielle: But I'm feeling really (3) _____.
Meena: Relax. What can go wrong?
Gabrielle: On a first (4) _____!? Plenty!
Meena: He's probably going to feel uncomfortable, too.
Gabrielle: Not as much as me. My hands are all (5) _____.
Meena: It would help if you could stop (6) _____ with your hair.

DICTATION

5 2.01 Write the sentences that you hear.

1 _____?
2 _____.
3 _____.
4 _____.
5 _____.
6 _____.

READ & LISTEN

6 2.02 Read and listen to the reading text *Liars!* on page 4 of the Student's Book.

1B Daily lives

PRESENT SIMPLE & PRESENT CONTINUOUS

1 Choose the correct verb forms to complete the interview.

I: Tonight I (1) *interview / am interviewing* the world famous model, Tania Brookes. Tania, welcome.
T: Thanks, James.
I: Now I'd like to start by asking you about this new reality TV programme you (2) *do / are doing* called *Swapping Jobs*.
T: Yep. Basically, I swap jobs for a week with someone … with Dot Bryce, in fact. Dot is a single working parent with three kids. She (3) *lives / is living* in a small flat and (4) *works / is working* as a cleaning lady.
I: And how does her life compare to yours?
T: To be honest, there's no comparison. Let me give you an example. In a normal photo shoot I (5) *make / am making* about £300 per hour. That is 50 times more than Dot makes in the same time!
I: Wow! Do you feel sorry for her?
T: Not at all. She's a terrific woman: strong, optimistic and fun. We actually (6) *like / are liking* each other a lot. And she (7) *has / is having* three lovely girls.
I: OK, tell us a little about your new job.
T: OK. I (8) *get / am getting* up at six and take the girls to school for 8.30. Then it's a bus ride to my first job. I seem to spend a lot of time on buses! Anyway, the work is non-stop. At the moment I (9) *do / am doing* stuff like washing dishes, cleaning floors, baths and toilets, hoovering carpets, tidying up rooms, and so on.
I: And (10) *do you enjoy / are you enjoying* it?
T: Is that a serious question!? No way!

VERBS WITH TWO MEANINGS

2 Complete the dialogue. Put the verbs in brackets into the present simple or present continuous.

Alan: I (1) _____ (think) about going on that *Swapping Jobs* programme.
Bob: I (2) _____ (not / think) they'll want you.
Alan: Why not? I (3) _____ (have) an interesting job.
Bob: Alan, forget it! You're a traffic warden. That is not an interesting job!
Alan: Well, you're wrong. Look at this. A letter from AVD TV.
Bob: What!?
Alan: Yep! I (4) _____ (see) them for a meeting tomorrow. Being a traffic warden is one of the most unpopular jobs in Britain, you know.
Bob: Yeah, I know. So?
Alan: Well, that means a lot of people would love to see someone famous doing my job.
Bob: Oh, I (5) _____ (see) what you mean. So the idea is to watch someone who (6) _____ (have) a really bad time for a week.
Alan: That's the idea.
Bob: I don't believe it!

TRANSLATION

3 Translate the sentences into your language.

1 I normally vote for the Liberal Democrats in general elections.
   _____.

2 What are you doing at the moment?
   _____?

3 She's trying to explain, but he doesn't seem to understand her.
   _____.

4 I'm thinking of going to Poland on holiday this summer.
   _____.

5 I'm working in a bar until I can find a better job.
   _____.

6 I think reality TV is usually complete rubbish.
   _____.

1c | Identity

SUBJECT & OBJECT QUESTIONS

1 How much do you know about Southeast Asia? Do the quiz to find out.

DO YOU KNOW ...

1 What is the official language in Brunei Darussalam?
  a) Chinese
  b) English
  c) Malay

2 Which of these Southeast Asian nations has never been colonized?
  a) Brunei Darussalam
  b) Malaysia
  c) Thailand

3 When did North and South Vietnam reunify?
  a) 1966
  b) 1976
  c) 1986

4 Where do most people in Cambodia live?
  a) Phnom Penh, the capital
  b) rural areas

5 What is the currency of Lao PDR?
  a) the baht
  b) the kip
  c) the rupiah

6 Who was the first president of Indonesia (1949–1966)?
  a) Habibie
  b) Suharto
  c) Sukarno

Which of the questions are subject questions (S) and which are object questions (O)?

2 Choose the correct verb form to complete the questions.

1 Which country *does lie / lies* on the equator?
2 Which country does the red flag with a yellow star *belong / belongs* to?
3 Which country *does use / uses* the ringgit as its national currency?
4 Which country *does have / has* a land area of 710 sq. km?
5 Which country *did win / won* three medals at the 2012 Olympics?

3 Choose the correct answers to the questions in exercise 2.

Brunei Darussalam	Cambodia	Indonesia
Lao PDR	Malaysia	Myanmar	Philippines
Singapore	Thailand	Vietnam

1 _____ 2 _____
3 _____ 4 _____
5 _____

4 Write a question for every answer.

1 What _____?
  Spiders and horror films frighten me.
2 Who _____?
  My best friend is Julie.
3 Where _____?
  I live in Myanmar.
4 Which language _____?
  I speak Chinese.

SELF-IMAGE

5 Complete the sentences in column A with a phrase from column B.

A	B
1 I consider myself lucky to have a job	a first and as Chinese second.
2 My children probably see	b but I love playing tennis.
3 I think of myself as an Asian	c because there is very little work around.
4 I would describe myself	d friend I have.
5 I don't see myself as a great player,	e me as an old dinosaur.
6 My wife is the best	f as open and friendly.

DICTATION

6 🔊 2.03 Write the sentences that you hear.

1 _____.
2 _____.
3 _____?
4 _____?
5 _____.

86

1D | First impressions

Describing people

1 Complete the dialogue between two friends, Jake and Anita, with words or phrases from the box.

> eyes   shaven   What does he look like
> pale   prominent   blond
> muscular   straight   what's his hair like

J: My new flatmate moved in today. His name's Neil.
A: Oh, right. (1) _____?
J: Well, he's tall and he's got a (2) _____ build. I think he goes to the gym a lot. And he's got a (3) _____ complexion.
A: So, he's really sporty?
J: Yeah.
A: Well, that's good. You like sport, too. Anything else? Does he have a really big, (4) _____ nose?
J: No, nothing like that. He's got a very ordinary, (5) _____ nose.
A: And (6) _____? Is he completely bald?
J: Well, actually, his hair is really short. He's got a (7) _____ head.
A: Oh, right.
J: Yes, and his hair's (8) _____. And he's got big, blue (9) _____.
A: Oh, right. Is he Swedish?
J: No, but I know what you mean.
A: OK. Well, he sounds OK. Hope you two get on together in the flat.

2 Read the dialogue again. Which picture shows Neil, A or B?

3 Underline the word that does not go with the noun.

1	**complexion**	pale	shaved	tanned
2	**build**	wide	muscular	average
3	**head**	bald	round	healthy
4	**eyes**	dark	blond	narrow
5	**hair**	wavy	prominent	shiny
6	**nose**	slim	pointed	prominent

4 Choose the correct phrase to complete the sentences.

1 Does she look *as if / like* her mother?
2 They look *as if / like* boyfriend and girlfriend.
3 My mother *looks like / looks* very tired. I think she works too much.
4 Are you OK? You *look as if / look* you have just seen a ghost.
5 He *looks like / looks* that film star, Orlando Bloom.
6 She *looks like / looks* French. I think it's because of her clothes.

Translation

5 Translate the sentences into your language.

1 What's your new flatmate like?
_____?

2 He looks as if he has had some very bad news.
_____.

3 What does his brother look like?
_____?

4 He's bald, quite muscular and tanned, and has got big green eyes.
_____
_____.

5 She's average build and has got dark brown hair and eyes, and a prominent nose.
_____
_____.

1 | Reading

You never get a second chance to make a first impression

When two people meet for the first time, physical impressions are immediate. Before they have a chance to say a word, their senses are in overdrive; they are picking up and storing information about each other.
5 They register looks, smell and body language. They use eye contact to support the process and to establish a relationship. Within a few seconds, they have made a mental picture of each other. On the basis of this tiny amount of data, they form opinions which they use in the future.

10 But just how reliable are first impressions? Take the story of Jake and Caroline. Jake didn't like Caroline when he first met her. 'She seemed cold and distant. She made almost no eye contact and she didn't seem to listen to me.' Six months later, they met again. 'Caroline was a completely different person.
15 She was warm, friendly and smiled a lot. When she told me that her father had died two days before we first met, that explained everything. It taught me to be more careful about making assumptions about people based on first impressions.'

However wrong they can be, first impressions are a necessary
20 survival mechanism. Thousands of years ago they helped people decide how to react in potentially dangerous situations. That is still true today, although in most cases it is not a question of life and death. According to some, we can learn to read first impressions better. We can also learn to create more
25 powerful first impressions. Professor Helen Trent, a specialist in interpersonal relations, has studied the practice of good communicators. 'Research shows that people who can make others feel good about themselves are excellent at creating positive first impressions. We call these people 'Powerful
30 Communicators' or PCs. You can tell when you meet one; you feel really good afterwards and you think "What a nice person." PCs immediately get in sync with the other person; they coordinate their body language and smiles with their partner. They also maintain eye contact and sound and look as
35 if they are interested, although sometimes they are not. These actions make the other person feel good about the experience.' PCs are winners in the first-impressions race. So if you want to be a PC, start training and remember, you only get one chance to make a great first impression!

1 Read the article. Complete the sentences 1–5 with the best answers a–c.

1 The moment two people first meet they …
   a) look at and talk to each other.   b) look at each other.
   c) look at each other and build a picture of each other.
2 The story about Jake and Caroline shows that …
   a) problems stop communication.
   b) we can make mistakes based on first impressions.
   c) they liked each other in the end.
3 Studying good communicators tells us that they…
   a) make us feel positive.
   b) make us feel friendly.
   c) make us feel like good communicators, too.
4 Powerful communicators …   a) do not always know the effect they have on the other person.
   b) are never honest.   c) are not always honest.
5 PCs are …   a) the best at running.
   b) the best at winning.
   c) the best at creating positive first impressions.

2 Match the words and phrases 1–6 to the definitions a–f. The line numbers are in brackets.

1 are in overdrive (3)   4 get in sync (32)
2 data (8)   5 survival mechanism (20)
3 reliable (10)   6 assumptions (18)

☐ a make two or more things happen at the same time
☐ b something that helps you stay alive
☐ c be very active or too active
☐ d information
☐ e something (or someone) that you can depend on
☐ f things that you think are true, but you cannot be certain

🎧 Read & listen

3 🎧 **2.04** Listen to Reading 1 *You never get a second chance to make a first impression* on the CD and read the article again.

2A Around the world

VOCABULARY FROM THE LESSON

1 Complete the sentences with words from the box.

| travels | trip | travel |
| adventure | journey | hitchhiked |

1 We haven't finished planning our _____ to Croatia yet, but we're going for two weeks.
2 My aunt made lots of trips to India and now she is writing a book about her _____ there.
3 My hobbies are sports and _____. Last year I went on a two-month trip around South America.
4 Travelling around Indonesia was an incredible _____ – we saw some amazing things and met some wonderful people.
5 I've _____ all over Europe. The best lift I ever had was from France to Hungary.
6 The _____ from Turkey to India was long and difficult.

PRESENT PERFECT & PAST SIMPLE

2 Find and correct six mistakes in the review.

> I've just finished *Long Way Round*, a book about an incredible around-the-world journey written by two British actors, Ewan McGregor and Charley Boorman. The story has started one day when McGregor was looking at a map of the world. He has realized that it was possible to ride all the way around the world by motorbike. He suggested the idea over dinner to his good friend, Boorman. Boorman has immediately agreed. The result, 20,000 miles and three months later, is a very entertaining travel book that I didn't want to put down. On the journey they have experienced terrible weather and road conditions and they have had all sorts of adventures, including a meeting with Mongolian nomads and gun-carrying Ukrainians. *Long Way Round* is action-packed and was a real success for the two actors.

3 Complete the dialogue between a mother (M) and her daughter (D). Put the verbs in brackets into the present perfect or past simple.

D: Hi, Mum! I (1) _____ just _____ (get back).
M: Oh, Amy, welcome home, darling! When (2) _____ you _____ (get back)?
D: Yesterday! The plane (3) _____ (land) at about 10pm.
M: Oh, I was so worried. The last time I (4) _____ (have) any news was that call from Tanzania. Where (5) _____ you _____ (be) since then?
D: Oh, everywhere. We (6) _____ (go) to Uganda, Malawi and Mozambique.
M: 'We'? Who's 'we'?
D: Oh, mum. I (7) _____ (meet) a fantastic man. His name is Brian.
M: That's wonderful, dear. Where (8) _____ you _____ (meet)?
D: On a safari in Kenya. And I've got some great news for you and dad. We (9) _____ (get married).
M: Married! When (10) _____ you _____ (get married)?
D: I'll tell you all about it when we see you tonight. Brian and I want to take you out for dinner.

DICTATION

4 2.05 Write the sentences that you hear.

1 _____.
2 _____.
3 _____?
4 _____.
5 _____.
6 _____.

READ & LISTEN

5 2.06 Read and listen to the reading text *Lawyer gives up job to cycle around the world* on page 14 of the Student's Book.

| 89

2B Unusual journeys

Phrasal verbs

1 The particles underlined are in the wrong sentences. Rearrange the particles to make the sentences correct.

1 We couldn't go to Brazil because we didn't have enough time to sort the visas <u>up</u>.
2 I came <u>off</u> this old lamp in a Moroccan market.
3 The medicine helped me get <u>off</u> the malaria.
4 After two days in the truck the driver dropped me <u>out</u>.
5 I waited for eight hours and eventually a car picked me <u>over</u>.
6 All my friends saw me <u>across</u> at the airport.

2 Complete the email with phrasal verbs from exercise 1 in the correct form.

Hi Mum and Dad,

Well, I've finally made it to New Zealand. I can't believe that it's eighteen months since you (1) _____ me _____ at the airport. But this is definitely the last leg of my journey because I've spent almost all my money. When I was in Vietnam, I (2) _____ a wonderful, antique vase in a market and I just had to buy it. It was quite expensive, so that's why I'm broke.

Anyway, I've been hitchhiking here in New Zealand. A lorry driver (3) _____ me _____ in Wellington and (4) _____ me _____ by the coast in the south of the country. So, that was really lucky. I've found a nice hostel to stay in and I've met two travellers from England and we're hanging out together. They've been quite unlucky on their trip. One of them had a problem with his passport, but, fortunately, he (5) _____ it _____ now. And the other had malaria. Fortunately, he (6) _____ it now. He's looking healthy again.

I'm flying home on Sunday.

Looking forward to seeing you.

Love,
Matthew xx

---

3 The particles in the sentences are in the wrong place. Put them in the correct place.

1 Did you get your illness over in a hospital?
2 The villagers offered to look my motorbike after.
3 Could you drop off us in Paris, please?
4 I came an old school friend in a tea house across in Darjeeling, India.
5 We sorted a lift to La Paz in Bolivia out.
6 The doctor's family looked me after when I got malaria in Pakistan.

Translation

4 Translate the dialogue into your language.

Andrew: Have you ever hitchhiked anywhere?
Darina: Yes, lots of places when I was younger.
Andrew: And where did you go?
Darina: Oh, I travelled around Europe and I went to America in 1992. And how about you? Have you ever hitchhiked?
Andrew: No, never. I've never liked the idea of hitchhiking. Did you ever have any problems on your trips?
Darina: Yes, once. When I was in Nebraska I waited for eight hours in the snow until someone stopped and gave me a lift.
Andrew: Really!?
Darina: Yeah. I've never been so cold in my whole life!

_____
_____
_____
_____
_____
_____
_____
_____
_____
_____

2c | Down under

Present perfect for unfinished time

1 Complete the phone dialogue between Pia (P) and Jenny (J) with the correct form of the verbs in brackets.

P: Hello? Jenny?
J: Pia? I thought you were in Greece.
P: We are. We (1) _____ (get) here five days ago.
J: Yes, you left on Saturday, didn't you? Are you enjoying the sailing?
P: Oh, yes. Absolutely amazing! We (2) _____ (visit) three islands in the last three days. And last night we (3) _____ (have) dinner on the beach. It was so romantic.
J: Lovely! And how's the weather?
P: It (4) _____ (be) very hot. It (5) _____ (be) so hot last night that we slept outside on the deck of the boat. I (6) _____ (never / see) so many stars.
J: Oh, that sounds beautiful.
P: Yes, very. Anyway, could you do me a favour, Jenny?
J: Sure. If I can.
P: I think I (7) _____ (leave) the back door open when we left the house.
J: Oh, dear. I've got your keys. I'll pop over and check.
P: Oh, thank you. I (8) _____ (be) so worried.
J: Well, stop worrying now. Just have a lovely time.
P: We will. Thanks again.

2 Choose the correct time expression to complete the sentences.

1 They flew to Tokyo *last week / over the last week*.
2 We've met some nice people *two weeks ago / during the last two weeks*.
3 I haven't been to Australia *last year / up till now*.
4 My sister has visited eight different countries *over the last two months / last month*.
5 They haven't been abroad *in 1990 / since 1990*.
6 Have you read any good travel books *recently / last summer*?

Vocabulary from the lesson

3 Complete the travel guide with phrases from the box.

> settle down   best-known monuments
> cultural and historical   popular destination
> landmark   so many things to see and do

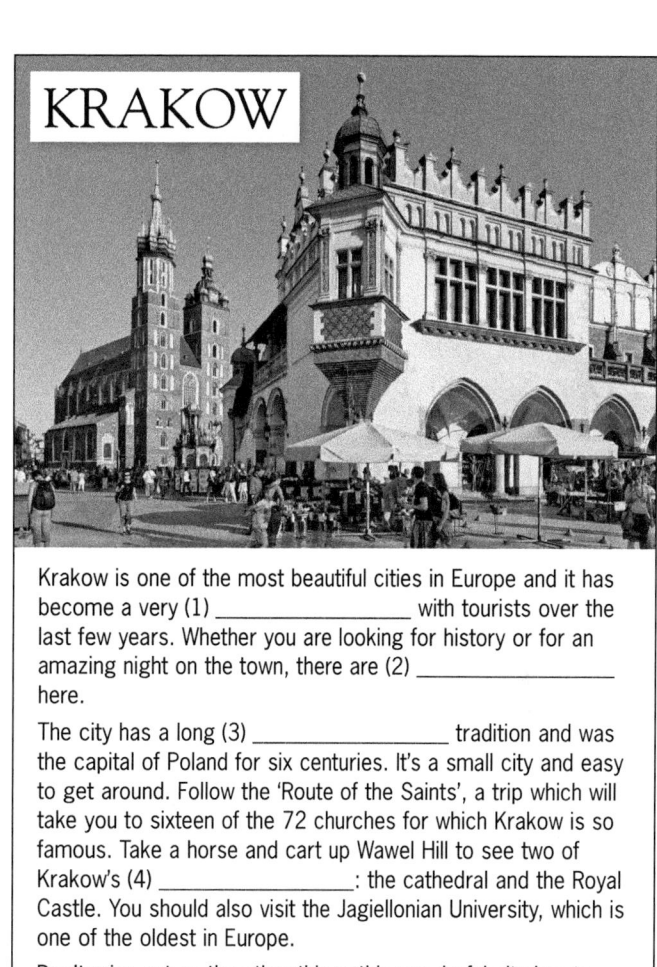

KRAKOW

Krakow is one of the most beautiful cities in Europe and it has become a very (1) _____ with tourists over the last few years. Whether you are looking for history or for an amazing night on the town, there are (2) _____ here.

The city has a long (3) _____ tradition and was the capital of Poland for six centuries. It's a small city and easy to get around. Follow the 'Route of the Saints', a trip which will take you to sixteen of the 72 churches for which Krakow is so famous. Take a horse and cart up Wawel Hill to see two of Krakow's (4) _____: the cathedral and the Royal Castle. You should also visit the Jagiellonian University, which is one of the oldest in Europe.

Don't miss out on the other things this wonderful city has to offer; the shopping is good and the nightlife is excellent. Finally, whatever you do, visit the Rynek Glowny, that other famous Krakowian (5) _____. It is the largest medieval square in Europe and the focus of much of Krakow's social life. So pull up a chair in one of the restaurants, bars or cafés, (6) _____ and watch the world go by.

Dictation

4 **2.07** Write the dialogue that you hear.

_____
_____
_____
_____
_____
_____
_____
_____
_____
_____

2D | Getting around

TRAVELLING

1 Rearrange the words to make sentences.

1 airport , please   to the   a single .
_____

2 tell me , please   the time of the next train could you   to Bristol ?
_____

3 a five-pound note   have you   change for   got , please ?
_____

4 we get to , please   tell me when   York Road could you ?
_____

5 a cab for   Dorset Road   I'd like   , please in Ealing .
_____

6 get a taxi   around here   anywhere   can I ?
_____

2 Imagine that you are studying English in a language school in London. Take this quiz in a school magazine and see how many questions you can answer.

How well could you survive on public transport in London?

1 You are at the train station and need to know what time the next train to Plymouth leaves. What do you say?
_____

2 You are in your hotel room and want a cab to go to Piccadilly Circus in London. What do you say to the receptionist?
_____

3 You get on a bus and you only have a five-pound note. What do you say to the driver?
_____

4 You are at the train station and you want a first-class return ticket to Manchester. What do you say?
_____

5 You are in the street and need to catch a taxi. You stop a person and ask for a taxi rank. What do you say?
_____

6 You are on a bus, but you don't know where the stop for Church Road is. What do you say to the person next to you?
_____

VERB COLLOCATIONS (TRAVEL)

3 Complete the story with verbs from the box.

get off	missed
arrived	take
drop	walk
catch	took

I flew to Paris once for an important business meeting and when I landed, I decided to (1) _____ the bus into town. I thought I had lots of time. Unfortunately, I (2) _____ the bus and had to wait twenty minutes for the next one. When it came, I got on, but the traffic was terrible. So I decided to (3) _____ and I (4) _____ a taxi instead. I asked the driver to take me straight to the meeting. After 40 minutes in the taxi, it was clear I was going to be late. I asked the driver to (5) _____ me off by the Pont Neuf, a bridge by the river Seine. I wanted to (6) _____ to the meeting because of the terrible traffic. I thought it would (7) _____ about 20 minutes, but I was wrong. The streets were full of people and I was carrying two heavy bags. I finally (8) _____ at the building an hour later and it was shut. Then I realized it was May 1 and a public holiday in France! The meeting wasn't until the next day! What an idiot!!

TRANSLATION

4 Translate the sentences into your language.

1 There are special tickets that allow you to get on and off the tour bus when you want.
_____.

2 Excuse me. Have I missed the 12.08 to Liverpool?
_____?

3 Could you tell me the time of the next train to Glasgow, please?
_____?

4 I'd like a cab for the Royal Plaza Hotel, please.
_____.

5 Did you get a single or a return ticket to Berlin?
_____?

2 | Reading

1 Read the article about Eddie Izzard. Tick the five achievements in the list below which, according to the article, Eddie has achieved.

- [ ] 1 He has performed his comedy show all over Europe.
- [ ] 2 He has been in well-known American films.
- [ ] 3 He has run over 40 marathons.
- [ ] 4 He has appeared in British TV series.
- [ ] 5 He has run a leading charity.
- [ ] 6 He has completed a marathon in Wales.
- [ ] 7 He has appeared in London theatres.
- [ ] 8 He has finished a triathlon.
- [ ] 9 He has won the London Marathon.

EDDIE IZZARD – THE MARATHON MAN!

Eddie Izzard is well known in the English-speaking world as a funny and talented comedian. He has performed his live comedy show to huge audiences and he has also appeared in a number of successful Hollywood films, including *Ocean's Twelve* and *Ocean's Thirteen*. He has played leading theatrical roles on London's West End and New York's Broadway, and he has even been in an American TV series, although he has never made a TV series for British TV. However, he has also achieved something quite incredible that nobody ever expected him to do – he has run 43 marathons in 51 days!

In 2009, Eddie decided he wanted to do something to raise money for Comic Relief, a popular charity which a lot of famous comedians support. He had only five weeks of training before he set out on his epic run around Britain, and when he ran the first marathon he found it really tough. It took him almost ten hours to complete the course, which is very slow. However, he got faster and faster as he continued to run marathons. Soon, he was running marathons in under five hours – which is not bad, especially as Eddie had never been a serious runner before!

Eddie started his marathon adventure in London in late July 2009 and headed west towards Cardiff. His plan was to run in England, Wales, Northern Ireland and Scotland, and to visit the capital cities of all four countries. He managed to do this – he also carried the flag of each country when he was running there! When he finished his last marathon, crossing the finishing line in Trafalgar Square in London, he had been running a marathon a day, six days a week for seven weeks. He ran over 1,700 kilometres!

Since running the marathons, Eddie has become more interested in keeping fit. He has competed in the Ironman triathlon and in other charity events, and he has pointed out that once you are really fit, it's a good idea to stay that way!

2 Read the article again and decide if the sentences are true (T) or false (F). Correct the false sentences.

1 Eddie usually performs in small theatres. ___
2 Eddie has only made two Hollywood films. ___
3 Eddie ran the marathons for charity. ___
4 Eddie spent months training to be ready to run the marathons. ___
5 It took him less time to run the last marathon than the first. ___
6 Eddie didn't run any marathons in Scotland. ___
7 Eddie has decided never to do any more tough endurance events. ___

3 Find words or phrases in the text that match the definitions 1–6. The paragraph numbers are in brackets.

1 very good at what he does (1)
2 very big (1)
3 difficult (2)
4 fairly good (3)
5 went in the direction of (3)
6 explained (4)

READ & LISTEN

4 2.08 Listen to Reading 2 *Eddie Izzard – the marathon man!* on the CD and read the article again.

3A Dream homes

MODALS OF OBLIGATION, PERMISSION & PROHIBITION (PRESENT TIME)

1 Four people are looking for somewhere to live. Read the two adverts and then read what the four people are looking for. Match the adverts 1–2 to the people a–d.

Advert 1

Looking for third person to share three-bedroom flat.

Rent £460 per calendar month for double room. Well-equipped: microwave, washer dryer, dishwasher, widescreen TV, etc. Very near tube and buses.

You don't need to pay any extra bills apart from phone, as all bills included in rent. Tenants are allowed to smoke in the flat. Please note that we can't accept pets because flat's too small.

Advert 2

Looking for fourth person to share large, quiet house with big garden.

Must be non-smoker and would prefer vegetarian.

£640 per month, including bills, for extra large double bedroom with view of garden. House not near public transport, but has off-street parking.

We have a cleaner, but you'll have to take care of your own room. Owner allows pets, providing they are small.

Please note that everyone has to turn down TV and music after 10pm as people have to get up early.

2 Choose the correct phrase to complete the sentences.

1 You *don't need to / can't* clean the house because we have a cleaner.
2 I'm sorry, but you *have to / aren't allowed to* smoke in the flat.
3 You *don't need to / are allowed to* pay a deposit.
4 I'm afraid that you *are allowed to / can't* park your car here.
5 You *can / don't need to* have visitors any time you like.
6 If you like, you *don't have to / can* park your car in the garage.
7 Your room has its own entrance, so you *are allowed to / don't have to* worry about disturbing others if you come home late at night.
8 You *can't / have to* pay your rent on the last day of the month at the latest.

Person a

I can afford up to £500 a month. I'd prefer a double, but I'm OK with a single room. It's really important that I'm near public transport as I haven't got a car. What else do I want? Oh, I love cooking, so the kitchen should be well-equipped. I'm a smoker! I also love football, so my dream place would have one of those massive screens. That would be just perfect.

Person b

I have a pretty busy life, so what I'm looking for is a bit of peace and quiet. I absolutely hate housework, so ideally want somewhere where I have to do the minimum and I'm prepared to pay for that – up to £1,000 a month, not including bills. Would be ideal if there was somewhere I could park my car, too. Finally, I'm into sports and have a healthy lifestyle, so no smokers, please!

Person c

Money's not a problem at the moment. Much more important is a big room with light as I'm a painter. Ideally I'd like a place which isn't noisy as I need to be able to concentrate. The other essential thing is Chloe, my little dog. Whoever I share with has to be OK about pets. I'm a vegetarian and I don't smoke. Finally, I've got a motorbike, so transport links aren't that important.

Person d

I'm happy to pay up to £450 plus bills, but I do want a big room. My last flat had nowhere to wash clothes, so this place must have a washing machine at the very least.

Another thing – I don't have transport, so this place has to be close to good public transport. What else? Well, I'm a social smoker, so I'd prefer a place where I can have the occasional cigarette without people making me feel bad. Oh, and one final thing: I'm allergic to animals!

DICTATION

3 🔊 **2.09** Write the sentences that you hear.

1 _____?
2 _____.
3 _____?
4 _____.
5 _____.

READ & LISTEN

4 🔊 **2.10** Read and listen to the reading text *Paradise Ridge* on page 25 of the Student's Book.

3B | Unusual homes

VOCABULARY FROM THE LESSON

1 Complete the sentences with a word from the box.

accommodation   share   facilities
move   detached   local

1 In addition to the usual _____, the hotel also offers internet access and conference rooms.
2 She's going to move into a flat that belongs to the _____ authority.
3 There are three people living in the flat. They _____ the facilities and the bills.
4 There is not enough _____ for students in this town.
5 We're going to _____ house next year. We want to live somewhere bigger in the country.
6 This marvellous _____ house is surrounded by an enormous garden.

ACCOMMODATION

2 Complete the sentences with a word or phrase from the box.

rented accommodation   terraced house
holiday home   mobile home   suburbs
apartment block   flat   tree house

1 My parents wanted to escape the English winters, so they bought a _____ in the south of Spain where they are going to live for four months a year.
2 We want to buy a house, but because we don't have enough money, we're living in _____.
3 Living in the _____ is so much quieter and greener than living in the town centre.
4 I live in a two-bedroom _____ on the third floor.
5 I hated living in an _____ because you had neighbours above and below you.
6 I like living in a _____ because you have neighbours on both sides of you.
7 The thing we love about our _____ is that we can drive wherever we want and always know we have our own beds to sleep in.
8 My dad built me a _____ at the bottom of the garden.

MAKE, LET & ALLOW

3 Choose the correct word to complete the sentences.

1 The prison guards *make / let* us play music until 10pm.
2 The prison *allows / lets* us to have one hour's exercise outside a day.
3 The prison doesn't *make / allow* us to smoke in our cells.
4 Prison regulations *let / make* us work hard ten hours a day.
5 If a prisoner wants to take exams, prison regulations *let / allow* them study for two hours a day.
6 They *allow / let* family and friends visit us regularly.
7 The prison guards *make / let* us surf the internet, watch TV or play games after dinner.
8 They *make / allow* us go back to our cells at 8.30 at night.

TRANSLATION

4 Translate the sentences into your language.

1 Some people prefer rented accommodation to buying a house.
   _____.
2 The owners don't allow smoking in the flat, but you can smoke in the garden.
   _____.
3 I want to sell my flat in the town centre and move out to the suburbs.
   _____.
4 Our holiday home allows us to spend four months a year in Italy.
   _____.
5 The owners make you pay a two-month deposit before you can move in.
   _____.

| 95

3c | Bedrooms

Verb collocations (sleep)

1 Complete the dialogue between a doctor (D) and her patient (P) with words from the box.

| feel | set | get | wake | nap | fall |

D: Take a seat, Mrs Patel. Now what seems to be the matter?
P: I'm always tired, doctor. If I sit on the sofa for more than five minutes, I (1) _____ asleep.
D: Oh, dear. How much sleep do you get?
P: Not enough. I go to bed at eleven, but I don't
(2) _____ to sleep before one. I
(3) _____ my alarm clock for six, but I
(4) _____ up at five.
D: I see. Have you tried having a (5) _____ during the day?
P: I should because I always (6) _____ sleepy.
D: Uh-huh. Mrs Patel, I think you have to … Mrs Patel? Mrs Patel! Wake up …

Modals of obligation, permission & prohibition (past time)

2 Complete the text with *were allowed to, weren't allowed to, had to, didn't need to, didn't have to* or *could*.

I went to a strict boarding school with rules for everything. Take, for example, the bedrooms. You (1) _____ make your beds and keep the room clean and tidy, although of course you (2) _____ clean the windows and floor. Obviously, you (3) _____ smoke in the bedrooms, but some older boys did. You (4) _____ read in bed until nine, but then the lights were turned off. Sundays were more relaxed. You (5) _____ wake up until eight and there were no lessons. You were free and you (6) _____ do what you wanted. Sunday was always my favourite day.

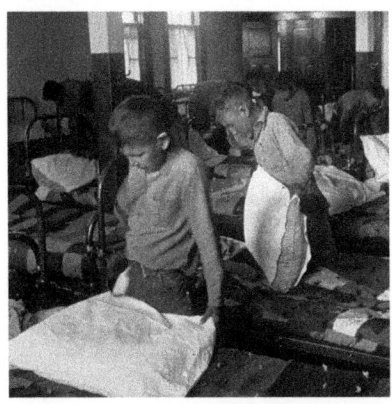

3 Choose the correct phrases to complete the dialogue between a granddaughter (GD) and a grandmother (GM).

GD: Gran, did you have to study for exams?
GM: Oh, yes. Children have always had tests and exams. But you're a lot luckier these days.
GD: Luckier? Why?
GM: Well, we (1) *didn't have to / had to* do so much housework. And our parents were much stricter.
GD: Do you mean that you (2) *could / had to* be home by six, or something?
GM: We (3) *were allowed to / had to* be home before it got dark. You can go out till ten or eleven!
GD: Yeah. But weren't you allowed to do anything?
GM: Of course. Generally speaking, we (4) *had to / were allowed to* do what we wanted. Parents weren't worried about children being hit by cars or attacked. We (5) *were not allowed to / could* walk out of the door on Saturday morning and come back at teatime and our parents didn't say a word.
GD: Fantastic.
GM: Yes. And we (6) *didn't have to / had to* worry so much about fashion – that's a terrible pressure nowadays.
GD: Yeah. But didn't you get dressed up for parties and stuff?
GM: No. I only had one party dress! So I (7) *had to / didn't need to* worry about that.

Vocabulary from the lesson

4 Underline the word or phrase that does not go with the verb.

1 **make** a bed   complain   a decision   a record
2 **have** rules   a conviction for drugs   sleepy   a cold
3 **be** a heavy sleeper   fresh and airy   sleepy   peace   a chance
4 **get** a visa for America   a good night's sleep   up in the morning   a disagreement
5 **go** through passport control   nowhere   bed   home

Dictation

5 🔊 **2.11** Write the sentences that you hear.

1 _____.
2 _____.
3 _____.
4 _____.
5 _____.

96

3D | Dinner invitation

Requests

1 Read the situations and choose the correct phrase to complete the sentences.

1 You're having something to eat at a friend's house. Ask him to pass you the salt.
   Do you mind / Can you pass me the salt?
2 You're in a newsagent's and you want to buy a magazine. What do you say?
   Do I / Can I buy this magazine, please?
3 A work colleague lives next to the post office. Ask her to post a letter for you.
   Could you possibly / Would you mind posting this letter for me?
4 You really need to take a day off work tomorrow. Ask your boss.
   I wonder if I could / Do you think you could take the day off tomorrow?
5 You're in a train carriage and it's very hot. Ask the lady opposite you if it is OK to open the window.
   Would you mind if I / Do you think I could opened the window? It's very hot.
6 You're late and need a lift to the station. Ask your friend if she can take you.
   Do you / Could you give me a lift to the station?

'Could you possibly…?'

2 Find and correct the mistake in each dialogue.

1 **Thomas:** Can I used your toilet?
  Catriona: Yes, certainly.
2 **Pierre:** Could you telling me how to get to Piccadilly Gardens?
  Mavis: No problem. It's straight ahead, past that school on the corner.
3 **Erika:** Is it alright if I to close this door? It's too noisy.
  Tom: Yes, of course.
4 **Victoria:** Could I borrow your pen? Mine's at home.
  Marion: I'm afraid you can. I'm using it.
5 **Chris:** Did you think you could lend me £5?
  Douglas: I'm sorry, but I haven't been paid yet.
6 **Lou:** Is it alright if I gone to bed early? I'm very tired.
  Andrew: Yes, go ahead.

3 Look again at dialogues 1–6 in exercise 2. Decide which are requests for permission (P) and which are requests for someone else to do something (D).

1 _____   2 _____   3 _____
4 _____   5 _____   6 _____

Translation

4 Translate the dialogue into your language.

Marjory: I wonder if I could leave my coat somewhere?
Frank: Feel free. There's a wardrobe in the bedroom. Do you need any help?
Marjory: Would you mind opening the door for me?
Frank: No worries. Just leave it there.
Marjory: OK. Thanks. Is it alright if I use this hanger?
Frank: Sure. Be my guest.

_____
_____
_____
_____
_____
_____

| 97

3 | Reading

1 Read the magazine article and choose the best title 1–3.

1. A life of no responsibility
2. A life of luxury
3. A travelling life

2 Read the article again and write question letters a–d in the correct spaces 1–4 in the text.

a. What's it like living in such a small space?
b. Do you ever have problems with local people or the police?
c. Why did you choose this lifestyle?
d. Do you work?

3 Decide if the sentences are true (T) or false (F). Correct the false sentences.

1. Mark has travelled all over the world. ___
2. The most important thing for Mark is the right to do what he wants. ___
3. He often has problems with residents or the police. ___
4. He doesn't think people have to work. ___
5. 'WWOOFs' are paid money for their work. ___
6. He doesn't mind living in a small place. ___

4 Find words or phrases in the article which mean the same as the definitions below. The paragraph numbers are in brackets.

1. a place where you always live (1) _____
2. limitations (2) _____
3. to annoy someone or cause them problems (3) _____
4. cut in a violent way (3) _____
5. popular performances of music that DJs do for money (4) _____
6. things (5) _____

🎧 READ & LISTEN

5 🎧 **2.12** Listen to Reading 3 on the CD and read the article again.

INTERVIEW

1
Mark Westgate is a traveller, that is to say, someone who lives on the road and doesn't have a fixed abode. For over 30 years he has lived in buses and coaches and visited every continent on the planet. His latest home is a small van that is just two metres wide and six metres long. I went to meet him and ask him a few questions.

Interviewer: (1) _____
2
Mark: The most important thing for me is freedom – freedom from the constraints that most people have, like a house and a steady job. I can move when and where I want to. Travel has allowed me to meet people and experience new cultures. I think my lifestyle is a reaction to my parents. They controlled me and I wasn't allowed to do a lot of things other children did.

Interviewer: (2) _____
3
Mark: No, not really. If you respect people, things are normally fine. The police make me move on from time to time, but that's OK – they have to do their job, too. People hassle me sometimes – you know, by saying that I shouldn't park somewhere, or that I should go back to my own country. I once woke up to find that I had two flat tyres because someone had slashed them during the night. But bad experiences like that are very, very rare.

Interviewer: (3) _____
4
Mark: Of course. I believe everyone has to do something. I'm a travelling DJ and I do gigs all over Europe – mostly for the peace movement or for friends. I also work as a 'WWOOF' – that's a 'Willing Worker On Organic Farms'. The workers aren't paid, but are given food and accommodation. The farmers always let me park my van in a field.

Interviewer: (4) _____
5
Mark: It's great! Everything is relative, isn't it? When I was a child, I had an enormous bedroom, but I wasn't happy. Now I live in one small room on wheels and I am very happy. The space doesn't worry me. I have to be organized, but I don't have much stuff and I'm a tidy person. My van is my bedroom, lounge, kitchen and bathroom. Sadly, I don't have a shower, but I am thinking of building a swimming pool under my bed.

4A Luck of the draw

Past simple & past continuous

1 Choose the best verb form to complete the sentences.

1 Jack was looking for a job when he *was winning / won* the lottery.
2 I *was crossing / crossed* the road, went into the shop and bought a lottery ticket.
3 I *was watching / watched* a game of tennis when my boyfriend phoned and told me I'd won £25,000.
4 I *was buying / bought* my lottery ticket on Saturday and as usual I didn't win a thing.
5 The gambling industry *was making / made* over £42 billion last year.
6 I *was listening / listened* to the radio when my winning numbers came up.
7 My sister *was living / lived* on nothing when she won £1,000,000.
8 I *was reading / read* the newspaper when I saw an article about an old school friend of mine who had won £12 million.

2 Complete the text with the correct form of the verbs in brackets.

My friend (1) _____ (tell) me a funny story the other day. When she was at university, she (2) _____ (share) a house with five other girls and none of them had any money. One day, they (3) _____ (talk) about ways to make money when one of them (4) _____ (suggest) they buy a lottery ticket. They (5) _____ (decide) to use the dates they were born as their 'lottery numbers'. The next Saturday, they (6) _____ (sit) in a café and (7) _____ (have) something to drink, when the winning numbers came up on the TV. They (8) _____ (have) all six winning numbers. The only problem was that they had forgotten to buy a lottery ticket!

Vocabulary from the lesson

3 Complete the dialogue with words or phrases from the box.

| scratchcards | jackpot | raise money | charities |
| a lot at stake | against the odds | win the lottery |

Alf: This is serious. The club now owes the bank £250,000. There's (1) _____ here. No money means no football club!
Brian: £250,000! How on earth can we (2) _____ of that sort?
Charlie: Easy! Rob a bank or (3) _____.
Alf: Our chances of winning the lottery are one in three million – totally (4) _____.
Charlie: How about (5) _____? I like them because you know straight away if you've won or not.
Brian: I've got an idea … maybe there are some (6) _____ that help sports clubs.
Alf: We're hardly a priority, are we? But maybe we could find a local business to sponsor …
Brian: Wait a second! Jason … Jason Sewell.
Alf & Charlie: From school?
Brian: Yeah. He won a lottery (7) _____ worth £7 million ten years ago. He's a billionaire now and a big football fan.
Charlie: Terrific! He's our man.

Dictation

4 🔊 **2.13** Write the story that you hear.

_____
_____
_____
_____
_____
_____
_____

Read & listen

5 🔊 **2.14** Read and listen to *Lottery winners and losers* on page 34 of the Student's Book.

| 99

4B Twists of fate

Past perfect simple

1 Look at these sentences. Write *1* by the action that happened first and *2* by the action that happened after it.

1 *When I got to the station* (2), *the train had already left.* (1)
2 She'd already left ( ) by the time I got to the party. ( )
3 The moment I opened the door, I saw ( ) that someone had broken into the flat. ( )
4 I didn't recognize her at first ( ) because she'd changed her hairstyle and hair colour. ( )
5 Unfortunately, we got to the cinema ( ) after the film had started. ( )
6 The football match was so bad that half the fans had left ( ) before the game finished. ( )
7 I'd read and replied to 87 emails ( ) by the time I stopped for lunch. ( )

2 Choose the correct verb forms to complete the story.

On August 1, Martin Wallis and Bob Cram (1) *went / had gone* to the Accident and Emergency Department of Sutton Hospital. Mr Wallis (2) *broke / had broken* his arm and burned himself badly. Mr Cram (3) *twisted / had twisted* his ankle, sprained his wrist and broken his nose.

Apparently, the two men had entered Mr Wallis' flat earlier in the day to do some DIY work. Mr Cram turned on the gas and was looking for some matches when he (4) *put / had put* his foot in a bucket of water that the cleaner (5) *left / had left* there earlier. He (6) *skidded / had skidded* across the kitchen and (7) *grabbed / had grabbed* at one of the kitchen wall units to stop his fall. Unfortunately, being a rather large man, he pulled all three wall units off the wall as he fell down.

Then Mr Wallis, hearing the commotion, (8) *entered / had entered* the kitchen with a lit cigarette in his mouth. The gas from the cooker instantly (9) *ignited / had ignited*. The explosion threw Mr Wallis across the room and burned all of his hair off. Luckily, Mr Cram was protected from the explosion because he (10) *was / had been* under the wall units.

Injuries

3 Complete the dialogues with injuries from the box.

| suffering | bleeding | black eye | sprained |
| unconscious | twisted | scratches | bruise |

1 **A:** Why can't you play football?
  B: Because I _____ my ankle.
2 **A:** Mum, I fell off my bike.
  B: I can see that, darling. You've got a big black _____ on your leg.
3 **A:** You're _____!
  B: Yes, I cut my finger when I was peeling the potatoes.
4 **A:** I think he's _____ from shock.
  B: Yes, he is. He's just received some very bad news.
5 **A:** She can't hear you, can she?
  B: No, that car just knocked her down and she's _____.
6 **A:** You've got _____ on your arm.
  B: Yes, it was that stupid cat!
7 **A:** Are you playing tennis on Saturday?
  B: I'm afraid I can't. I _____ my wrist.
8 **A:** How did he get that _____?
  B: Oh, he was in a fight.

Dictation

4 2.15 Write the sentences that you hear.

1 _____.
2 _____.
3 _____.
4 _____.

4c Bad luck stories

Time linkers

1 Choose the best time linker to complete the sentences.

1 Kate phoned *the moment / while* you were having a bath.
2 *The moment / While* I found the bag, I phoned the police.
3 I'd had three different job offers *while / by the time* I left my old job.
4 *While / As soon as* they met, they fell in love.
5 *As / By the time* I was driving to Cornwall, the countryside became more beautiful and green.

2 Read the two articles. Find and correct six mistakes with time linkers. More than one answer is possible.

> A couple decided to go away for the weekend in their motor home. By the time they were taking a walk, a thief paid them a visit. While they got back, they noticed that something was wrong, so they took a look around. They found a man in the bushes being violently sick. It appeared that the thief had tried to steal petrol from the motor home using suction and a plastic tube. Unfortunately, he'd connected the tube to the toilet tank instead of the petrol tank. As soon as the police arrived, the ambulance had already taken the thief away.

Two ten-year-old girls were seriously reprimanded by the police yesterday for playing tricks on customers of the Garden Café in Swansea. The girls would wait while customers ate their sandwiches. While they threw away the plastic boxes the sandwiches came in, the girls would secretly refill them with 'new' sandwiches made of grass, leaves and flowers. The two would then go into the café and by the time the staff was not looking, they would put the 'new' sandwiches back on the cool shelves. The girls would then go back outside and watch as customers ate their sandwiches. Kate Waters and Pia Fine said they were sorry and hadn't wanted to hurt anybody. They confessed, 'It was so funny to watch the faces of people as they tried the sandwiches. One man had eaten half a sandwich the moment he noticed he was eating grass.'

Vocabulary from the lesson

3 Complete the bad luck stories with words from the box. Write the verbs in the correct form.

| lock out | cut off | get away |
| hang out | jump onto | put on |

1 The moment Sophie Miller _____ her washing _____ to dry, a huge lorry drove by and covered the washing with dirt …
2 As Penny Fisher was leaving a lift, the doors closed and her long ponytail was caught between the doors. She had to _____ _____ her hair with her nail scissors to escape …
3 Thieves who stole over $10,000 worth of diamonds believed they had _____ _____ with their crime until police identified them from CCTV footage …
4 The moment Patrick Hughes walked out through the front door in his pyjamas to pick up his post, a gust of wind blew the door shut and _____ him _____. He had no key and had to wait five hours until his wife came home …
5 Doreen Smith had spent hours laying the table for Christmas dinner. Five minutes before the guests arrived, her cat _____ _____ the table, knocked over a bottle of wine, and ruined everything …
6 On her way to an interview, Molly Clarke tried to _____ her make-up _____ while she was travelling on the underground. The train stopped suddenly and she had lipstick all over her face …

Translation

4 Translate the sentences into your language.

1 I was running for the bus when I fell over and twisted my ankle.
   _____.
2 Christine and I had been married for eighteen months when Richard was born.
   _____.
3 By the time I returned to the kitchen, the children had eaten all the cake.
   _____.
4 It suddenly started to rain when they were walking in the park.
   _____.
5 When I got home, I realized that I had left my keys in the office.
   _____.

4D Fancy that!

BOTH & NEITHER

1 Complete the online chat room dialogue with words and phrases from the box.

> We're both from Edinburgh   neither of us liked
> Neither did I   I do
> Both of us are divorced   both of us

ladybug187:	Hi, superchap.
superchap249:	Hi, ladybug. Where are you from?
ladybug187:	I'm originally from Scotland.
superchap249:	Oh, really? So (1) _____ are Scottish. Whereabouts?
ladybug187:	Edinburgh.
superchap249:	Wow! (2) _____. Do you still live there?
ladybug187:	No. I moved to York and then to Birmingham.
superchap249:	What a coincidence! I used to live in York, but I'm in Bristol now. Didn't like York.
ladybug187:	(3) _____. It wasn't a good time of my life.
superchap249:	So, (4) _____ York.
ladybug187:	Crazy! So, do you have any hobbies?
superchap249:	I used to play a lot of tennis, until I got divorced.
ladybug187:	You're divorced? So am I! (5) _____.
superchap249:	No fun is it? Still, at least I don't have to play tennis anymore. I don't like tennis.
ladybug187:	(6) _____. Your name is Jerry, isn't it?
superchap249:	Yes. How did you know that!?
ladybug187:	We were married for ten years, you idiot!

2 Complete the table using the dialogue in exercise 1 to help you.

Prompt	Both superchap and ladybug	Neither superchap or ladybug	Only superchap	Only ladybug
(1) From Scotland?	✓			
(2) From Edinburgh?				
(3) Lived in York?				
(4) Liked York?				
(5) Moved to Birmingham?				
(6) Moved to Bristol?				
(7) Divorced?				
(8) Like tennis?				

TALKING ABOUT SIMILARITIES & DIFFERENCES

3 Match the sentences 1–6 to the responses a–f.

1 I've just won something on the lottery!
2 This time last year, I was celebrating the win.
3 That looks horrible. I'm not eating that.
4 I've never won a penny on the lottery.
5 I can't understand people who gamble.
6 My parents allowed me to smoke when I was fourteen.

☐ a No, neither am I.
☐ b So was I. Weren't we lucky!
☐ c I can. I was addicted to it once.
☐ d That's incredible! So have I.
☐ e Really! Mine didn't.
☐ f No, neither have I. It's such a waste of money.

4 Choose the incorrect response to the first sentences.

1 **A:** I didn't go to the cinema on Friday.
  B: *Neither did I. / Neither didn't I. / Me neither.*
2 **A:** I saw the new Brad Pitt film on Saturday.
  B: *So do I. / Me, too. / So did I.*
3 **A:** I love chocolate.
  B: *Me, too. / I too. / I don't.*
4 **A:** I haven't seen Tom for ages.
  B: *Neither I have. / I have. / Me, neither.*
5 **A:** I'm reading Harry Potter.
  B: *Me, too. / So I am. / I'm not.*
6 **A:** I can't understand the problem.
  B: *I can. / Neither can I. / I can, too.*

TRANSLATION

5 Translate the text into your language.

I was living in Warsaw when I first met Kasia. She was sitting in a café and we just started chatting. It was small talk at first: 'I don't like the traffic.' 'Neither do I.' 'I have a brother.' 'So do I.' But there were some real coincidences. For example, both of us were born in the same year, on the same day and in the same hospital. And neither of us had ever fallen in love. And all that was 40 years ago.

_____
_____
_____
_____
_____
_____

4 | Reading

A WIN ON THE HORSES

1

Horse racing is big business in the UK. There are a number of race meetings on every single day of the week, and thousands of people attend the biggest meetings. National Hunt racing, in which the horses jump over fences, takes place from autumn to spring, whereas the Flat racing season starts in the spring and ends before the winter. Both types of racing attract professional gamblers who are experts at understanding the form of the horses and playing the odds. However, they also attract ordinary people who go to the races with friends and enjoy trying their luck even though they usually lose.

2

Steve Whiteley, a heating engineer in his sixties, was just one of those ordinary people when he headed to the racecourse in Exeter with seven of his friends in March, 2011. However, by the time the day was over, Steve had won the biggest jackpot in horse racing history and was £1.4 million richer. What was even more amazing was that on the day of the win he very nearly didn't go to the race meeting because he was a bit short of money. He only decided to go when he realized that entrance to the racecourse was free on that day and he could use his bus pass to get to the meeting without having to pay anything!

3

Steve's winning bet was fairly complicated. He didn't just place money on one horse to win. There were six horse races at Exeter on that day, and he chose which horse he thought would win each race. He then placed a £2 bet on this happening. He needed all six horses he had selected to win their races before he won any money. Of course, the odds against predicting the winners of all six races were huge. That was why he won so much when, amazingly, every single horse passed the finishing line in first place.

4

As soon as the sixth horse had won, Steve became a celebrity. Everybody at the racecourse was cheering him, and journalists were keen to interview him. They asked him what his secret was, but, of course, he didn't have one. He explained that he had chosen the winning horses at random. For example, the winner of the fourth race had the same name as a friend of his, and the winner of the fifth was named after a town he knew. When journalists asked him what he intended to do with the money, Steve explained that his first priority was to buy a present for his girlfriend because it was her birthday. Before the race meeting, he hadn't had enough money for a present, so he had only got her a card! Now, she could look forward to something special!

1 Read the article. Match the headings a–d to the paragraphs 1–4.

a The man who won £1.4 million
b How to pick a winner
c The popularity of horse racing
d How Steve's bet worked

2 Read the article again and choose the correct answer, a or b.

1 Which type of racing takes place during the winter months in the UK?
 a) National Hunt
 b) Flat
2 What type of people tend to go to Flat racing?
 a) mostly professional gamblers
 b) all types of people
3 Why did Steve almost miss the day at Exeter racecourse?
 a) He didn't have much money.
 b) He thought he had to work that day.
4 How much did it cost Steve to go to the races in the end?
 a) It didn't cost anything.
 b) It only cost him his bus fare.
5 How many races did Steve win in order to become a millionaire?
 a) just the one
 b) six in a row
6 How did he choose the horses that he placed the bet on?
 a) He chose horses with good form.
 b) He chose horses with names he recognized.
7 What had Steve bought his girlfriend for her birthday before he won £1.4 million?
 a) just a card
 b) a cheap present

3 Find words or phrases in the text that mean the same as the definitions 1–9. The paragraph numbers are in brackets.

1 go to (1)
2 appeal to (1)
3 not unusual (2)
4 went to (2)
5 not simple (3)
6 selected (3)
7 shouting and saying 'well done' (4)
8 enthusiastic (4)
9 in no order or for no reason (4)

READ & LISTEN

4 **2.16** Listen to Reading 4 *A win on the horses* on the CD and read the article again.

| 103

5A Hard sell

ADJECTIVES (ADVERTISING)

1 Match the adjectives from the box to the products 1–6.

| comfortable | delicious | efficient | fashionable |
| healthy | popular | reliable | strong | stylish |

1 furniture _____
2 a car _____
3 food _____
4 clothes _____
5 a washing machine _____

2 Complete the sentences with the adjectives from exercise 1.

1 *Triton Trainers* are so _____ to wear that your feet will feel warm and relaxed all day.
2 *Cherokee Cycles* sells more bikes than anyone else! We're the world's most _____ bike manufacturer.
3 *Sheng Cheng Hong* restaurant has tasteful, modern, elegant décor. In fact, it's one of the most _____ restaurants in London.
4 The *Country Cruiser* is a car that will never break down and will always start in the morning. It's an extremely _____ vehicle. Test drive one today!
5 At *Dovey Accountancy*, we are professional, well-organized and do everything on time. We are a very _____ company.
6 *Brady Boots* are new and have come straight from the shows in Paris. All the film stars are wearing them. They are so _____!

COMPARISONS 1

3 Match the adjectives 1–8 to the nouns and noun phrases a–d.

1 short
2 heavy
3 cheap
4 big   a size
5 small   b battery life
6 light   c weight
7 long   d price
8 expensive

4 Read the review of two smartphones. Complete the sentences comparing the phones using the adjectives 1–8 in exercise 3.

WHICH SMARTPHONE?
This week's latest smartphones

▶ **XTC Wave**
Battery life: 18 hours
Weight: 0.15 kilos
Size: 12 x 8 cm
Price: £50
Expert's view: ★★★ stars

▶ **OMD Cloud**
Battery life: 12 hours
Weight: 0.18 kilos
Size: 11 x 7 cm
Price: £80
Expert's view: ★★★★★ stars

1 The XTC Wave lasts _____.
2 The OMD Cloud is _____.
3 The XTC Wave is _____.
4 The OMD Cloud is _____.
5 The XTC Wave is _____.
6 The experts think the OMD Cloud is _____.

DICTATION

5 🔊 **2.17** Write the sentences that you hear.

1 _____.
2 _____.
3 _____.
4 _____.
5 _____.

READ & LISTEN

6 🔊 **2.18** Read and listen to the reading text *Catch them young* on page 44 of the Student's Book.

5B Cold calling

COMPARISONS 2

1 Rewrite the sentences using the appropriate form of the word in brackets so that the meaning is the same.

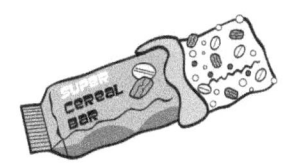

1 No other cereal bars are as good as *Super cereal* bars. (*good*)
  Super cereal bars are better than any other cereal bars.
2 Other cereal bars are not as fruity as *Super cereal* bars.
  Super cereal bars are _____.
  (*fruity*)
3 *Super cereal* bars are not the same as other cereal bars.
  Super cereal bars are _____.
  (*different*)
4 *Super cereal* bars are the healthiest bars on the market. No other cereal bar is _____.
  (*healthy*)
5 Other cereal bars are not as popular with children.
  Super cereal bars are _____.
  (*popular*)
6 *Super cereal* bars are the least expensive you can buy. No other cereal bar is _____.
  (*cheap*)

2 Correct the mistake in each sentence.

1 Branded trainers are often the same quality that normal trainers, but just more expensive.
2 I don't think that your mobile is so good as mine.
3 Yuck! That fizzy drink is not as best as *Koola Kola*!
4 That new digital camera isn't very different of the older version.
5 I think the new XP3 smartphone is much gooder than the XP2.
6 Why did you buy that DVD player? It's very similar the one you already have.

ADJECTIVES (NEGATIVE PREFIXES)

3 Complete the table with the adjectives from the box.

believable   sufficient   patient   lucky
prepared   honest   successful   accurate
polite   correct   convenient   satisfied

dis-	un- *unbelievable*	im-	in

4 Complete the sentences with a negative adjective from exercise 3. Not all the adjectives are used.

1 I'm sorry to phone so late. Is it an _____ time?
2 I buy lottery tickets all the time, but I never win anything. I'm very _____.
3 Does advertising tell the truth? No way. Most of it is _____.
4 I told him I didn't want another credit card and he hung up. How _____!
5 I'm very _____ with the service you offer, so I'm going to find another bank.
6 I was _____ for the exam, so I didn't pass it.
7 Please just wait for a second! You are so _____ at times.
8 Unfortunately, his attempt to reach Antartica on foot was _____.

TRANSLATION

5 Translate the sentences into your language.

1 Advertisers are very aware of the fact that girls are much bigger spenders than boys.
  _____.
2 This mp3 player's hard drive isn't nearly as big as the other one.
  _____.
3 Children are one of the most important markets for advertisers.
  _____.
4 When I was a child, advertising was much less sophisticated than it is now.
  _____.

5c | The office

COMPARING NOUNS

1 Choose the correct words to complete the dialogue between Alison (A) and Barbara (B).

A: So, who should we promote?
B: Well, who has the (1) *most / more* experience, Simon or Kate?
A: Simon, definitely. He's the (2) *long / longest* serving member of staff.
B: True. But is he the (3) *good / best* person for the job?
A: Well, I think so. He's one of the (4) *hardly / hardest* workers in the department; he works (5) *longest / longer* hours than anyone else.
B: Yes, I agree with all of that. I'm not sure those are the (6) *more / most* important qualities at the moment though. I feel this new job is for someone who has (7) *more / the most* vision than the rest; and someone who can make the right decisions and make them quickly.
A: So you don't feel Simon is right for the job?
B: To be honest, no. Kate is different though. I've been watching her. OK, she's made a couple of bad decisions, but she's the (8) *quick / quickest* learner I've seen for years. She's also made the best decisions in the team.
A: Simon is the most popular person in the team.
B: He is. But does that make him a leader? He's (9) *lesser / less* respected than Kate, don't you think?
A: True. And he tends to shy away from leadership.
B: Yes, I agree.

OFFICE ACTIVITIES

2 Complete the sentences with a noun or phrase from the box. Remember to put the verbs in the correct form!

| make write receive make send make |
| report phone calls photocopies coffee |
| emails call |

1 I'm going to the kitchen. Can I _____ you a _____?
2 I'll _____ a detailed _____ and have it on your desk first thing Monday morning, sir.
3 Could you _____ me five double-sided _____ of this letter, please?
4 I've just arrived back from holiday to find 231 _____ have been _____ to me while I was away.
5 I'm sorry, I have to go now. I've just _____ an urgent _____ from the hospital.
6 While I'm flying I won't be able to _____ any _____, so I'll contact you when I get there, OK?

VOCABULARY FROM THE LESSON

3 Complete the sentences with a word or phrase from the box.

| get some work experience   colleagues |
| at my desk   a staff   cell phone |
| laptop   boss   9 to 5 |

1 I wish I had an exciting job, not just a regular Monday to Friday _____.
2 My work _____ are great fun, but the _____ is an idiot.
3 She works from home a lot, but she'll pick up your emails on her _____ or you could ring her on her _____.
4 I'm off for lunch but will be back _____ by 2pm.
5 Yeah, it's a pretty small company. We've only got _____ of eleven, but we're growing fast.
6 I'm here for six weeks to _____ before I go to university.

DICTATION

4 🔊 **2.19** Write the sentences that you hear.

1 _____.
2 _____?
3 _____.
4 _____.
5 _____.

READ & LISTEN

5 🔊 **2.20** Read and listen to the reading text *Office Stereotypes* on page 48 of the Student's Book.

5D | Paperwork

OFFICE SUPPLIES

1 Find ten office objects in the word search.

n	o	d	a	p	a	p	e	r	c	l	i	p	u	p
f	y	r	l	o	x	i	w	a	u	c	n	e	z	d
a	m	u	k	r	s	d	h	i	p	y	g	n	r	h
p	t	b	i	r	o	m	r	u	t	h	a	c	l	i
z	a	b	n	e	k	g	o	p	i	n	k	i	a	g
t	i	e	k	s	v	r	i	s	k	s	b	l	o	h
o	g	r	c	r	t	g	u	d	p	e	x	s	e	l
d	r	e	a	m	s	l	o	g	h	l	g	h	y	i
h	i	t	r	u	g	p	m	o	n	l	d	a	b	g
p	o	s	t	i	t	s	a	t	w	o	b	r	i	h
l	f	u	r	m	r	o	s	e	w	t	i	p	e	t
f	e	t	i	p	p	e	x	r	n	a	x	e	t	e
m	o	r	d	r	a	w	i	n	g	p	i	n	s	r
a	p	u	g	e	j	i	n	o	b	e	r	e	t	a
n	o	t	e	p	a	d	g	r	e	y	t	r	i	p

ON THE PHONE

2 Complete the phone dialogue between a caller (C) and a secretary (S) with sentences or phrases from the box.

> Could you tell him   will he be back in the office
> Could I take a message
> I don't think he'll be back until tomorrow morning
> I'll call back then   Could you say that again

C: Could I speak to Mr Vaswani, please?
S: I'm afraid he's not in the office this morning.
(1) _____?
C: Yes, please. (2) _____ Mr Chowdri phoned?
S: I'm sorry. (3) _____, please? I'm afraid it's a bad line.
C: Yes, it is, isn't it? The name's Chowdri. C-H-O-W-D-R-I.
S: Thank you, Mr Chowdri.
C: When (4) _____?
S: (5) _____.
C: Tomorrow morning? OK, (6)_____.
S: Thank you, Mr Chowdri. I'll tell him you called. Goodbye.

3 Read the telephone dialogue between a caller (C) and a secretary (S). Why does the secretary seem to be unfriendly?

C: I want to speak to Ms Horne.
S: Who's calling, please?
C: John Stratford from Stratford Cars.
S: I'm sorry, but Ms Horne's not at her desk. Would you like to leave a message?
C: Yes. Tell her to call me.
S: Excuse me!?
C: Get her to call me when she gets back, OK?
S: Well ... yes. Do you have a number?
C: Yes. It's 0267 3416.
S: 0267 3416?
C: That's right.
S: I'll pass the message on.
C: Good.

4 Underline the parts of the dialogue that seem impolite. Rewrite them so that they are more polite than the original.

TRANSLATION

5 Translate the telephone dialogue into your language.

A: Could I speak to Ms Harvey, please?
B: I'm afraid she's not in the office at the moment.
A: Do you know when she'll be back?
B: I think she'll be back tomorrow morning. Can I take a message for her?
A: No. I'll call her tomorrow. Thank you.
B: You're welcome. Goodbye.
A: Goodbye.

_____
_____
_____
_____
_____

| 107

5 | Reading

1 Match the words 1–5 to the definitions a–e.

1 takeaway food
2 stationery
3 fare
4 expenditure
5 confectionery

a money that you spend on something
b sweets and chocolate
c ready-to-eat food that you take away from a restaurant
d things that you use to write with, like paper and pens
e the price you pay to travel on a bus, train, etc

2 Look at this quiz for parents of seven to fifteen-year-olds in the UK. The quiz asks them about their children's expenditure per week in the UK. Can you guess the answers?

Do you really know what your kids spend their money on?

① Seven to fifteen-year-olds spend an average of
a) £10.70 b) £12.00 c) £11.40 a week.

② Boys spend a) more money than b) less money than c) the same amount of money as girls a week.

③ The biggest expenditure for boys and girls is …
a) bus and train fares. b) clothes and shoes.
c) takeaway food and snacks.

④ The smallest expenditure for boys and girls is on …
a) confectionery and snacks. b) fares.
c) mobile phones and charges.

⑤ The two areas that boys and girls spend the same amount of money on are … a) sporting and cultural activities, music accessories. b) fares, sporting and cultural activities. c) mobile phones and charges, takeaway and snack food.

3 Check your answers to exercise 2 by looking at the table.

Items 7–15-year-olds spend their money on
(as a percentage of the total)

Items	Boys	Girls	All aged 7–15
takeaway and snack food eaten away from home	24%	23%	24%
clothing and footwear	12%	22%	17%
games, toys, hobbies, pets	19%	6%	12%
of which computer software and games	12%	1%	6%
magazines, books and stationery	5%	6%	6%
music accessories (CDs and DVDs)	7%	4%	5%
sporting and cultural activities	4%	4%	4%
mobile phones and charges	3%	5%	4%
confectionery and snacks	3%	4%	4%
fares	2%	2%	2%
other expenditure	21%	24%	22%
all expenditure (=100%) (£ per week)	10.70	12.00	11.40

4 Complete the summary with information from exercise 3.

A year ago, a survey in the United Kingdom discovered that seven to fifteen-year-old girls spent about 12% more money than boys. Girls spent an average of £12.00 compared to £10.70 for boys. Boys and girls spent most of their money on (1) _____. Girls spent almost the same as boys: 23% and 24% respectively.

In all the other major areas except for (2) _____, children spent the same or very similar amounts of money. For example, boys spent the same as girls on sporting and cultural activities (4%) and on bus and train fares (3) _____.

The biggest difference between the two groups was in the area of games, toys, hobbies, pets. In this category (4) _____ spent much, much more on computer software and games. In fact, they spent (5) _____ of their money on these items, which was twelve times more than girls spent.

108

6A | Summer holiday

Future 1 (future plans)

1 Choose the correct verb forms to complete the email.

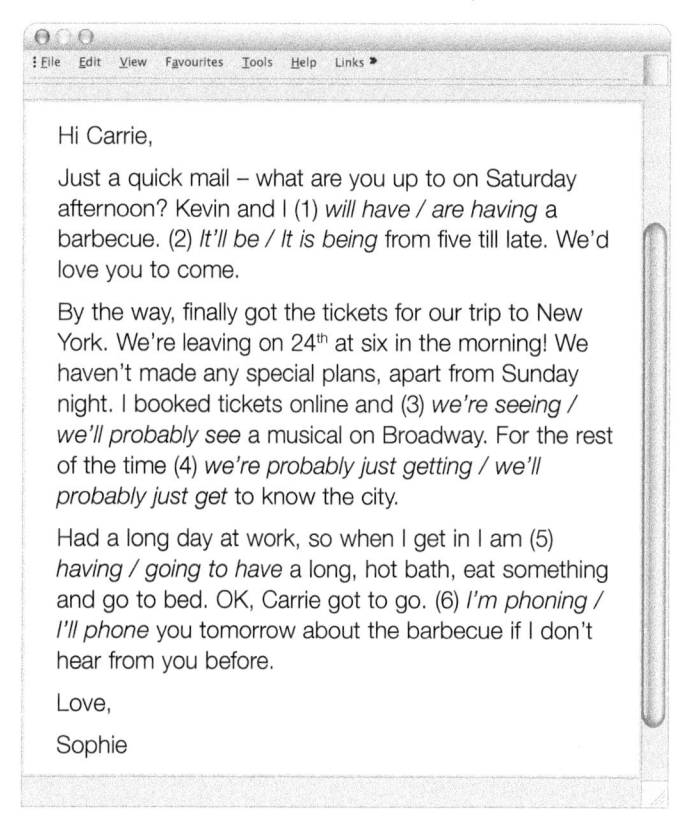

Hi Carrie,

Just a quick mail – what are you up to on Saturday afternoon? Kevin and I (1) *will have / are having* a barbecue. (2) *It'll be / It is being* from five till late. We'd love you to come.

By the way, finally got the tickets for our trip to New York. We're leaving on 24th at six in the morning! We haven't made any special plans, apart from Sunday night. I booked tickets online and (3) *we're seeing / we'll probably see* a musical on Broadway. For the rest of the time (4) *we're probably just getting / we'll probably just get* to know the city.

Had a long day at work, so when I get in I am (5) *having / going to have* a long, hot bath, eat something and go to bed. OK, Carrie got to go. (6) *I'm phoning / I'll phone* you tomorrow about the barbecue if I don't hear from you before.

Love,

Sophie

2 Read Carrie's reply to Sophie's email and correct the six mistakes in verb forms.

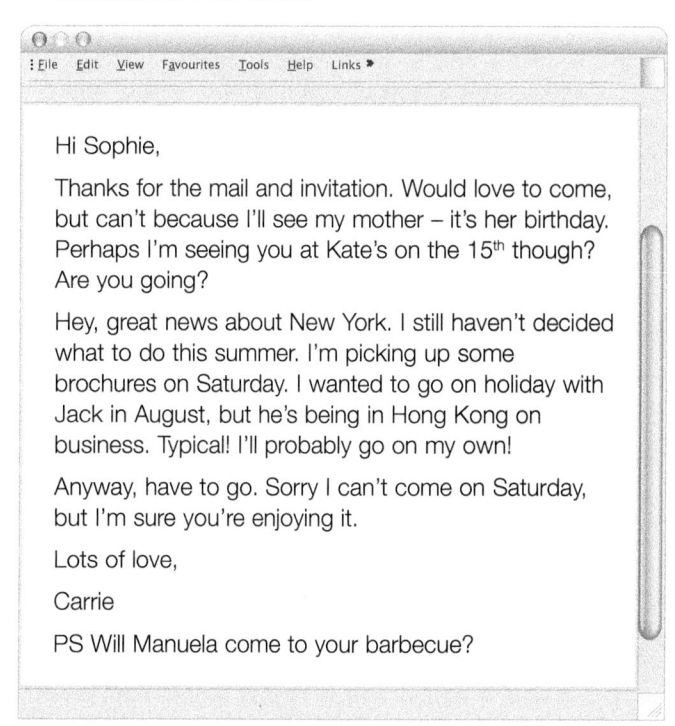

Hi Sophie,

Thanks for the mail and invitation. Would love to come, but can't because I'll see my mother – it's her birthday. Perhaps I'm seeing you at Kate's on the 15th though? Are you going?

Hey, great news about New York. I still haven't decided what to do this summer. I'm picking up some brochures on Saturday. I wanted to go on holiday with Jack in August, but he's being in Hong Kong on business. Typical! I'll probably go on my own!

Anyway, have to go. Sorry I can't come on Saturday, but I'm sure you're enjoying it.

Lots of love,

Carrie

PS Will Manuela come to your barbecue?

Holidays 1

3 Complete the dialogue between a customer (C) and a travel agent (T) with phrases from the box.

| picked up a brochure   pay a deposit |
| do the packing   chosen a destination |
| find your way around   book the flights |

T: Travel Direct. Jenny speaking. How can I help?

C: Good morning. I (1) _____ from your travel agency yesterday.

T: OK, and have you (2) _____?

C: Yes, it's the *Bellavista Real Hotel* in the Algarve. It's on page 128.

T: Ah yes. It's a very pretty resort. Not too big, so you can (3) _____ very easily. It's a fishing village with a sandy beach.

C: Oh, that sounds lovely. Are there any family rooms for four left for the first week in August?

T: Let me just check … yes. I can reserve one for you, but you'll have to (4) _____ of 10%.

C: 10%? OK. And can I (5) _____ with you, too?

T: OK … yes, accommodation plus flights for four … that comes to £1,200.

C: Oh, great! How exciting. I think I'll (6) _____ tonight.

T: Tonight!? But the holiday doesn't start for another three months!

C: Yes, I know, but you haven't seen my shoe collection!

Dictation

4 🔊 **2.21** Write the sentences that you hear.

1 _____.

2 _____.

3 _____?

4 _____.

5 _____?

| 109

6B Getting away

Holidays 2

1 Complete the holiday advertisements with phrases from the box.

> the beaten track   laid-back atmosphere
> magnificent white beaches   cosmopolitan guests
> crowded beach parties   range of water sports
> secluded beach   exclusive, upmarket hotel
> unforgettable beach parties   picturesque mountains

Coral Retreat, Phuket ★★★★★

One of Phuket's best-kept secrets, this fabulous five-star hotel is one of the finest on the island. Set on a hill overlooking kilometres of (1) _____, the hotel sits in a beautiful coconut grove. Loved by the (2) _____ who fly in from all over the world, Coral Retreat has everything you'd expect from a five-star (3) _____. There is a wide (4) _____ such as snorkelling and seakayaking. The hotel also has a beautiful swimming pool, tennis courts and gym. Coral Retreat is famous for its (5) _____ on Friday night when the rich and famous dance on the sand till sunrise.

Mermaid Beach, Mauritius ★★★

In an area said to enjoy the best weather on the island, this hotel is set on a (6) _____ that looks out to a small island. Behind and up above the hotel are the (7) _____ of the south-west coast. This small family-run hotel is off (8) _____, so no lively clubs or (9) _____ here. Enjoy a week just relaxing in the (10) _____ – doing nothing but listening to the rhythm of the sea.

2 Match what the tourists said about their holidays 1–6 to the travel representative's replies a–f.

1 'I didn't worry about a thing while I was there. The atmosphere was so relaxing.'
2 'We've met people from all over the world here.'
3 'We sunbathed and swam and didn't see a single person all day.'
4 'I'm happy paying a lot more because it means we can avoid those horrible mass-tourist destinations.'
5 'It was hard to get here, but it's worth it to be away from the rest of the world.'
6 'I love this place because it's so pretty.'

☐ a 'Yes, it's a very cosmopolitan resort, isn't it?'
☐ b 'Yes, it's a very secluded beach, isn't it?'
☐ c 'Yes, it's very laid-back, isn't it?'
☐ d 'Yes, it is off the beaten track, isn't it?'
☐ e 'Yes, it's a very picturesque village, isn't it?'
☐ f 'Yes, it's a very exclusive resort, isn't it?'

Future 2 (predictions)

3 Complete the sentences with *will* or *going to* and the verb in brackets.

1 I think I _____ (own) my own travel company one day.
2 Jamie has eaten all that chocolate! He _____ (be) sick!
3 We're already late! We _____ (miss) the train.
4 Don't ask me why, but, in my opinion, Simon _____ (not / pass) the exam.
5 Who do you think _____ (win) the pop talent show?
6 The boys are playing football in the garden. They _____ (break) a window if they aren't careful.

6c | Perfect day

PRESENT TENSES IN FUTURE TIME CLAUSES

1 Complete the description of a day trip with clauses from the box.

> you'll meet   before the coach leaves at six
> You'll have a chance   we'll take a studio tour
> you'll visit some of the   Once the tour is over

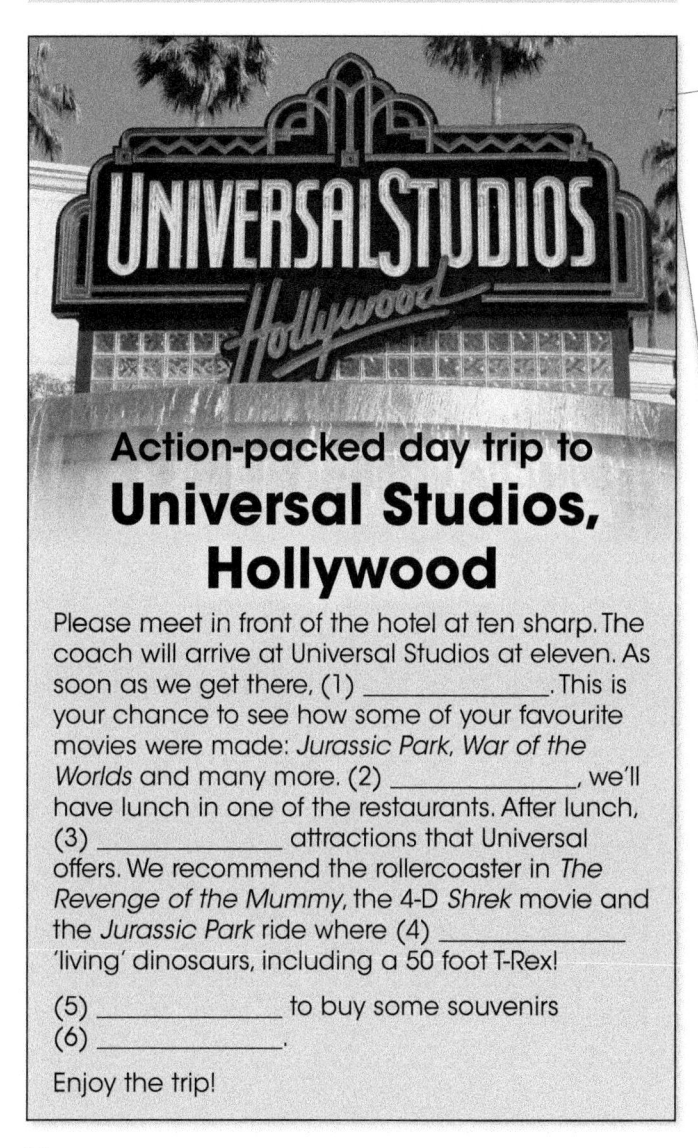

Action-packed day trip to Universal Studios, Hollywood

Please meet in front of the hotel at ten sharp. The coach will arrive at Universal Studios at eleven. As soon as we get there, (1) _____. This is your chance to see how some of your favourite movies were made: *Jurassic Park*, *War of the Worlds* and many more. (2) _____, we'll have lunch in one of the restaurants. After lunch, (3) _____ attractions that Universal offers. We recommend the rollercoaster in *The Revenge of the Mummy*, the 4-D *Shrek* movie and the *Jurassic Park* ride where (4) _____ 'living' dinosaurs, including a 50 foot T-Rex!

(5) _____ to buy some souvenirs (6) _____.

Enjoy the trip!

VOCABULARY FROM THE LESSON

2 Underline the word or phrase that does not go with the noun or verb.

1 **go**   out for the day   on an excursion
                 on a romantic holiday   rock-climb
2 **take**   a tour of Ireland   tourists to Dublin
                 drink   you for a pony ride
3 **have**   sightseeing   a look around
                 lunch with friends   a swim in the sea
4 **see**   the dramatic west coast   the packing
                 breathtaking scenery   a concert
5 **travel**   agent's   guide   land   rep
6 **tourist**   destination   attraction   resort   car

3 Complete the postcard with phrases from the box.

> holiday makers   a taste of   feel in the mood
> hire bikes   guided tour of

Dear Jude and Dave,
Having a horrible time here! On our first day we took a guided tour of churches. I'll certainly never go on one again! It was boring and the bus was hot and full of retired (1) _____ from England!

We'll probably go to a local restaurant tonight for (2) '_____ our town's best seafood'. It'll probably be fish and chips!

Tomorrow we're going on a (3) _____ the island, but I don't want to - I don't (4) _____. I'd prefer to (5) _____ and cycle around instead.

Can't wait to get home!

Love,
Your unhappy friend,

Annie xxx

DICTATION

4 🔊 **2.22** Write the sentences that you hear.

1 _____.
2 _____.
3 _____.
4 _____.
5 _____.

READ & LISTEN

5 🔊 **2.23** Read and listen to the reading text *Emerald Tours* on page 58 of the Student's Book.

6D Travel plans

INDIRECT QUESTIONS

1 Tick the correct questions. Correct the incorrect questions.

1 And can you tell me if that's a direct flight?
2 I wonder you have flights going from London, Heathrow to Vietnam.
3 I'd also like to know if I can book a hotel through you.
4 Do you know how long does the flight take?
5 Do you think you could tell me how much Business and Economy cost?
6 Could tell me how much do the flight costs, please?

2 Read the dialogue between a customer (C) and a travel agent (TA). Complete the dialogue with the indirect questions in exercise 1.

TA: Good morning, Freedom Travel. How may I help you?
C: Good morning. (1) _____?
TA: Yes, sir. Where are you travelling to?
C: The capital, Hanoi.
TA: Yes, that's no problem.
C: Good. (2) _____?
TA: Just one second. Yes, that's ... that's fifteen hours and 45 minutes with Thai Airways.
C: Oh, that's a long flight. (3) _____?
TA: Bear with me ... no, sir. There's a stopover in Bangkok, Thailand. So London to Bangkok is eleven hours and 30 minutes. Then a two-and-a-half hour wait ... and then another one hour and 45 minutes to Hanoi.
C: OK. (4) _____?
TA: Certainly. Return or single? First, Business or Economy, sir?
C: Return. (5) _____?
TA: Sure ... just one second. Yes, here we go ... a return in Business is £1,740.90 and in Economy it's £1,050.90.
C: Oh, a big difference. I think I'll go Economy.
(6) _____.
TA: Yes, of course. There are a number of good hotels in Vietnam.

COLLOCATIONS WITH *SOUND*

3 Imagine someone is talking about their holiday. What would you say to the person? Choose the best option to complete the phrases.

1 And you could eat as much as you wanted for $3.00!
  That sounds *great / painful*.
2 We were dancing on the beach and I cut my foot on a broken bottle.
  That sounds *funny / painful*.
3 And at dinner this silly man talked about himself nonstop for an hour!
  That sounds *fascinating / boring*.
4 We sat in a hot bus for five hours.
  That sounds *uncomfortable / wonderful*.
5 We had dinner together and watched the sun go down.
  That sounds *romantic / too bad*.
6 And the guide explained how they built this 98-metre church 2,000 years ago.
  Wow! That sounds *much fun / fascinating*.

TRANSLATION

4 Translate the sentences into your language.

1 Could you tell me where the post office is, please?
_____?
2 Does that sound like a good idea to you?
_____?
3 Do you know what time the guided tour starts, please?
_____?
4 I'd like to know if there are any non-smoking restaurants near here.
_____.
5 Waiting for a bus for two hours doesn't sound much fun.
_____.
6 Do you think you could tell me how much a return flight costs?
_____?

112

6 | Reading

1 Read the article and match the paragraphs 1–4 to the headings a–d.

- [ ] a The real solutions
- [ ] b 'Carbon-neutral' tourists
- [ ] c The problem
- [ ] d A solution

WHAT IS THE REAL PRICE OF TOURISM?

1 Tourism is the largest and fastest growing industry in the world. By 2020, 1.6 billion people will be taking holidays abroad – mostly by plane. Increased flights lead to more pollution, especially the production of
5 carbon dioxide. Carbon dioxide, or CO_2, is a gas and is one of the main causes of climate change. To give an example, a return flight from London to New York creates 1.22 tonnes of the gas per person. Multiply this by the number of people flying around the world and
10 it's easy to see what a terrible effect flying has on the environment.

2 Now most of us happily take flights without realizing the damage we are causing. A small but growing number of tourists, however, are taking responsibility
15 for the CO_2 produced by their holiday. These 'carbon-neutral' travellers want to offset or 'neutralize' all the carbon dioxide their holidays produce. They do this in a number of ways, for example, by turning off air conditioning when it's not needed or asking a hotel
20 not to change towels and bedding every day. But how do you offset a return flight to New York for a family of five that produces over six tonnes of CO_2!?

3 One answer lies with a growing number of not-for-profit companies that offer to balance the negative
25 effects of CO_2 by planting trees. Trees naturally take in CO_2 and give off oxygen and this process helps to balance out the problem. So, for that return flight that produces over six tonnes of CO_2, the family gets a company to plant ten trees for them. The trees
30 neutralize the effects of the flights on the environment. It doesn't cost very much and the family, in this case, have paid the real price of their flights by becoming 'carbon-neutral'.

4 Sadly, planting trees will not solve the problem. Non-
35 governmental organizations (NGOs) like Greenpeace, an environmental pressure group, are helping by fighting for a cleaner, safer world. National governments are also acting, although they could do more. For example, they could tax airplane fuel and
40 they could get tourists to pay an 'environmental' tax. The best hope, however, lies with international organizations working together. If not, tourism will suffer. Rising sea levels are already threatening those idyllic island beach holidays and rising temperatures
45 are slowly melting the snow on those fantastic ski resorts. It's time to act!

2 Read the article again and decide if the sentences are true (T) of false (F). Correct the false sentences.

1 Planes produce CO_2, which damages the environment. ___
2 In 2020, one and a half million people will go on holiday abroad. ___
3 Most travellers know that planes are bad for the planet. ___
4 Carbon-neutral travellers want to eliminate the CO_2 they generate by flying less. ___
5 Trees help to reduce CO_2. ___
6 If you plant five trees, it neutralizes the effect of around six tonnes of CO_2. ___
7 Trees will take care of the situation. ___
8 The ultimate answer to the CO_2 problem lies with governments. ___

3 Match the speakers 1–6 to what he or she might say a–f.

1 an average tourist
2 a carbon-neutral tourist
3 a spokeswoman from an organization that works to make things better, but doesn't make any money from what they do
4 a representative from an environmental NGO
5 a government spokesperson
6 a spokesperson for an international environmental organization

a 'Governments in 141 countries have signed this agreement to reduce the production of CO_2.'
b 'I didn't know that airplanes caused so much pollution!'
c 'You don't need to change the sheets. I'm happy to use them all week during my stay.'
d 'We are going to raise taxes on all air travel.'
e 'So if you plant one tree, that will cover your return flight to Rome.'
f 'We're putting pressure on the government to stop its road-building plans.'

4 Match the words from the text 1–4 to the definitions a–d. The line numbers are in brackets.

1 offset (21)   a gas or diesel used to drive a vehicle
2 tonnes (22)   b balance the effect of something
3 take in (25)   c absorb
4 fuel (39)   d units used for measuring weight, equal to 1,000 kilograms

READ & LISTEN

5 🔊 **2.24** Listen to Reading 6 *What is the real price of tourism?* on the CD and read the article again.

1 | A description of a best friend

Me and my best friend

1 My best mate is Greg. (1) *I first met him* at school over 20 years ago when we were eleven. I remember that it was in the playground while we were playing football. (2) *To begin with, he seemed* very arrogant, and I didn't like him at all. But he made a joke about what a terrible footballer I was, and it was so funny that I had to laugh. We've been close friends ever since, although there have been times when we haven't seen each other for years.

2 Many people find it hard to understand Greg. (3) *He comes across as being* very serious, but he loves having fun and meeting people. He's really good company and he's got a great sense of humour, although he doesn't like telling jokes. He's also a very good listener. Over the years he has helped me when I've had a problem by sitting and listening. Because he's very easy to talk to, we chat for hours about stuff like football, politics and relationships.

3 Physically, he is average build and quite tall. He has got a pale complexion and blond curly hair, but (4) *the first thing you notice about him is* his moustache. (5) *I wouldn't describe him* as good-looking, but he has an interesting face. He has lively blue eyes and a prominent nose that lots of women seem to like.

4 (6) *He's into* lots of things, especially music, but he hates dancing! (7) *He's got a real talent for* the guitar and he plays a lot when he's alone at home. He is quite an active guy and he enjoys sport, although he can't play football any more. He loves going out to concerts, the pub and exhibitions. One of his greatest loves is food and wine. Now that's another reason why I like him so much – he's an excellent cook!

READING

1 Read the article and match the paragraphs 1–4 to the headings a–d.

☐ a What he looks like
☐ b What he likes
☐ c What he is like
☐ d How we met

2 Look at the writer's plan for the article. Cross out the three pieces of information which he did not include in the article.

1	2
don't see each other all the time / met at school / arrogant / much bigger than me / joke about me	seems serious / really fun / good company / hates telling jokes / good listener / we chat a lot / a bit impatient
3	4
the moustache! / looks like his father / blue eyes / women like his nose / height / pale / hair	guitar / dancing Ugh! / sport / his cooking / concerts, etc

LANGUAGE FOCUS

1 Match the phrases in italics in the article 1–7 to the phrases a–g.

☐ a At first, I thought he was
☐ b He gives the impression of being
☐ c He's really good at
☐ d He's really keen on
☐ e His most prominent feature is
☐ f The first time we met was at
☐ g You can't really say that he's

114

2 Complete the phrases in exercise 1 about your best friend. Change *he* to *she* if necessary.

3 Insert capital letters and full stops in the paragraph below.

> physically, he is average build and quite tall he has got a pale complexion and blond curly hair, but the first thing you notice about him is his moustache I wouldn't describe him as good-looking, but he has an interesting face he has lively blue eyes and a prominent nose that lots of women seem to like

Check your answers in the article.

4 Use the notes below to write a short paragraph. Choose the best order in which to present the information.

> Dave / short / in his forties / fair hair / going a little bald / very fit / old-fashioned clothes / still thinks he's good-looking! / small round glasses / muscular

5 Check that you have included capital letters and full stops in the correct places in the paragraph that you wrote for exercise 4.

Writing

1 Use the paragraph organization in Reading exercise 2 to write a plan for a text about your best friend.

1	2
3	4

2 Look at your plan and decide …

- if there is any extra information that you want to include.
- if there is any information that you do not want to include.
- the best order to present the information in each of the paragraphs.

3 Write an article entitled 'My best friend'. Use the points below to help you.

1 Look again at the phrases in Language focus exercise 1 and in the article about Greg. Do you want to use any of these phrases in your article?
2 Check that you have used capital letters and full stops where necessary.

115

2 | A description of a town or city

Madrid

(1) ___ Visitors are attracted by the city's history, excellent museums, wonderful food and unbelievable nightlife. Add marvellous weather and the open friendliness of its people and it's not too difficult to understand why Madrid is one of the most popular places to visit in Europe.

(2) ___ Madrid was just a small town in the centre of Spain until King Philip II made it the capital in 1561. The city rapidly became the political and cultural centre of Spain. One of the most popular places with visitors is the impressive Plaza Mayor (Main Square), which was built in Madrid's early days. Other interesting historical landmarks include the Royal Palace and the Cibeles Fountain (18th century), and the Toledo Arch, a national monument built in 1817. When the weather is good, why not escape the city and spend some time in the beautiful Retiro Park? Families with young children will enjoy strolling around the park or boating on the lake.

(3) ___ A must for all visitors is the spectacular Prado Museum with its first-rate collection of European art. If you have a little more time, you should definitely go to the Thyssen-Bornemisza Museum and the Queen Sofia National Centre for the Arts. Apart from these three exceptional museums, there are a lot of smaller art museums housing superb collections.

(4) ___ Many Madrileños (i.e. people from Madrid) love going out to the cinema, the theatre or a concert. Others enjoy going from one bar to another, meeting friends along the way. Food is really important to people here and you can eat very well in bars, cafés and restaurants. The city has an outstanding live music scene and the choice is enormous: rock, pop, flamenco, reggae, hip hop, and much more. For people looking for a night out, there are hundreds of clubs and many of them are open all night. People here enjoy life and there is definitely something for everyone.

Reading

1 Read the text about Madrid and choose where you would see it 1–3.

1 a history book
2 a guidebook
3 a description of a holiday

2 Complete the spaces 1–4 with the topic sentences a–d.

a If you love history, Madrid has a lot to offer.
b Madrid is famous for its nightlife and at night the city explodes into action.
c Madrid is the capital of Spain and a great destination for a short weekend break or for a longer trip.
d The city is well known for its marvellous art museums.

3 Tick the information that is included in the text.

1 There are many good reasons for visitors to go to Madrid.
2 It's easy to get around the city on the public transport system.
3 Madrid was not always an important city.
4 Tourists like going to the city's Main Square.
5 The city has a rich collection of museums.
6 Madrid has first-class shopping centres, as well as many interesting small shops.
7 There are plenty of things to do in the evening.
8 Sports fans should try to get tickets for a football match at the Bernabéu Stadium.
9 People who enjoy good food will not be disappointed.

Language focus

1 Complete the phrases so that they are true for a town or city in your country.

1 One of the most popular places with visitors is …
2 Other interesting historical landmarks include …
3 When the weather is good, why not …
4 Families with young children will enjoy …
5 A must for all visitors is the …
6 If you have a little more time, you should definitely …
7 For people looking for a night out, there are …

2 Look at the thesaurus box and find the adjectives in the text about Madrid. Which nouns do the adjectives describe?

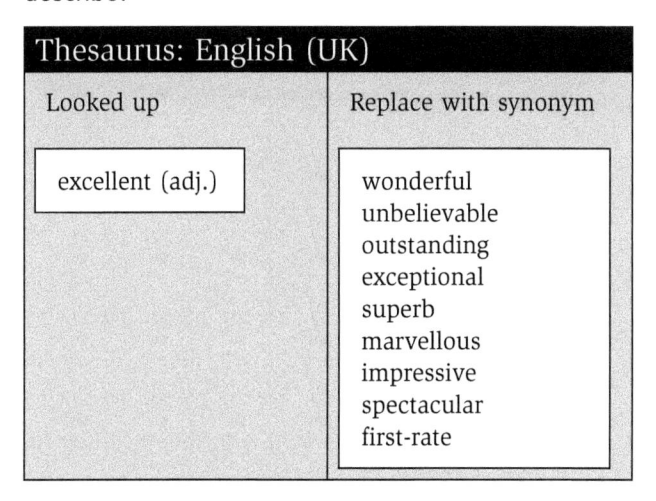

Thesaurus: English (UK)	
Looked up	Replace with synonym
excellent (adj.)	wonderful unbelievable outstanding exceptional superb marvellous impressive spectacular first-rate

3 For each adjective in the thesaurus box, write the name of something you could describe in a town or city in your country.

4 Read the information in the box.

> **Use capital letters for …**
> - names of people and places.
>   *Madrid, Toledo Arch*
> - countries, nationality adjectives and languages.
>   *Spain, Spanish*
> - titles.
>   *King Philip II, Queen Sofia, Dr Gardner, Sir Elton John*
> - days of the week and months of the year.
>   *Saturday, December*

5 Rewrite the text using capital letters where necessary.

> If you're in brussels in april or may, don't miss a visit to the royal palace at laeken with its beautiful gardens and greenhouses. The greenhouses were built for king leopold II of belgium, who was also responsible for the nearby japanese tower, which sometimes houses temporary exhibitions.

WRITING

1 You are going to write a guide to your town or city, using the following instructions.

1. Choose a town or city in your country and make notes about its attractions to visitors.
2. Organize your notes into three paragraphs.
3. Select the three or four most important reasons for visitors to come to this place and write a short introductory paragraph.
4. Then write the three paragraphs that you planned in point 2.

Below are some notes on paragraph writing.

> When we begin a new paragraph, we can (1) leave a line before starting the new paragraph, or (2) leave a short space at the beginning of the new paragraph.

> responsible for the nearby Japanese Tower, which sometimes houses temporary exhibitions.
>
> Another interesting place to visit outside the town

> responsible for the nearby Japanese Tower, which sometimes houses temporary exhibitions.
> Another interesting place to visit outside the town

2 Look at what you have written. Can you improve it in any way?

1. Are there any phrases in Language focus exercise 1 that you could use in your guide?
2. Have you used an interesting variety of adjectives?
3. Check that you have used capital letters and full stops where necessary.

3 | Advantages and disadvantages

Reading

1 Read the composition and choose the best summary 1–4.

1 It is better for students to live off campus.
2 There is no important difference between living on and off campus.
3 Living on campus is better for students.
4 On or off campus?

2 What reasons does the writer give (1) for and (2) against living on campus?

Language focus

1 Find five words or expressions in the composition to complete the table.

ordering points in a composition		
making your first point	making additional points	making your final point
Firstly, In the first place, _____ _____	Moreover, On top of that, _____ _____	Lastly, _____

2 In the paragraph below, insert expressions from exercise 1 so that the text is easier to follow.

> There are many good reasons for studying a foreign language in the country of the language. You are surrounded by the language and can learn a lot without really making any effort. There are many opportunities to learn about the culture, and this can be extremely interesting. The progress that you make will probably be much faster.

There are a lot of advantages to living on a university campus. For a start, life is usually cheaper. For example, food and accommodation are often subsidized by the university and students who live off campus have to pay normal prices for everything. Secondly, you don't have to deal with things that go wrong in rented accommodation, such as washing machines breaking down or gas cookers that don't work properly. The most important reason for living on campus is the time you save being so close to places like the library. As a result, you have much more time to study.

However, there are some disadvantages, too. First of all, it is easy to spend all your time on campus and because of that you can lose contact with the 'real world'. What is more, you don't have as much independence or freedom on campus as off. For instance, you normally can't choose what and when to eat. Finally, if you live on campus, it isn't necessary to develop the same life skills as you do living off campus – skills like managing the day-to-day running of a house.

To sum up, I believe that the main reason for being at university is to study. Living on campus allows students more time to study without the distractions and responsibilities of rented accommodation. As a result, I would recommend people to live on campus if they have the chance.

3 Correct nine spelling mistakes in the sentences below.

1 It normaly costs a lot of money to study in a foreign country.
2 I beleive that it is often a good idea to find accomodation with a host family.
3 It is usualy neccesary to plan your stay very carefully.
4 With more independance, you may also have responsabilities which you do not have at home.
5 I would certainly reccomend looking for a part-time job during your stay.
6 With so much to do, manageing your time can be difficult.

Find the correct spellings in the composition about living on campus.

Writing

1 Look at the title of a composition and the notes that a writer has made. Mark the notes A (advantages) or D (disadvantages).

The advantages and disadvantages of studying abroad

1 Make new friends/meet different kinds of people ___
2 No support from family and friends when things go wrong ___
3 Learn about a new culture ___
4 Foreign language may cause problems ___
5 Difficult to study with so many distractions ___
6 Improve your foreign language skills ___
7 Looks good on your CV ___
8 Helps to develop self-confidence ___
9 Usually more expensive ___
10 Hard to adapt to different food and customs ___

---

2 Choose three advantages and three disadvantages that you think are the most important. What is the best order in which to present these ideas?

3 Write a composition called *The advantages and disadvantages of studying abroad*.

Paragraph 1: present the advantages
Paragraph 2: present the disadvantages
Paragraph 3: sum up the argument and give your personal opinion

Use the points below to help you.

1 Remember to use a variety of expressions to present the order of your arguments.
2 Check your spelling. If you are using a computer, set the computer language to English and use the spelling checker.
3 Check that you have used capital letters and full stops where necessary.

STUDY ABROAD

Beijing, China   London, England   Bonn, Germany
Dublin, Ireland   Oxford, England   Rome, Italy
Kenya, East Africa   Paris, France   Washington, DC

4 A narrative: lottery winner

The UK's BIGGEST Lottery Win

1 'Ooh, I've won. That's nice,' Iris Jeffrey said to her family when she learned that she had become the UK's biggest-ever lottery winner, with a jackpot of £20.1 million. However, the Belfast woman almost missed out on her big win. She had put the winning ticket in a cupboard and forgotten about it. It was only a month later when she was watching TV with her husband, Robert, that she heard that the winner of a jackpot had not claimed their prize. She checked her numbers and found that she had all six correct. At first, the mother-of-two still couldn't believe she had won, and she asked her daughter, Wendy, to check again. In the end, she had to accept the news. 'I had a glass of milk and went to bed,' said the lucky winner when she described her reaction to becoming a multi-millionaire.

2 For 58-year-old Iris, the win came at an important time. Earlier this year, she discovered that she was suffering from cancer. She was waiting for an operation when her numbers came up, so the money will help in her fight against the disease. Elder daughter Wendy told reporters, 'With all the money, we can go anywhere in the world to get the very best treatment.'

3 With her winnings, the UK's latest winner says that she wants to look after her friends and family. Her younger daughter, Karen, is expecting a baby, and the grandmother-to-be is looking forward to spoiling them both. First of all, however, she plans to buy a new washing machine. After that, there will be a new car for Robert. And finally, she would like to go to Las Vegas with her husband. Having just heard from her doctor that the cancer is responding well to treatment, Mrs Jeffrey now has two reasons to celebrate.

Reading

1 Read the newspaper article about a lottery winner and match the paragraphs 1–3 to the summaries a–c.

☐ a What she plans to do with the money
☐ b How she won
☐ c The winner and why the win was so special

2 Put the events in the correct order.

☐ Her health improved.
☐ She decided how to spend the money.
☐ She discovered that she had won the jackpot.
☐ She had a glass of milk to celebrate.
☐ She learned that she had cancer.
☐ She put her lottery ticket in a cupboard.
☐ She watched TV with her husband.

3 Match the things people said 1–5 to the people a–e.

1 'Good news! Things seem to be improving.'
2 'Yes, I'd love a new BMW.'
3 'I've got something to tell you both – I'm pregnant.'
4 'It could be me – wait a minute – I'll go and find that ticket.'
5 'Yes, you've definitely got all six numbers, mum.'

☐ a Robert to Iris
☐ b Iris to Robert
☐ c Wendy to Iris
☐ d doctor to Iris
☐ e Karen to Iris and Robert

Language focus

1 Read the information in the box.

> We use *first of all*, *at first* and *initially* to talk about the first of a series of actions. *At first* and *initially* suggest a contrast with later actions.
>
> *First of all, she plans to buy a new washing machine.*
> *At first, she couldn't believe she had won.*
>
> We use *finally*, *in the end* and *eventually* to talk about the last of a series of actions. *In the end* and *eventually* suggest that the series of actions was long or difficult.
>
> *Finally, she would like to go to Las Vegas.*
> *In the end, she had to accept the news.*

2 Choose the best expressions to complete the text.

> A few years ago, I started buying lottery tickets.
> (1) *At first / First of all*, my husband thought it was a waste of money, but then I started winning.
> (2) *Eventually / First of all*, I won just a small amount – £50 – but then I got another £40 two weeks later. My husband still thought it was stupid. I continued to win small amounts, but after four months, I (3) *finally / initially* won quite a lot – £2,000. After winning nine times in six months, my husband (4) *at first / eventually* agreed that the lottery wasn't such a bad thing after all.

3 In order to avoid repeating 'Iris Jeffrey', the writer uses seven other ways to refer to her, other than 'she'. Find and underline them.

4 Use your imagination to replace the words in italics.

> Richard Pratt appeared in court yesterday with debts of over £90,000. *Richard Pratt* had spent it all on the lottery. He first tried his luck with a single ticket over a year ago, but each week he gambled more and more.
> After spending more than £500 a week on tickets, *Richard Pratt* soon ran out of money. Sure that he would soon have a lucky break, *Richard Pratt* sold his car and, finally, his house. Outside the court, *Richard Pratt* told reporters, 'It wasn't worth it.'

5 Look at the examples. Then rewrite sentences 1–6 with correct punctuation and capital letters.

> *'I had a glass of milk and went to bed,' said the lucky winner.*
> *Wendy told reporters, 'With all the money, we can go anywhere in the world.'*

1 And the final winning number is 49 said the man on the radio
2 I thought I'd give it a go, but I never thought I'd win he said
3 I used my parents' birthdays to choose the numbers he explained
4 He turned round to his passenger and said I've just won the lottery
5 You're kidding he said
6 The most incredible thing happened to me today he told his wife

WRITING

1 You are going to write the story of another lottery winner. Divide the information below into two paragraphs.

> John Townsend / 24 / taxi driver / from Glasgow, Scotland / prize £15 million / never played before / the six numbers were his mother and father's birthdays / driving in taxi / heard lottery results on the radio / had to stop his taxi because he was so shocked / explained to passenger / asked him to take another cab

2 Write the story.

Use the information in exercise 1 for the first two paragraphs.

Decide the order in which you want to present this information.

Use your imagination in the third paragraph to decide what he did (or plans to do) with the money.

Use the points below to help you.

1 Remember to use a variety of ways to refer to Mr Townsend.
2 Check all the past tenses (past simple, past continuous, past perfect) that you have used.
3 Remember to use time expressions to show the connections between different events.
4 Check your spelling and punctuation.

5 | An advertisement

TO RUSSIA WITH LOVE

Travelling to Moscow or St Petersburg?
Looking for low fares & quality services?

1 MillanAir's reliable and efficient new service between London Heathrow and Russia offers you unbeatable choice at unbeatable value. Two departures a day, seven days a week, 52 weeks a year. With a journey time of just under four hours, you'll be in Russia before you know it.

For travellers going further, our network of partner airlines provides a full range of onward flight connections.

2 And like any good airline, we also offer hotel booking, travel insurance and car hire services. All of this at discount rates.

For convenience, comfort and care, fly MillanAir.

3 With MillanAir's modern fleet of stylish A320 aircraft, you are sure to arrive relaxed and happy, and our in-flight service is second to none. And naturally, we are more than happy to look after passengers with special needs.

4 You can rely on us to make your journey a memorable experience. Delicious meals prepared by top-class chefs. An incredible choice of ten music channels and the very latest movies. Duty-free shopping at unbelievable prices. And if there's anything we've forgotten, our friendly and professional staff will be only too pleased to help.

5 Whether you're travelling on business or for pleasure, MillanAir is the choice for you. With prices starting at £150 one way, you won't find a better deal. But that's only the beginning. Regular flyer discounts. Early booking reductions of 10%. Last-minute offers.

It all adds up to one thing: we'll take you to Russia with love.

MILLANAIR.COM

READING

1 Read the advertisement and match the paragraphs 1–5 to the headings a–e.

- [ ] a   Food and entertainment
- [ ] b   Other services
- [ ] c   Prices
- [ ] d   Routes and connections
- [ ] e   Type of aircraft

2 Compare the MillanAir service with the service of Wilson Air, another company. Mark each feature *M* (if MillanAir's service is better) or *W* (if Wilson Air's service is better).

Wilson Air

Direct flights to four top destinations (Moscow, St Petersburg, Novosibirsk, Vladivostok) ____
Ten flights a day ____
Journey time 4 hours 10 minutes ____
Basic fare £180 ____
Free travel insurance ____
Book early and get 5% off ____
Sandwiches and snacks served on board ____

LANGUAGE FOCUS

1 Complete the adjectives by putting the missing letters in the spaces.

1   r e l i _ _ _ _
2   e f f i c i _ _ _
3   u n b e a t _ _ _ _
4   s t y l _ _ _
5   m e m o r _ _ _ _
6   d e l i c _ _ _ _
7   i n c r e d _ _ _ _
8   u n b e l i e v _ _ _ _

Check your answers in the advertisement for MillanAir.

2 English sentences contain a subject and a main verb. Which of the following are not full sentences?

1. Journey time only 30 hours.
2. Light meals are served on board.
3. Our award-winning website makes booking easy.
4. Prices start at an unbelievable £60 one way.
5. Special rates for group travel.
6. Total satisfaction guaranteed or your money back.
7. We never forget you have a choice.

3 Rewrite the phrases below as full sentences with a subject and a verb. Use the words in the boxes to help you.

Subjects

| there | we | you |

Verbs

| is | are | offer |

1. Two departures a day, seven days a week, 52 weeks a year.
2. Looking for low fares & quality service?
3. Last minute offers.
4. All of this at discount rates.
5. Delicious meals prepared by top-class chefs.
6. An incredible choice of ten music channels and the very latest movies.
7. Travelling to Moscow or St Petersburg?

4 Complete the sentences with words from the box.

| before | at | for | like | on | only | with | to |

1. We offer you unbeatable choice _____ unbeatable value.
2. You'll be in Poland _____ you know it.
3. _____ any good travel operator, we also offer a variety of additional services.
4. Our service is second _____ none.
5. You can rely _____ us to make your journey a memorable experience.
6. Our friendly and professional staff will be _____ too pleased to help.
7. Whether you're travelling on business or _____ pleasure, this is the choice for you.
8. _____ prices starting at £150, you won't find a better deal.

Check your answers in the advertisement for MillanAir.

WRITING

1 You are going to write an advertisement for MillanTours Coach Travel. Below is the first paragraph. Insert one missing word in each of the lines below.

Poland is only a click away with MillanTours Coach Travel

MillanTours now offers three departures a week from London Victoria six top destinations in Poland (Warsaw, Krakow, Gdansk, Katowice, Poznan Wroclaw). When you arrive, we can help you hotel bookings and we can arrange connections to than 50 other destinations. With journey time of thirty hours between London Warsaw (including the regular rest stops), is no better or more convenient way to travel.

2 You are going to complete the advertisement in exercise 1. Decide in which order you want to use the information below.

- onboard video
- panoramic windows
- toilet and washroom facilities
- one way £60, return £100
- hotel bookings
- travel insurance
- air conditioning
- light snacks, hot and cold drinks served
- no extra charges
- onboard telephone
- non-smoking
- access for disabled passengers
- easy internet booking system
- money back guarantee

3 Write the rest of the advertisement. Use the points below to help you.

1. Is your information organized in a logical way?
2. Have you used an interesting variety of adjectives?
3. Are there any phrases in Language focus exercise 4 that you could use in your advertisement?
4. Look at all the nouns in your advertisement and check that you have used articles where they are needed.
5. Check your spelling and punctuation.

123

6 | An extract from a holiday brochure

ST LUCIA –
WHERE YOU DON'T HAVE TO DREAM

1
Our exclusive hotel, *The Coconut Club*, is situated near Marigot Bay, on the west coast, only a short drive from Castries. Set in 70 acres of palm trees and with stunning views of the bay, *The Coconut Club* offers excellent facilities. The hotel has its own private beach, as well as two swimming pools and a gym. (1) ___ If you enjoy food as well as (or instead of) sport, there are two superb restaurants, one of which serves traditional local dishes like Callaloo soup or Creole curry. (2) ___ Although you probably won't want to leave the hotel, it's only a short walk to the bars and restaurants in the village of Marigot Bay. For a special night out, The Shack, for example, is one of the most memorable restaurants in the area.

2
When you feel like a day away from the beach, it's easy to find activities for all the family. (3) ___ Take your pick from our huge range of excursions, including pony rides through the banana plantations, a morning at the breathtaking Diamond Waterfalls and a cruise around the island's fishing villages.

(4) ___ If you're looking for an action-packed holiday, you won't be disappointed either. With dozens of sports to choose from (windsurfing, mountain-biking, water-skiing and rock-climbing, for instance), there is sure to be something for you.

3
Located between Martinique and St Vincent, St Lucia is one of the Caribbean's best-kept secrets. With its beautiful white beaches, its tropical rainforests and its dramatic volcanic mountains, St Lucia's stunning beauty is everything you would expect of a Caribbean island. (5) ___ In the many pretty villages and towns, such as the picturesque capital, Castries, the islanders' warm welcome makes St Lucia the perfect holiday destination.
(6) ___

READING

1 Read the extract from a holiday brochure and match the paragraphs 1–3 to the headings a–c.

☐ a The island
☐ b The resort
☐ c Things to do

2 Read the extract again and insert sentences a–f in the spaces 1–6.

a A trip to the weekly market in the capital will be a must for all your holiday souvenirs.
b In addition to tennis and squash courts, *The Coconut Club* also has a brand-new health spa.
c In fact, the only problem is that you won't have enough time to do everything that we offer.
d It is nothing less than a dream come true.
e The hotel's own beach bar also offers light snacks and drinks.
f Unlike many of its neighbours, the island has not been ruined by tourism.

3 Read the extract again and match the adjectives 1–7 to the nouns a–g.

1	our exclusive	a	capital
2	stunning	b	facilities
3	excellent	c	hotel
4	superb	d	restaurants
5	the breathtaking	e	views
6	pretty	f	villages
7	the picturesque	g	waterfalls

Read the extract again to check your answers.

LANGUAGE FOCUS

1 Insert a missing apostrophe in each of the extracts from the tourist brochure. Use the notes in the box to help you.

> 1 Put the possessive apostrophe before the *s* with singular nouns.
>   The **hotel's** private beach has its own bar.
> 2 Put the possessive apostrophe after the *s* with plural nouns.
>   It's impossible to forget the **mountains'** beauty.
> NB *its* = possessive form of *it*
>   *it's* = short form of *it is* or *it has*

1 Although you probably won't want to leave the hotel, its only a short walk to the bars and restaurants in the village of Marigot Bay.

124

2   When you feel like a day away from the beach, its easy to find activities for all the family.
3   Take your pick from our huge range of excursions, including pony rides through the banana plantations, a morning at the breathtaking Diamond Waterfalls and a cruise around the islands fishing villages.
4   Located between Martinique and St Vincent, St Lucia is one of the Caribbeans best-kept secrets.
5   In the many pretty villages and towns, such as the picturesque capital, Castries, the islanders warm welcome makes St Lucia the perfect holiday destination.

Read the extract again to check your answer.

2 Look at the extract again and underline examples of the language in the box.

X is	situated located	near … not far from …
	on the north/south/east/west coast.	
	set in …	
	a short drive from/walk to …	

3 Use the language in exercise 2 to write five sentences about a beach resort that you know.

4 Complete the sentences with words or phrases from the box.

for example   including   like

1   There are two restaurants, one of which serves local dishes _____ Callaloo soup.
2   The Shack, _____, is one of the most memorable restaurants in the area.
3   Take your pick from our range of excursions, _____ pony rides through the banana plantations or a morning at the Diamond Waterfalls.

Read the text again to check your answers.

Writing

1 Use the notes to write an extract from a tourist brochure. Use the points below to help you.

Maui Sunrise Hotel, Maui

Maui – biggest island in Hawaiian chain / middle of Pacific Ocean / volcanic island / tropical forests / long sandy beaches / cosmopolitan resorts (eg Kapalua and Makena)

Hotel: The Maui Sunrise / Four-star / close to beach / west coast / views of ocean / golf course, tennis centre, swimming pool, two restaurants, two bars and nightclub / relaxed but elegant

Haleakala National Park, home of the biggest dormant volcano in the world / mountain bike down volcano at sunrise / go whale-watching / take a helicopter tour / walk the streets of the old capital Lahaina / wide range of water sports: kayaking, sailing, windsurfing

Remember to …
- present the information in a logical order.
- think how you're going to describe the location of the island and the hotel – have you used an interesting variety of adjectives?
- use the language in Language focus exercise 4 to help give you examples of the points you make.
- check your spelling, punctuation and use of capital letters.

Useful language to improve your writing

Language for describing

Describing people
He gives the impression of being …
She's really keen on …
He's really good at …
Her most prominent feature is …

Describing towns & cities
One of the most popular places with visitors is …
Other interesting historical landmarks include …
When the weather is good, why not … ?
A must for all visitors is the …
For people looking for a night out, there is/are …

Discussion language

Advantages & disadvantages
There are a lot of advantages to …
For a start, …
For example, …
Secondly, …
The most important reason for … is …
However, there are some disadvantages, too.
First of all, …
What is more, …
Finally, …
To sum up …

Narrative language
First of all … .
Initially … .
Eventually … .
In the end … .
Before long, … .
After a few minutes, … .
Later that afternoon, … .
After a while, … .
Seeing the sign, regular customers were not surprised.
Finding no trace of him, they pronounced him dead.

Advertising language

Advertising a service
We offer you unbeatable choice … .
Our service is second to none.
Our friendly and professional staff will be only too pleased to help.
You can rely on us to make this a memorable experience for you.
With prices starting at £10, you won't find a better deal.
All of this at discount rates.
We never forget you have a choice.

Advertising a holiday
X is situated near …
X is located not far from …
X is on the west/east/south/north coast.
X is set in …
X is a short drive from/to …

Irregular verbs

Infinitive	Past simple	Past participle
be	was/were	been
beat	beat	beaten
become	became	become
begin	began	begun
bend	bent	bent
bite	bit	bitten
blow	blew	blown
break	broke	broken
bring	brought	brought
build	built	built
burn	burned/burnt	burned/burnt
burst	burst	burst
buy	bought	bought
can	could	been able
catch	caught	caught
choose	chose	chosen
come	came	come
cost	cost	cost
cut	cut	cut
deal	dealt	dealt
do	did	done
draw	drew	drawn
dream	dreamt	dreamt
drink	drank	drunk
drive	drove	driven
eat	ate	eaten
fall	fell	fallen
feed	fed	fed
feel	felt	felt
fight	fought	fought
find	found	found
fly	flew	flown
forget	forgot	forgotten
forgive	forgave	forgiven
freeze	froze	frozen
get	got	got
give	gave	given
go	went	gone
grow	grew	grown
hang	hanged/hung	hanged/hung
have	had	had
hear	heard	heard
hide	hid	hidden
hit	hit	hit
hold	held	held
hurt	hurt	hurt
keep	kept	kept
kneel	knelt	knelt
know	knew	known
lead	led	led
learn	learned/learnt	learned/learnt
leave	left	left

Infinitive	Past simple	Past participle
lend	lent	lent
let	let	let
light	lit	lit
lose	lost	lost
make	made	made
mean	meant	meant
meet	met	met
must	had to	had to
pay	paid	paid
put	put	put
read /riːd/	read /red/	read /red/
ride	rode	ridden
ring	rang	rung
rise	rose	risen
run	ran	run
say	said	said
see	saw	seen
sell	sold	sold
send	sent	sent
set	set	set
shake	shook	shaken
shine	shone	shone
shoot	shot	shot
show	showed	shown
shrink	shrunk	shrunk
shut	shut	shut
sing	sang	sung
sit	sat	sat
slide	slid	slid
sleep	slept	slept
smell	smelled/smelt	smelled/smelt
speak	spoke	spoken
spell	spelt/spelled	spelt/spelled
spend	spent	spent
spill	spilled/spilt	spilled/spilt
spread	spread	spread
stand	stood	stood
steal	stole	stolen
stick	stuck	stuck
swear	swore	sworn
swim	swam	swum
take	took	taken
teach	taught	taught
tear	tore	torn
tell	told	told
think	thought	thought
throw	threw	thrown
understand	understood	understood
wake	woke	woken
wear	wore	worn
win	won	won
write	wrote	written

Macmillan Education
4 Crinan Street, London N1 9XW
A division of Macmillan Publishers Limited

Companies and representatives throughout the world

ISBN 978-1-786-32047-6 Student's Book plus Workbook

Cover photograph by Corbis/Lois Ellen Frank, Getty Images/Doug Chinnery, Alamy/Robert Harding Picture Library Ltd, Corbis/Roger Tidman, Corbis/Gerolf Kalt, Alamy/Images & Stories

Text © Philip Kerr, Ceri Jones, John Waterman and Mike Sayer 2013
Design and illustration © Macmillan Publishers Limited 2013

First published 2006

All rights reserved; no part of this publication may be reproduced, stored in a retrieval system, transmitted in any form, or by any means, electronic, mechanical, photocopying, recording, or otherwise, without the prior written permission of the publishers.

For the Student's Book

This edition designed by eMC Design Ltd.
Original design by Oliver Design
Cover design by eMC Design Ltd. and Andrew Magee Design Ltd.
Illustrated by Nigel Dobbyn pp64, 66; Javier Joaquin p39; Gary Kaye p57; Roger Penwill pp38, 44, 54; Norbert Sipos p30.
Picture research by Sally Cole

Authors' acknowledgements
The authors would like to thank Nicola Gardner for her sterling work as Content Editor. They would also like to express their debt of gratitude to Nicola Stewart, editor for Level 2B, the designers at eMc Design Limited, Sally Cole for picture research and James Richardson for the sound recording, who all played vital roles in the development of this new edition. Finally, they would like to thank Katy Wright and the late David Riley, the driving forces behind the first edition of *Straightforward*.

The publishers would like to thank all the teachers from around the world who provided invaluable comments, suggestions and feedback on the first edition. The publishers would also like to thank the following people for their help and contribution to the second edition:
Tatiana Baytimerova (Russia), Lenka Boehmová (Czech Republic), Dr. Manuel Padilla Cruz (Spain), Svetlana Elchaninova (Russia), Jennifer Díaz Green (Dublin), Elena Mokeeva (Romania), Lynn Thomson (freelance editor), Amany Shawkey (Macmillan Egypt), Maria Teresa Rius Villaplana (Spain), Natalia Vorobyeva (Russia).

The authors and publisher are grateful for permission to include the following copyright material:
Page 29: Material from 'Bedrooms through the Ages' by Richard Wood, copyright © Richard Wood. Published by Hachette Children's Books;
Page 38: Extracts from 'World's luckiest man wins the lottery' 16.06.03; 'Toddler locked mum out on balcony' 15.10.03; 'Man fired after being stranded on mountain top' 04.11.03 and 'Fried egg cost teenagers' mum £675.00' 04.11.03, all taken from Ananova.com.;
Dictionary extracts taken from the Macmillan Essential Dictionary, copyright © Macmillan Publishers Limited 2003, used with permission.

The authors and publishers would like to thank the following for permission to reproduce their photographs:
Alamy/J.Arnold Images Ltd pp55, 56(A), Alamy/S.Belcher p44(D), Alamy/F1online digitale Bildagentur GmbH p60, Alamy/A.Bramwell pp18-19(b), Alamy/N.Cannon p16(D), Alamy/M.Caruana p67(mr), Alamy/T.Cordoza p44(C), Alamy/I.Dagnall p60(insert), Alamy/Robert Harding Picture Library p59(b), Alamy/R.Jahns p56(B), Alamy/Motoring Picture Library p16(E), Alamy/S.Outram p17(map), Alamy/T.Simon p51, Alamy/TongRo Image Stock p44(B), Alamy/Vario Images GmbH & Co p16(B), Alamy/G.Vurtis p21(tr); **Alvaro Neil** the biciclown pp14(a),14(b); **Archive Photos** pp37, 41(m), 46(br); **Brand X** p10(bl); **Corbis**/Abode/Beateworks p29(br), Corbis/T.Brakefield p16(F), Corbis/R.Cousins p26(B), Corbis/Destinations p58, Corbis/H.Diltz p10(tr), Corbis/Construction Photography p26(tl), Corbis/E.Ghioldi p10(tml), Corbis/Imagmore Co.Ltd p26(ml), Corbis/ImageSource p10(tl), Corbis/Platform/Johner Images p10(tmr), Corbis/B.Lewis.In Pictures p18(insert), Corbis/M.Longhurst p26(C), Corbis/K.Maack/Nordicphotos p39(mr), Corbis/National Geographic Society p58(insert), Corbis/C.Pizzello/Reuters p40(tl), Corbis/H.Scheibe p40(br), Corbis/V.Streano p25(mr), Corbis/G.Thomas/Loop Images p26(F); **Digital Vision** p20(B); **Europic**/CEN p36(r); **Getty**/ R.Kaufman /L.Hirshowitz p65(bl), Getty/M.Rochon p10(mr); **Getty Images Entertainment** p6(ml); **Tony Hawks** p15;

Hulton Archive pp29(mr), 41(mr); **Iconica** p20(A); **Photodisc** p9(tml), 9(tr), 20 (C); **Macmillan Publishers Ltd** p9(tl), 9(tmr), Macmillan Publishers Ltd/D.Ryan pp16(A), 49, 50, Macmillan Publishers Ltd/D.Tolley/R.Judges p17(money); Cover of The Secret Life of Walter Mitty reproduced with kind permission of **Penguin Books** p5; **Photoalto** p17(compass); **Photographers Choice** pp34-35(b); **Photolibrary**/J.A. Castellano p20(ml), Photolibrary/Corbis p16(C), Photolibrary/East Photo p17(sunglasses), Photolibrary/R.Edwards 26(A), Photolibrary/Food Collection p45(br), Photolibrary/Imagebroker p18(m), Photolibrary/ImageSource p8(t), Photolibrary/Image100 p18(ml), Photolibrary /D.Johnston pp24-25(b), Photolibrary/J.Klee p66(mr), Photolibrary/J.Osmond p26(E), Photolibrary/L.Pampalone p44(A), Photolibrary/D.Gair Photographic p21(br); **Rex Features** /Action Press p31, Rex Features/Everett Collection p4(br), Rex Features/N.Jorgensen p26(D); **Stockimage** p10(ml); **Taxi** p10(m); **The Bridgeman Art Library**/Louis XIV (1638-1715) receiving the Papal Legate at Fontainebleau on 29 July 1664 (colour litho), Le Brun, Charles (1619-90) (after) / Bibliotheque des Arts Decoratifs, Paris, France / Archives Charmet p29(ml); **The Conservative Party** logo p7(mbr); **The Labour Party** logo p7(br); **The Liberal Democrat Party** logo p7(tm).

For the Workbook

Designed by eMC Design Ltd.
Illustrated by Paul Daviz, Darren Lingrad, Peter Lubach, Mark Ruffle, Martin Shovel.
Cover design by eMC Design Ltd. and Andrew Magee Design Ltd.
Picture research by Suzanne Williams

Author's acknowledgements
I would like to thank Janet Castro and Nicola Stewart for their support on this project.

The publishers would like to thank all the teachers from around the world who provided invaluable comments, suggestions and feedback on the first edition. The publishers would also like to thank Mike Sayer and the following people for their help and contribution to the second edition:
Tatiana Baytimerova (Russia), Lenka Boehmová (Czech Republic), Dr. Manuel Padilla Cruz (Spain), Svetlana Elchaninova (Russia), Jennifer Díaz Green (Dublin), Elena Mokeeva (Romania), Lynn Thomson (freelance editor), Amany Shawkey (Macmillan Egypt), Maria Teresa Rius Villaplana (Spain), Natalia Vorobyeva (Russia).

The author and publishers are grateful for permission to reprint the following copyright material:
Page 107: Statistical information from HMSO website www.statistics.gov.uk used with permission.

The authors and publishers would like to thank the following for permission to reproduce their photographs:
Alamy/67photo p94, Alamy/Jon Arnold Images Ltd p115, Alamy/Richard Cooke p110, Alamy/David Fleetham p123(b), Alamy/Gavin Hellier/Robert Harding World Picture Library Ltd p110, Alamy/Juice Images p87, Alamy/Art Kowalsky p109, Alamy/Laurence Mouton/ PhotoAlto p117, Alamy/Chris Rout p86(tl), Alamy/Stella/Imagebroker p109; **Bananastock** p118(cr,cl); **Corbis**/Ron Dahlquist/Terra p123(t), Corbis/Kurt Hutton/Hulton-Deutsch Collection p95, Digital Stock/Corbis p118(c,br); **Getty Images** p118(bl), Getty Images/Able Images/Photodisc p122, Getty Images/BLOOM Image p107, Getty Images/Buena Vista Images/The Image Bank p123, Getty Images/Grant Faint/ The Image Bank p118(t), Getty Images/Bruno DeHogues/Photographers Choice p90, Getty Images/Robert Harding/Digital Vision p121, Getty Images/Tim Hawley/ Photographer's Choice p103(c), Getty Images/Martin Harvey/Gallo Images p89, Getty Images/Bruce Hershey/Workbook Stock p97, Getty Images/Davis McGlynn/Photographer's Choice p100, Getty Images/Thomas Northcut/Photodisc p103(t), Getty Images/Charriau Pierre/Photographer's Choice p102; **PA Photos**/Hayden West/PA Archive p119; **Photolibrary**/David Harrigan/Ableimages p86(tml); **Rex Features**/Geoff Pugh p92, Rex Features/Mike Webster p88.

These materials may contain links for third party websites. We have no control over, and are not responsible for, the contents of such third party websites. Please use care when accessing them.

Although we have tried to trace and contact copyright holders before publication, in some cases this has not been possible. If contacted we will be pleased to rectify any errors or omissions at the earliest opportunity.

Printed and bound by CPI Group (UK) Ltd, Croydon, CR0 4YY

2020 2019 2018
10 9 8 7 6 5 4 3